# *Australian Women at War*

PATSY ADAM-SMITH is one of Australia's best-known and best-loved authors. Awarded the OBE in 1980 for services to literature and the Order of Australia in 1994 for services to recording oral history, she has written thirty books, all of which have topped or appeared on the best-seller lists. Among her most popular books are *Hear the Train Blow* (the story of her childhood), *The Shearers, Heart of Exile, There Was a Ship, Outback Heroes* and *The Anzacs*, which was joint winner of The Age Book of the Year Award in 1978. *Prisoners of War* received the prestigious triennial Order of Australia Association Book Prize in 1993. Her most recent book, the autobiographical *Goodbye Girlie*, appeared to great acclaim in 1994.

# BY THE SAME AUTHOR

*Rediscovering Tasmania: the North-West Coast* (1955), with Piet Maree
*Hear the Train Blow* (1964)
*Moonbird People* (1965)
*There Was a Ship* (1967)
*Tiger Country* (1968)
*Hobart* (1968), with Max Angus
*The Rails Go Westward* (1969)
*Folklore of the Australian Railwaymen* (1969)
*Across Australia by Indian–Pacific* (1971)
*No Tribesman* (1971)
*Port Arthur* (1971), with Max Angus
*Tasmania* (1971), with Max Angus
*Footloose in Australia* (1973)
*Romance of Australian Railways* (1973)
*The Barcoo Salute* (1973)
*Launceston* (1973), with Max Angus
*The Desert Railway* (1974)
*Trader to the Islands* (1977)
*The Anzacs* (1978)
*Islands of Bass Strait* (1978)
*Victorian and Edwardian Melbourne from Old Photographs* (1979)
*Romance of Victorian Railways* (1980)
*Outback Heroes* (1981)
*The Shearers* (1982)
*When We Rode the Rails* (1983)
*Heart of Exile* (1986)
*Australia, Beyond the Dreamtime* (1987), with Thomas Keneally and Robyn Davidson
*Prisoners Of War: From Gallipoli to Korea* (1992)
*Trains of Australia* (1993)
*Goodbye Girlie* (1994)

# Patsy Adam-Smith

# *Australian* WOMEN *at* WAR

Penguin Books Australia Ltd
487 Maroondah Highway, PO Box 257
Ringwood, Victoria 3134, Australia
Penguin Books Ltd
Harmondsworth, Middlesex, England
Viking Penguin, A Division of Penguin Books USA Inc.
375 Hudson Street, New York, New York 10014, USA
Penguin Books Canada Limited
10 Alcorn Avenue, Toronto, Ontario, Canada M4V 3B2
Penguin Books (N.Z.) Ltd
182–190 Wairau Road, Auckland 10, New Zealand

First published by Thomas Nelson Australia 1984
This edition published by Penguin Books Australia Ltd 1996

1 3 5 7 9 10 8 6 4 2

Copyright © Patsy Adam-Smith, 1984, 1996

All rights reserved. Without limiting the rights under copyright reserved above, no part of this publication may be reproduced, stored in or introduced into a retrieval system, or transmitted, in any form or by any means (electronic, mechanical, photocopying, recording or otherwise), without the prior written permission of both the copyright owner and the above publisher of this book.

Typeset in Galliard by Midland Typesetters, Maryborough, Victoria
Printed in Australia by Australian Print Group, Maryborough, Victoria

National Library of Australia
Cataloguing-in-Publication data

Adam-Smith, Patsy, 1926– .
Australian women at war.

Bibliography.
Includes index.
ISBN 0 14 025843 4.

1. Women and war – Australia. 2. Women – Australia – History – 20th century. 3. Women in war – Australia. 4. World War, 1914–1918 – Women – Australia. 5. World War, 1939–1945 – Women – Australia. 6. Women – Australia – Social condition. 7. Women – Employment – Australia – History – 20th century. I. Title.

994.0082

# Contents

Preface vii

Introduction 1

1. Soldiers of the Queen 7
2. The Rose 19
3. All Men are Brothers 36
4. Socks, Socks and More Socks 41
5. A Great and Glorious Sisterhood 48
6. The Yearning Heart 63
7. The White Feather 79
8. The Bride Ships 84
9. People in the Storm 87
10. Après la Guerre est Finie 90
11. Would my Heart Tell Me? 99
12. No Foe Shall Gather our Harvest 106
13. Australia is Fighting Mad 110
14. From Tobruk to Tokyo 118
15. The Ultimate Crime 125
16. RAAFNS 131
17. RAANS 136
18. The VAs who became AAMWS 139
19. Calls for Blood and Serum 150

| | | |
|---|---|---|
| 20 | Persons and Practitioners | 155 |
| 21 | Gallant Sailor-girls | 156 |
| 22 | They Keep them Flying | 172 |
| 23 | The True Glory | 186 |
| 24 | 'Sigs' | 202 |
| 25 | The Petal and the Bee | 207 |
| 26 | That Branch of Physiology | 213 |
| 27 | A Boy from Alabama | 221 |
| 28 | Down on the Farm | 226 |
| 29 | Anything and Everything | 232 |
| 30 | Shells, Bombs and Depth Charges | 239 |
| 31 | The Invisible Crew | 247 |
| 32 | The String Bag Cometh | 249 |
| 33 | War in the Outback | 261 |
| 34 | What Did you Do in the War, Grandma? | 269 |

| | |
|---|---|
| Appendixes | 279 |
| Bibliography | 283 |
| Some Abbreviations Used in Text | 287 |
| Acknowledgements | 289 |
| Index | 291 |

# *Preface*

One of the rarest cavalcades Australia has known occurred in 1995 – the fiftieth anniversary of the end of World War II – when about a thousand ex-servicewomen came to Darwin en masse – to remember, and to meet friends not seen since fifty years ago, when we were young.

These women – all happy to announce that they were over seventy years of age – travelled the thousands of kilometres from each State and Territory and corner of the map of Australia. Some drove cars and station wagons 'up the track' to reach the Top End of Australia, others flew in, but it mattered little how they reached this distant outpost: they were coming to celebrate with friends who can never be forgotten, comrades they hadn't seen for half a century, women who had forged a bond they could never forget.

To talk with these women is not only to speak of the past (for there was little glory) but to remember, often vividly, how we all worked, some of us sleeping in tents for the whole of our service days and sometimes unsleeping on duty for 12 hours, night or day, when 'the whips were cracking'.

They were brave, cheerful, strong, cheeky young girls and women, whose loyalty was not that which some today play down, but was a certain determination to see it through, every hour, every day, until it was done, and thoroughly done.

'Who's your mate?' they used to ask in the Services. Everyone had a mate, you couldn't manage without a mate. Men have always been said to have mates but it cannot be said that they were the only people in wartime who had a mate. We all did, and many, most, either vaguely remember or are still in contact with that girl or woman who starched your collar when you were running late for duty, or embraced you and dried your tears when word came that a brother, or a friend, or one of the boys you nursed, or went on duty with, was later reported 'missing'.

It was this cameraderie that bonded all the Services, the Navy, Army and Air Force, and later the people back home, who changed their whole lifestyle to work in factories, on the land, in machinery and tool making, milking cows, ploughing, canning foodstuffs and making munitions. There was an enormous variety of things that suddenly had to be done that would never be thought of in peace time.

During World War I there was little that women could do to help but 'wait and pray', as the saying went. But in World War II there was an avalanche of needs for the nation. By 1941 there was a demand for labour and service. Young women were not only volunteering to go to war but many were volunteering to work in civilian jobs once believed to be fit only for men. Thousands of women, dressed in denim overalls, toiled in factories amid grease and deafening machinery all day. There was nothing genteel about it, it was all-in war, even though they had never worn denim before.

In one strange way war was a great relief, a chance for some young women – and men – to leave an often uninteresting, drab life in a country scarcely out of the dreary, poverty-struck Depression that had dragged on for almost all that life-sapping period. Many men and women leapt at the chance of leaving home and going – anywhere but the unpromising past – whilst others were imbued with a sense of loyalty and a deep pride in serving their country.

For whatever reason, we came to 'the call of the colours', as male soldiers have done from time immemorial. Whatever drove us to enlist, though, we immediately knew that war was more costly than any of us had envisaged.

When the last bugle blew and we were sent home with few or no plaudits, it mattered little to all of us: for we knew what we did in those years, and this will remain with us for all time.

But it didn't end there in 1945. Fifty years later, long after the war was ended, two young Darwin women, Toni Kelly (ex-US Navy) and Robyn Smith (Darwin), and Robyn's mother Nola wrought a miracle.

'Wouldn't it be great,' said Nola to the two girls, 'if you got a real gathering of ex-servicewomen up here to Darwin, to remember.'

It was 1993 when they sent out the feelers. In the way miracles happen a totally unknown but soon to be a unique event was taken up and swept along. The two young women began writing letters and phoning to all States. Within a week 50 women had responded with enthusiasm, and eventually almost 1800 approaches were made. The result was that 960 drove or flew up, and Darwin sent off a heart-warming and true end to the war.

The Vietnam veterans honoured us with a rip-roaring motor cycle escort from the city out to the Adelaide River. Here the victims of war, men and women who were killed in this vicinity, are buried, and here we said goodbye.

The badge pinned to our jackets read **Women Are Vets Also**.

Patsy Adam-Smith
1996

# *Introduction*

In writing such a book as this, one regrets that many groups' endeavours, many stalwart individuals must be left out. *No* history can tell everything about its subject. And this subject had been so grossly ignored that there was a surfeit of magnificent women to select from. In 1972, when I first discussed this work with Colonel Sybil Irving (Controller of the Australian Women's Army Service in World War II), she advised me: 'Try to tell your countrymen what they don't know. Answer their unthought-of questions. Build your book on that framework.'

How did Australian women rise to the challenge – and the opportunities – presented by their country being at war? What were their feminine strengths and weaknesses? What did Australian men think of women in traditionally masculine jobs? And did our Constitution, our trade unions and, later, our Manpower Priorities Boards recognise the value of women's services, or merely use them in work uncongenial to men and as emergency shop-girls when the enemy was already hammering at the gate? Was the work of tens of thousands of young Australian girls in uniform of any significance in their country's struggle; how did civilian women react to the pressures on them? Lastly, did this tremendous upheaval and experience, this reversal of women's roles, leave us any guidance for future emergencies?

My main aim in *Australian Women at War* was to record the many instances of endurance, devotion, bravery and self-sacrifice while some of these women were still alive; in tapping their memories, I wished to honour them.

Most of the brave, modest, forgotten women in this book were ageing. One I visited in Western Australia was a paraplegic, another was legless. One ex-officer had cancer, some were crippled with arthritis, or near-blind, or hobbling; some were still pained in the deep well of the heart from an old bereavement. Those still fit had one thing in common with the ailing: they all denied they did anything extraordinary. But for their leaders, I would never have known what splendid years women gave to Australia, and to the army, the navy and the air force. I knew each of the leaders, the supremos, of the three armed services in which women were enlisted in World War II, and each spoke of their 'girls' as any male commanding officer would speak of his 'boys'. 'Brave, loyal, tireless and cheerful.'

There is one group of women I have not treated with the space and detail they merit: the Australian Army Nursing Service. This service is set apart, different from any other. They know it, all mankind knows it, but in particular, the soldier knows it. Army nurses have been written and sung about, lauded, since Florence Nightingale walked among the wounded from the Crimea in 1857. Theirs is the oldest service; their uniform honours the women in past ages who tended the sick and dying. I am writing of these women, of the years they spent in prisoner of war camps in World War II, in a later book. I wrote of them earlier in the *The Anzacs*.

I have met none of the group of nurses who sailed off to the Boer War, these harbingers of the Australian Army Nursing Service, but I have known many women, including my mother, her sisters and my two grandmothers, who remembered the *men* riding off to 'give those Boers gyp'. My mother, then in her late eighties, most remembered the horsemen. 'Remounts were bought from our Gippsland farm for the Empire army in India. We supplied horses for South Africa also. When the boys came back to Gippsland, Frank O'Connor bent down from his saddle and lifted me up in front of him, and we galloped away, chasing Boers across our home paddock,' she said.

'I know it was really nothing much, but I can still remember the excitement. Seventy years later, when Rolf Harris sang the song "Two Little Boys", I wept, thinking of the stories told by the boys who came back from the veldt, about boys and their horses, "over there". All women my age have these feelings.'

Apart from the nurses, women were scarcely noted during the 1899–1902 Australian involvement in the Boer War. Women prayed in churches for victory, but the charnel-house of Bloemfontein was not mentioned in the service. It was here that 16 nurses, the first group of Australian servicewomen to travel overseas, were sent and no nurses since have entered a more fearful scene.

The 1914–1918 war may have launched many women on the path to emancipation, but the Great Depression, that greyly blanketed the country from the late twenties until the late thirties, smothered most of the advantages women had gained. World War II saw a grudging recognition of women's capabilities and their capacity for both concentrated and sustained repetitive work. In the services they drove ambulances and trucks, chauffeured officers, underwent the same training in over a hundred trades as the men; they manned anti-aircraft guns, serviced planes, were wireless-telegraphists, naval decoders – in all, there were over two hundred separately graded musterings, few of which had previously been available to women.

On the home front, life was no less changed for civilian women. Many waited until the end of the war not knowing if they were wives or widows, with their men reported *Missing, Believed Prisoner*. Housewives learned to carry their own shopping home, coped with rationing, brought up their children alone and worked ceaselessly to raise funds to help their men 'overseas'.

Those not tied to the house worked in factories, munitions and explosives centres; they built planes, ships and weapons carriers; they delivered ice, milk, bread – all erstwhile tasks for men only.

There was another side to women at war; and if women are to be considered as having equal rights with men, we must also examine the valid stance of those women who acted in a manner not attractive to us today. During World War I women, unable to show their loyalty and patriotism by dying on a battlefield for their country, came out in their thousands, ferociously, to support conscription. Their vicious actions and cruel speech were in total contrast to the love and labour they gave to the absent men – a surprising dichotomy which perhaps gives us a more pertinent peep at what war really does do to non-combatants.

At the opposite pole of the womanly war effort were women such as Vida Goldstein, a noted anti-conscriptionist during that war. Vida had early fought for the vote for women; from 1914 to 1918 she fought for the ending of hostilities. She was tenacious, courageous, magnificent in her determination, as were the other women involved with her: for these women stepped straight out of the accepted role for females of the time. To do what they saw as their duty, they threw off the mantle of safety and protection hitherto given to women by society and the law.

There was little need to mention women in manpower regulations during World War I, as women were scarcely in the workforce. The manners of Victorian England still prevailed. The propriety of women working was clearly defined. Women had worked in factories since the industrial revolution, but not *nice* women just *poor* women. In wartime, munitions work might just be acceptable, but women must go no further. The use of women as warriors 'threatens the whole of our society'. No, there was much more 'womanly' work for those women who waited here,

10 000 miles from the scene of battle and their sons, fathers, husbands and hoped-for husbands, in the age where spinsterhood was the 'long death' for that sex which had no money of their own.

Sydney newspapers published lists of addresses and objects of fund-raising groups which included: 'Old Gold and Silver War Fund for collecting and selling in aid of the War Chest and Sheep Skin Funds; Serbia-Montenegro Relief; Soldiers' Entertainments to provide concerts and lectures in Camps; Tanned Sheepskin Clothing Committee; Blue Cross, Veterinary Association for Disabled War Horses; Central Sandbag Committee for making, receiving and despatching sandbags; Fruit and Vegetable Gift Scheme for wounded or sick soldiers or their dependents'. The list was never-ending. 'No woman need be idle,' cried the Sydney *Sun*.

The girls who grew to womanhood in the Depression went into World War II with a quite different approach from that taken by their mothers in the earlier conflict. Indeed, from September 1939, when Australia went to war, the attempts women made to serve embarrassed both the Government and the Labor Opposition, who were agreed in their fears that women, given the opportunity, would take men's jobs.

In several cases, approval was passed for temporary employment of women on men's work where vacancies occurred through men enlisting for active service. There was permission given to vary the hours of work for women in textiles because it was clear that 'men are unavailable for this work and unless female employees are engaged, the result will be loss of employment for a large industry and a loss of export trade in an important commodity'. A government survey indicated a sharp decline in the first few months of war in the employment of women in domestic service – in country areas, the only employment open to most girls and to a lesser degree in the cities also. It noted that women were replacing men in 'less essential occupations'. (A survey of census figures showed 137 000 in domestic service in 1933. This figure had fallen to 60 000 by 1947, two years after the war ended.)

Primary industry was hard-hit as farm boys escaped from drudgery into the forces, and this led to the formation of the 'Fourth Women's Army' (after the Navy, Army and Air Force), the Australian Women's Land Army.

All these women were caught up in the passionate years the young can move through. There is no telescoping of emotions and the senses so immediate as in the days lived within the vortex of a war. There was always the chance that there would be no tomorrow. Always the urgency, always the fear there would be no forever after, no marriage, no lover.

Biros had not been invented; there were no television sets or transistors (although radio had been introduced between the wars, as had the first of the early coloured movies). There was no nylon, no plastics, no plastic bags; pantihose had not been made, nor had drip-dry fabrics. Wool was sold by the skein and had to be wound into balls before being knitted. The contraceptive pill was unknown and girls did not leave home and set up house in apartments or flats of their own. The gulf between their era and that of the 1980s was as great as if they had been living in the seventeenth century.

The Manpower Priorities Board discovered that there were as many resolute women as there are determined men. There were vast transfers of labour, mostly considered to be a step upwards by those moving, as well as a drawing into employment of many who would not normally have entered the workforce, those girls who would have been expected to 'leave their father's household only to pass into that of their husband'. From 1939 to 1941, women beat a path to the doors of the authorities, begging to be allowed to assist, to help win the war, to give of their talents. They were ignored. When the Japanese over-ran the Pacific islands during December 1941 and in February 1942 captured almost the whole of the Australian 8th Division at Singapore and bombed Darwin, Wyndham and Broome, the same women were needed as never before. The drear belief of centuries as recorded by Charles Kingsley was ended:

> *For men must work, and women must weep*
> *And sooner it's over, the sooner to sleep.*

The women did weep, but they now worked as never before: beside men.

# CHAPTER 1

# *Soldiers of the Queen*

The first of these pioneer women were early nurses who sailed off to the Boer War. From the home front it seemed to be glorious. For the first time, a largish body of Australian men dressed in uniforms were riding their sprightly, magnificent Australian horses through the streets on their way to war. Small numbers of Australians had served in Egypt and the Sudan (1882–98) but in numbers too small to enthuse a populace.

Now, with little encouragement from Britain, we were sending men off as though the result of that most questionable campaign in another colony was dependent on us. There was much to enthuse a people who were scarcely out of one devastating drought and about to go into another, people who had experienced the first onslaught of workmen striking for reasonable conditions and, worst of all, the depression and bank crashes of the 1890s. Perhaps the songs and the music were the greatest bloodstirrers. This was the peak of that era of arm-swinging, memorable, marching-time music backed by lyrics.

> *Oh Britannia, the pride of the ocean,*
>   *The home of the brave and the free*
> *The shrine of each patriot's devotion*
>   *No land can compare unto thee.*

And we, of course, were still British to the core.

> *When you're born by the red, white and blue*
>   *(white and blue!)*
> *When you're born by the red, white and blue*
>   *(white and blue!)*
> *And so shall we proudly sing forever,*
> *We are born by the red, white and blue!*

The Tommies were singing it in Pretoria, Australians were singing it in Sydney, Melbourne and anywhere else people gathered. (And they were still singing it through the 1930s and into the first years of the 1939-45 war.) During the Boer War even 'God Save the Queen' had great appeal, as the by-now-disgruntled little heap of an ageing queen neared her end and was still loved by her people. 'The event of the evening was the rendition of "God Save the Queen",' cried newspapers.

But the song with the most splendid martial air was 'The Soldiers of the Queen'. The words and music were not only catchy and easy to remember, but had the added magic of a foot-tapping score.

> *It's the soldiers of the Queen my lads,*
> *Who've been, my lads, who've seen, my lads,*
> *In the fight for England's glory lads,*
> *Of its world-wide glory let us sing.*
>
> *And when we say we've always won,*
> *And when they ask us how it's done,*
> *We'll proudly point to every one*
> *Of England's soldiers of the Queen!*

'After all my other memories of Bloemfontein have passed away I think I shall continue to hear the almost chant-like singing of the "Soldiers of the Queen" by the soldiers . . .' wrote an American war correspondent.

The attempted emancipation of women had begun before the nurses' departure to the Boer War. Throughout the 1890s women had been moving. Among the spontaneous interest in all states the cause of women became tied firmly to that of the men who were struggling for one man, one vote,

> *The women's cause is man's,*
> *They rise or sink together,*
> *Dwarfed or Godlike,*
> *Bond or free.*

So sang the New South Wales Women's Suffrage League when they first met on 22 April 1891. In Queensland, splendid Mrs Emma Miller led the struggle for the women's franchise.

Yet, one cannot say that women were in any way emancipated. It took another two world-wide conflicts to bring any change to their position in time of war.

Before the so-called 'Boer' War, few women were used in the medical corps of the nations, although 40 years had passed since Florence Nightingale pioneered nursing in the field at the Crimea.

Medical Officers early in 1899 urged that women nurses be sent, but the reluctant Army Department believed that soldiers preferred to be nursed by male orderlies and that women would interfere with the wounded soldiers' freedom. South Africa was said to be 'not a proper place' for women in wartime, and that flirtations would occur. Despite these peculiar objections, before that war ended the pattern for nursing in all future wars was decided. Florence Nightingale's great work was being carried forward and the War Office had agreed to the establishment of a permanent Army Nursing Service. For all that, the Service in South Africa sorely needed a champion such as Nightingale, 'who could have championed the cause of the sick against the prejudice and ineptitude of the controlling authorities'.

The first two Army Medical Corps sent to the conflict were from New South Wales. No nurses were with the first contingent and 'only strong, lusty men' were accepted or trained as stretcher bearers.

Lady Superintendent Ellen Julia Gould and 13 nurses accompanied the second contingent in the *Moravian* on 17 January 1900. (Of these, four remained in South Africa after the war, the Lady Superintendent and the other nurses returned to Australia. Nursing Sister Elizabeth Nixon was awarded the Royal Red Cross, and Nursing Sister Mary Annie Pocock was mentioned in despatches.)

On arrival, on 22 February 1900, the members of the New South Wales Nursing Service Reserve were sent to hospitals at Cape Town, East London and Sterkstroom. The medical corps was so urgently needed that when the *Moravian* anchored off Cape Town it was promptly despatched to sea again within a few hours for East London; when the nurses disembarked they headed inland to Sterkstroom. Miss Gould was given charge of nursing in the Orange River District which embraced Bloemfontein, considered to be the most undesirable posting in that war. 'A wretchedly dirty and out-of-repair structure', reads the official report of the hospital there.

Bloemfontein, 'the fountain of flowers', was a pestilential city, 'a pesthole of enteric fever and other illness'. Dead horses and human sewage had infected the water and the army. Field-Marshal Lord Roberts had rested his men and horses there for seven weeks while he waited for supplies and, in this time, upwards of 1000 men died. The carts carrying their blanket-wrapped bodies rumbled down the streets by day and night. The sick tents were crowded, the unwashed and despairing sick men lay on the floor in their stained uniforms with their one service blanket to cover them. An 'all pervading faecal odour' filled the makeshift hospital.

Into this setting came the 14 Australian nursing sisters with the New South Wales Medical Corps, a most distinguished body. So well known was the corps that it was said that English soldiers sewed a scrap of material inside their uniform with a legend, 'If wounded, please take me to N.S.W.A.M.C.'.

The 3rd Contingent, the 'Bushmen's', was drawn from farmers and bushmen. 'Hardy riders, straight shots, accustomed to finding their way about in difficult country and likely to make an expert figure in the vicissitudes of such a campaign' as was being conducted. 'There was an enormous number of candidates for enlistment.' They were untrained in military matters, many of them from bush farms or bush occupations and had no difficulty with 'the strict test in riding and shooting'. Preference was given to unmarried men.

Ten nursing sisters, all single, accompanied these men when the Bushmen's Contingent sailed from Melbourne in the *Euryalus* on 10 March 1900. The report states: 'They did excellent work in the hospitals, developing the best qualities of professional nurses. Sister Hines died in South Africa. Sister Rawson was awarded the Royal Red Cross. Sister Ivey was mentioned in Commander-in-Chief's despatches, 26 June 1902.'

The Bushmen fought their way to Elands River, where they were attacked and besieged and all their horses killed. Their casualties were heavy and the hardships great for the thirteen days they were encircled and, after the garrison was relieved, they marched on foot – having no horses – to Mafeking. Here they were partially re-equipped and within a week moved off to Kimberley, the Transvaal and Pretoria, fighting most of the way. What with the sick, wounded and dead they left along the way, the contingent was sadly weakened when they were ordered to march to help stop the Boer generals from invading Cape Colony. This long journey became 'a swift and impressive march. When other columns were tired out or withdrawn the 3rd [Bushmen] were with General De Wet to the last and lost heavily on their attacks on the enemy. Only 60 men answered the roll call when the orders came for the 3rd to be withdrawn.' They had fought on 'short rations' – six biscuits for six days. It was men such as these who succumbed to the diseases and fevers that filled the hospitals where the nurses worked.

All six colonies of Australia sent nurses to the Boer War, but the records are scanty. The Records of the Australian Military Contingents to the War in South Africa* say of the South Australian nurses: 'It may be mentioned that Nursing Sisters M.S. Bidmead, Glenie, and N.S. Harris, proceeded from Adelaide to South Africa at an early stage of the war. Sister Bidmead obtained the Royal Red Cross (Despatches, *London Gazette*, 10 September 1901). Sisters Bidmead and Glenie were presented with Devoted Service Crosses at the Review on Coronation Day, 26 June 1902. Sister Harris returned by the transport *Tongariro* from Cape Town, leaving on 31 March 1901. No further records of S.A. Nursing Sisters could be obtained.' Yet other sources say at least seven women left for South Africa from South Australia.

All nurses were under command of the officer commanding the unit to which they were attached, their Lady Superintendent holding a position little different from that of an intelligent duenna, adviser, labourer and supervisor.

The Bearer Company of the Australian Army Medical Corps had for transport 1 water cart, 2 buckwagons, 1 scotch cart, 2 horse ambulances, 1 ox cart and 2 mule wagons, and with this equipment followed the regiments as well as they could into battle. Often they were so busy with the wounded (searching for them in the rugged country, finding water, scavenging for food for the animals and men), they were left behind and must find the battle when they could catch up. On many occasions they had to quickly load the men they were tending on the ground and gallop back the way they had come because the Boers were fighting through them.

They were often under fire, sometimes for days at a stretch. Even the field hospitals had, on occasions, to evacuate the wounded and sick to the shelter of trees miles away when the hospital was under fire. When too many men needed attention and there was no accommodation, they bivouacked under trees and shelters made of tent flies and wagon covers. Blankets and waterproof sheets were always in short supply because of the weight involved in transporting them when on the march.

Transport was difficult. There were few made roads outside the large towns and distances were vast. The troops marched or rode overland. The single line rail tracks were over-taxed and the only way of conveying medical and surgical stores to the forward clearing stations or hospitals was by loading boxes of drugs and dressings on every supply wagon that left the western rail line for the front. Supply wagons spread with straw took

---

*Published by the Government Printer, Melbourne 1911.

the sick back to the line from the field hospitals – there were no ambulances to spare for this, as the two per brigade were insufficient for the advance and it was not possible to bring more forward, as all transport animals were needed to haul supplies to the troops. At Kimberley, on the railway from Cape Town to Bulawayo, hospitals could accommodate 380 sick men. But at times the train could not clear these, particularly when 800 sick men passed through Kimberley hospitals in one week in March 1900 (and this figure does not include those already in the hospital). Down the line at Modder River and Orange River those too ill to send on to Cape Town were off-loaded to hospitals. All the hospital trains carried smaller stores up in large quantities because of the congestion on goods traffic, but larger needs, such as beds, were always in short supply.

Fourteen more sisters arrived in Bloemfontein with the second half of the New South Wales ambulance in February and were thrown into the rigorous work which the fever beginning to rage through the battle lines generated. That 'all-pervading faecal odour' filled the make-shift wards, where many men lay on the floor in their clothes, covered with one blanket; 'unfed, unwashed, unhappy men will never cease to linger in one's memory', wrote a man about the 'crowded sick tents'. There were 24 nurses in the town when the medical corps entered; by May there was a total of 56, some of whom had travelled there by carts and wagons. By the end of April there were 123 nurses in the fever-stricken wards.

The troops were unusually susceptible to disease at the time they arrived in the endemic area. Suffering from lack of good food and water, footsore, some of the English with heat exhaustion and sunstroke, they arrived to a sad town – although its name led them to believe otherwise. Two churches, they say, were packed with Boer prisoners suffering from fever, and each day the burial carts rattled by . . .

The official report on the medical arrangements of that war state that 160 sick and wounded Boers who were prisoners were carried to safety from 'the Boer Laager' nine days after the men had been wounded. 'Many of the wounded had received their injuries in the engagement of the 18th, and had received no attention since; naturally they were in a terrible condition. These cases were carried to the drift by a party of some 200 men of two regiments, taken across the drift by the bearer companies, and thence removed by ambulance.'

And then the true horror of that quite horrible war began. 'It should be noted here that among the cases removed from the laager were at least 10 well marked cases of enteric fever: All these prisoners stated that [enteric] fever had been prevalent in the laager, and that a good many deaths had occurred from it there. The laager itself was indescribably filthy. The Boer force of about 4000 with some women and children, had been confined with their horses and oxen in a limited area for 10 days in a climate alternately hot and wet. Men, cattle, and horses had died; some of the bodies had been carried down by the swollen river and stranded below the laager, others remained on the banks. The sanitary arrangements of the Boers are, at the best, of the most primitive description, and in this impossible situation things were even worse than usual. Hence, a condition of which our troops were sensible before seeing the laager, when the breeze blew from that foetid spot to our trenches.'

'The difficulty of dealing with these men', wrote Surgeon General W. D. Wilson, 'was extreme, both in camp and hospital. Their disregard of elementary cleanliness made it impossible to maintain things in a satisfactory sanitary state and this was undoubtedly an important factor in the epidemic of enteric fever which developed . . . contracted while they were in the laager at Paardeberg.'

This last-mentioned town was in the region of Bloemfontein towards which the New South Wales Field Hospital was approaching with the army. The men fought, and marched. On one day after a long, hot march, though the men survived, some of the mules died on the way. The rocky, broken ground was so difficult, and the shortage of ambulances so acute, all the wounded could not be got to the field hospital by the time the moon set at 2 a.m. Fires were lighted at dressing stations and the wounded placed around them and given Bovril. On these battlegrounds, the Royal Engineers, when possible, went on ahead to lay hoses with hand pumps to the dams; one side of the dam was reserved for men, the other for animals, but the beasts, uncontrollable through thirst, rampaged and stirred the mud and fouled the water.

Thus they fought their way to Bloemfontein. Bloemfontein, the old capital of the Orange Free State, is on latitude 28 degrees, well within the area of summer rains. Two-thirds of the annual rain falls within the five months of December to April and one-sixth of the total rain occurs in March; it was in March that the attacking force came to the old town. Cape Town was 1000 kilometres away; the Boers, where they did not control the railway, blew up the bridges so that, for the first 16 days after the occupation of the 'fountain of flowers', not one rail truck reached it and no train came until the last two days of the month. Outside the town boundary were no made roads. The waterworks of the town were occupied by the Boers on the night of 31 March and by 3 April the town was reduced to the supply from polluted wells. There were no large cooking vessels, nor even enough firewood to permit the boiling of water.

Bloemfontein had had a bad reputation for the prevalence of enteric fever for some years before the war when it had appeared annually, after the first rains. In recent years, enteric fever had been increasingly prevalent in the smaller towns and farms round Bloemfontein.

Sanitary problems received very little attention. 'Among the Boer and native population no attention whatever is paid to these matters, while even in the English colonies, outside the coast ports, the conditions approximate to those obtaining in England a century ago. A water-carriage system for the removal of excreta would be very difficult to arrange. Irrigation schemes hardly exist. It is not recognised that expenditure on sanitary matters is profitable, hence, the usual method is a more-or-less unsatisfactory pail system, and this was in use in Bloemfontein.

'In addition to these well-defined sources of danger, the suspicious water supply, and the imperfect removal system, there was, as usual, a total disregard of any attempt at cleanliness in the surroundings of the houses, and, more important, of the wells. It is also important to note that whatever little may have been done in the town to improve these conditions, the small dorps and farms remained in a state of primitive filth.'

To this endemic area with impure water and bad sanitary conditions came Lord Roberts and his army of 33 954 men and 11 540 horses and all the debilitated men, exhausted and weakened from excessive exertion on a reduced diet and scanty water, many already infected by the Boer prisoners.

In the field hospitals around Bloemfontein, there were 327 cases when they arrived early in March, 110 of which were fever. By the third week in April admissions to hospitals exceeded 1400 and continued to rise. Field hospitals are equipped to give only temporary succour and are not suited for the continued treatment of serious cases, having neither beds nor blankets, utensils nor clothing, for the sick.

The serious cases increased more rapidly than beds could be found for them in the temporary hospitals in the town, and this in spite of the evacuation of such cases as were fit to move. Because of the destruction of bridges, it was impossible at first to send any but slight cases, which were in the minority in the hospitals housed in buildings, so that though the evacuation lessened the actual number under treatment in Bloemfontein, it did little to assist with treating the more severe cases. At first, only the limited number of cases able to walk across the pontoon bridge at Norval's Pont could be sent. After the resumption of traffic, by 6 April it was possible to send about sixty at a time by the ordinary trains, which then ran across the repaired bridge. The first hospital train arrived in Bloemfontein on 5 April and left for the base two days later, while another arrived in Bloemfontein on 8 April and left on 10 April with 144 of all ranks, sick and wounded. From this date the evacuation proceeded steadily.

As the April rains fell, rheumatism and bowel complaints began among the men who were not yet in tents. It is difficult to envisage any worse situation for nursing staff to encounter. As well as the men of Lord Roberts's command, the wounded and sick from the battles around the Orange Free State came into Bloemfontein, as did reinforcements which doubled the strength of men in the town. Official records declared it to be 'extremely improbable that any true estimate of the sick and wounded in the town would ever be assumed'. No. 9 General Hospital treated 7800 cases between 20 April and 27 July. As for the nurses, 'the energy and devotion of these ladies was beyond all praise; they never spared themselves while anything remained that could be done for the sick.'

Articles such as bedpans and urinals were not available in sufficient quantity until the end of May. The army was marching on Pretoria and took the field hospitals with them, leaving the general hospitals in Bloemfontein to cope as best they could. Betwen 16 March and 27 July there were 1134 deaths in Bloemfontein, of which 964 were from enteric fever.

The official records of 1911 give some small mention of the work the nurses did in this early, terrible theatre of war. 'Special mention must be made of the nursing Sisters from the over-seas Colonies. Sisters came from Queensland, Victoria, New South Wales, South Australia, Western Australia, Tasmania, and New Zealand, while Canada also sent Sisters.

'Most of these Sisters were originally sent free of expense to the Imperial Government, their services having been engaged either by their respective Governments or by private societies which sent them out. Others came with recommendations from their colonies, and were engaged immediately on their arrival in South Africa. All these ladies were, without exception, full of zeal and energy, and were anxious to get as far as possible to the front. Many of them served throughout the whole campaign, and all did most excellent service.

'It is impossible to say too much of the services which the nursing Sisters rendered in South Africa. Their devotion to duty, often under very trying conditions, was only exceeded by their kindness to their patients, many of whom owed their lives to the attention of these ladies. As regards the quality of their work, while the general average was very good, there were, of course, variations, and the best Sisters were undoubtedly those from the staffs of large hospitals at home. Those who had been engaged in private nursing were not so efficient as a class, and their employment is not to be recommended if Sisters can be obtained direct from the hospitals.'

After this war was ended a committee was convened to furnish a report, 'utilizing the experiences of these officers who were actually in charge of general hospitals in South Africa'. This report made the first assessment of needs for military hospitals in the twentieth century, including the nursing establishment, such as suggesting one nursing sister for every 40 patients, assisted by one staff nurse and four orderlies. As well, 'It is considered advisable that the operation theatre should be under the direct charge of a Nursing Sister, specially trained for this duty, as they are much neater, cleanlier, and tidier in their methods and habits, especially in handling and care of surgical instruments and appliances. She should have an attendant as assistant for rough work, scrubbing floors, &c., and cleaning utensils and instruments, to act under her orders. Nusing Sisters held these appointments in many general hospitals during the South African Campaign with satisfaction to all concerned and credit to themselves.

'The appointment of trained masseurs to general hospitals during active service would be advisable, their services being most useful. Nursing Sisters or nurses with masseur training and qualifications might be appointed for this special duty.'

A housekeeper to look after mess, catering and quarters was needed for the sisters. 'The Nursing Sisters' Camp, situated to the right front of the hospital, should consist of a hut combining mess and sitting rooms, kitchens, scullery, and pantry. If hut cannot be provided two tents, large size, are necessary, also a kitchen, scullery, and pantry built as in Officers' camp. The living tents recommended for these ladies' use are the Indian Field Officers' tents, with bath attachment. These would be far more comfortable and convenient for them than the double circular. Each nurse should have a tent to herself. The latrine is situated about 50 yards to the left of camp. In general hospitals at base we recommend that Nursing Sisters live in huts.'

Whilst this report was very advanced for its day, it gives latter-day readers a frightening insight into the conditions of the last century if the following suggestions are thought to be an advance on what had gone before: 'Disinfecting sheds are necessary, where all clothes are steeped in chemical disinfecting solutions and wrung out. Another where the foecal [sic] soiled clothes and others requiring it are boiled, and another for Thresh's steam disinfecting apparatus.

'The floor of this entire shed should be of concrete, 4 inches thick. The first should have three wooden tubs, about 3 feet by 3 feet in size, with a wooden tap in each, close to the bottom, for emptying them. A small open drain, commencing at first tub each side, made in the concrete, in connection with a portable cistern, sunk at back of hut, is also necessary if main system of drainage does not exist.

'Excreta and Slops: The second shed for disinfection and sterilisation of all infected discharges and slops from infectious division, should have a sink in one corner, drained into a cistern outside at back of hut, for washing bed-pans and urinals in after chemical disinfection. At one end of hut a large 100 gallon (or 150 gallon) ordinary boiler set in brick fireplace should be erected, for sterilising all infected discharges and slops. The walls all round should only extend 6 feet high, leaving a space of 1 foot below to allow for free circulation of air.

'The clothes boiler, excreta steriliser, and outside cistern should be emptied by hand buckets into sanitary carts as frequently as necessity demands. All these sheds should be lime-washed inside frequently, and floors washed with disinfectants daily. An incinerator for burning used dressings, infected and worn-out clothing, and all refuse generally found in camps, is a necessity.'

Thus by reading what is seen to be the ideal for the future, we understand a little what these gallant, unsung heroines had borne before this time.

There is but one reason for the paucity of records on nurses and their work at this war: nursing was not yet sociably acceptable work for ladies. The conditions in which they laboured ('that all-pervading faecal odour') in South Africa would have been enough to have them ostracised from respectable society had it been publicly known. But most of all, female civilian nursing itself was still battling to achieve respectability. The image of women working in hospitals was viewed as 'somewhere on a par with prostitution from a moral point of view' as Beverley Kingston tells in her work, *My Wife, My Daughter and Poor Maryann*. Working women would not take on nursing because factory conditions and pay, as well as self-respect, were far superior to those in hospitals.

Though professionally organised, any profession dominated by women in those days was doomed to have the lowest status and image of women in society at large. The utmost in ladylike behaviour was required before any professional work for women outside the home would be acceptable – even if this behaviour must have crippled many a spirit and crushed initiative in all but the most brave and resilient. When Florence Nightingale sent her first Nightingale nurses to Australia, Lucy Osburn described the women she found acting as nurses at Sydney Hospital as '... dirty, frowsy old women, slatternly, untidy young ones with their greasy hair, with ragged stuff dresses that required no washing. The doctors habitually stamped and raved at them. In the wards the patients called them to do the most menial work for them. The dirt, in spite of all the stamping and raging, seemed ever increasing. The noise and prank in the wards were too dreadful.'

To remedy the public distaste for these women, the Nightingale system had to exaggerate even more acutely the unblemished, drawing-room qualities insisted on for acceptance as nurses. Miss Nightingale had an impeccable background; so must her nurses, if the profession was to succeed.

Equally important were the conditions and remuneration if the service was to achieve status. This took time and constant courage; several of the women who were matrons and senior sisters in the AANS in World War I were in the forefront of this brave march. The popular nineteenth century cartoon of a nurse was 'Sairy Gamp' with her red nose, straggly hair, little black bag and brolly, and this image had to be extinguished.

Everything seemed to be against these magnificent women. Hospitals were regarded as places for poor people to die; any respectable family nursed and buried their sick from home. Antiseptics were scarcely known. Nurses' accommodation was ten women to a room (and they *must* live and sleep in); Prince Henry's Hospital nurses' quarters in Melbourne were known as the Buggery, presumably because of bed bugs tormenting the nurses; Melbourne Hospital was known as the Rattery. Yet these first white collar women, middle-class girls taking advantage of the opportunity to escape from home to a profession, persisted.

It was not until World War I that they achieved the praise and acceptance they richly merited. When this war began in 1914, nurses were working longer hours for less pay and less personal freedom than any female domestic servant would tolerate.

Perhaps the catalyst was a popular song that swept the music halls and was on everyone's lips during and after that war: 'The Rose of No-man's Land'.

# The Rose

*Through the war's great curse,*
*Stands the Red Cross nurse.*
*She's the Rose of no-man's land.*

The Australian Army Nursing Service originated in New South Wales on 13 August 1898 when 26 nurses, led by a 'Lady Superintendent', were formed into the Australian Nursing Service of New South Wales. With their lady superintendent, 13 of these women went to South Africa in 1900 and served in the Boer War as part of the British Army. With the coming of Federation, the Service became Commonwealth-wide as the Australian Army Nursing Service Reserve on 1 July 1902.

The uniform worn by those first gallant ladies brushed the floor – or the dirt, as was discovered by those in South Africa nursing in earth-floored tents – and a huge cape draped over this; a clumsy little bonnet with long ribbons was tied coyly in a bow beneath no-longer-young chins, and another ribbon down the back anchored the bonnet to the wide leather belt.

Some of the nurses setting off in 1914 still sported these outfits, but Miss Oram, the World War I Lady Superintendent, soon had them in the uniforms that have not changed much to this day: grey dress for the wards, with white veil and red flannel cape.

In World War I, 2030 Australian nurses served abroad (with reinforcements bringing the number to 3000) in Egypt, Palestine, the Persian Gulf, England, France, Italy, Burma, India, Vladivostok, Abyssinia and on hospital ships and transports.

The Army Nursing Reserve was established at the invitation of the Army Medical Corps, who suggested to Miss Hannah Glover that she form a reserve of 25 prominent nurses. It was from this reserve that the matrons of World War I were appointed. Hannah Glover was a trained nurse who was director of two residential homes for nurses and the first secretary of the Trained Nurses' Club Ltd, Melbourne. She had been largely instrumental in introducing the Nurses' Registration Act in Victoria to determine the professional status of nurses and protect the public.

The Service was to consist of 'those trained nurses who are qualified and willing to serve with stationary field hospitals and base hospitals when required upon a national emergency'.

The first group of AANS to see overseas service in World War I sailed with the troop-ships that left Melbourne on 20 October 1914, only three months after the outbreak of war, and departed Australian waters on 1 November. When news of the war had arrived, 24 nurses had been chosen from the AANS Reserve and from civil appointments to leave for 'the front'.

At the beginning of the war, many men and women from the colonies went away at their own expense to help bring in the wounded. 'Audrey Chirnside, "a plucky Australian girl", brought over her own car in which she drove the wounded to hospital through hair-raising risks and adventures,' wrote Miss C. Baxter of the International Women's Relief Committee about individuals' efforts in France. Others, already abroad when hostilities began, enlisted. In August 1914, Sister E. McDowell RRC was sent to Serbia with the British Army; she was there when revolution broke out, but eventually escaped to Switzerland.

Also in August, eight Australian nurses enlisted in London and left two weeks later 'under secret orders for an unknown destination' as part of the Lady Dudley Field Hospital. They were nurses Anderson, Armit, Baxter, Byrne, Dalziell, McGregor, McKenzie, and Reay.

Lady Dudley, the estranged wife of a former Governor-General of Australia, had been born Rachel Gurney and the poet, Banjo Paterson, described her as 'a singularly beautiful woman, graceful, and with a voice that had the range of an organ'. While in Australia, she had attempted to set up a chain of bush nurses, but her plan aroused the enmity of doctors and this halted the donations she needed for the scheme; she then returned to England.

When war broke out she called a meeting of Australians in London to form a hospital and then got her hospital across the Channel to France, where it was set up in Wimeraux. Soon, 'all the great consultants of the military medical world made it their meeting place'. Following the disastrous Battle of Mons, the wounded filled this Australian hospital, with stretchers in the golf house and Wimeraux Castle. According to Paterson, 'her hospital was the busiest and most important private hospital on the Boulogne front ... Followed by an orderly with a bucket of hot water, she walked the wards like a duchess and insisted on washing the faces of the dirtiest men'. Banjo Paterson drove an ambulance here for a short time. 'She should have been a general,' he wrote. In 1914 she was awarded the Royal Red Cross (RRC) and appointed a Commander of the British Empire.

Mr Frederick Bird, a prominent Melbourne surgeon, decided to enlist in the Medical Service and form a unit of four nurses; he was joined by Matron Muriel Robertson, who had worked constantly with him in a private hospital. He made all arrangements and the unit departed from Melbourne for Egypt, where they were stationed at Mena House Hospital adjoining an AIF camp.

In 1915, the unit joined the hospital ship *Cecilia* and sailed to Mudros with the transports carrying troops to Gallipoli. The *Cecilia* stood off the beaches and received patients, giving what attention was possible under the very poor conditions. Once the ship was loaded, it shuttled to and fro from Mudros to Alexandria and Malta until that December. *Cecilia* was next stationed at Salonika, transporting wounded and sick British soldiers to base hospitals.

In 1917, it was thought that the sisters should join the AANS, but it was found they were ineligible unless they first returned to Australia. They took the alternative of joining the Queen Alexandra Imperial Military Nursing Service and were sent to the hospital ship *Grantully Castle*, which worked in the Persian Gulf and up the Tigris from Buzza to Baghdad. Later, the nurses transferred to India, North West Frontier, and from there to England, where they served in the Royal Naval Base Hospital. (The small unit was the last of the 'gentlemen's' units to go home when it left for Australia on RMS *Ormonde* in March 1920.)

Along with four nursing friends from Tasmania, Elsie Gibson sailed to war on the *Kyarra*, the first hospital ship to leave Australia. Some nurses had already gone on the troop-ships carrying the early AIF battalions, but on the *Kyarra* were 80 doctors and 164 nurses, and a military hospital for Egypt. On 7 April 1915, Elsie, with six other sisters, joined the famous Colonel Bird and his four nurses plus 'one Imperial Sister' and travelled to Alexandria in Red Cross horse-drawn ambulance wagons. 'Motorboat conveyed us to ship HMS *Cecilia* owned and serviced by the Indian Government.

'We sailed for Lemnos on 12 April and arrived 15 April at 5.30 p.m. In the harbour there were many troop-ships, dreadnoughts. Hospital ship *Indian*, 1st Clearing Hospital. *Queen Elizabeth*, super-dreadnought, Battle Ship *Agamemnon* in harbour. 1st Stationary Hospital on shore.

'*April 23* Ordered to go on Hospital Ship *Gascon*. Sailed into bay nearer Dardanelles: anchored outside. First patients from Dardanelles commenced to pour in ...'

Of the many diaries written during the Gallipoli campaign between 25 April and 24 December 1915, none are greater than that kept by Sister Alice Kitchen. This woman was an original reservist of the AANS when it was formed after the Boer War. When World War I began, she was called up. She was then aged 42. On 20 October 1914, she sailed to war on the troop-ship *Benalla* and among her postings was the hospital ship *Gascon*.

Along with a handful of other hospital ships, the vessel collected the wounded from the beaches at Gallipoli and transported them to hospitals on the islands of Imbros, Mudros and Malta as well as to Alexandria – anywhere, in fact, that could move existing patients out and make room for the vast numbers that were carried from the wasteful battles against the Turks.

In August 1915, when the battles of Lone Pine and The Nek were tumbling the Australian dead, dying and wounded back onto those living who were gamely trying to 'go over the top' to attack the enemy, Alice Kitchen kept her diary. In the summer heat, she nursed down below the ship's water-line and often on deck among the stretchers laid side by side when below decks was full. Dressed in the thick, ankle-length uniform, with compulsory starched collar and cuffs, she worked her long shifts 'until I had all my boys fixed up', then wrote: 'Spent the day struggling with a poor abdominal – in vain. The poor boy died tonight, had no op. He was too bad. If they are operated on they die and they mostly die if nothing is done.'

Day after long day she nursed in the 'tropical heat ... I was in a state of dripping moisture'. She comments that 'The staff is not adequate for the heavy demands on it, especially the night when the wounded always come in. [They could not be moved off the beaches to the ship in daylight.] When I think of all the fuss and bother and all the "technique" we used to have over a clean abdominal operation, I wonder. These poor ones often have to do with such scanty nursing when there is a rush and two or three are urgently ill or even dying, you feel torn in two or three to have to leave them at all.'

And still they came on board, batch after batch of wounded men. 'A busy day as usual ... one abdominal amongst them; quite a huge wound – and awful gore everywhere; two other abdominals in, dying. They seem so hopeless ... a bad haemorrhage leg came in also which looks ominous ... [About thirty] stretchers came in at 9.30 p.m. ... we had to put them on the hatchway. We stayed with a dying man making the third that day and one later in the night. Tonight we were up till late trying to straighten things out a little ... [Then] we took on nine more cases on the hatch, or "the 'atch" as the boys call it, making 40 in all. Got the dressings finished.'

The ship rolled around on their journeys across and back on the Mediterranean and she was always searching for Worcestershire sauce or 'Mothersill' to try to prevent sea-sickness.

Laundering uniforms was a constant problem, as no facilities were provided on these ships. Some days she had several changes of dress: 'A leg haemorrhage, very bad, so much blood in one lot makes me feel sick.'

Whenever she had the opportunity to go ashore, she did her ironing with a box iron – a hollow iron box filled with red-hot coals. It was three months since mail had been delivered to her. On one day, 6 August 1915, she wrote that she saw 'six to eight' hospital ships leaving Mudros Island for Gallipoli. 'Also cruisers, transports, etc. and it looks as if a big attack is to be made.'

Next day, the *Gascon*, with Alice Kitchen and her fellow nurses on board, joined the others at Anzac Cove. 'Five other hospital ships anchored here and one went out tonight, also another as we came in.

'*August 9th* Was awakened at 1 a.m. and told that a large number of wounded were arriving in spite of the fact that about six other hospital ships were in the vicinity. Got up and worked till 4 a.m. Got in 50 or 60 cases, mine all being Gurkas ... all were frightfully dirty and dry and hungry. They say this time ... anything up to 4000 casualties ... At 5 a.m. ... such a cannonade going on I got up and found all the "monitors" and torpedo destroyers banging away at a great rate. During the day we filled up rapidly ... About dinner-time tonight we went over to Imbros Island. Many ships are here and we are to put off all our cases on to transports to go on either to Mudros Bay or elsewhere.'

She comments the next day that they had put through 650 patients in two days, and the men told her that the 'casualties have been frightful. Dead lying about everywhere while wounded have often been 48 hours before being got out of their position ... Truly this is a dreadful war ... more like wholesale murder.'

Even worse was to come. They worked from 7 a.m. until 11 p.m. on 11 August. 'We had often 3 boat-loads of stretcher cases alongside at once and 2 or 3 coming up, and as fast as they moved off another 2 or 3 boat-loads ... the men today are more badly injured and all in a fearful state of dirt, sand, blood dried, caked and smelly all over them and their clothes ... they were simply mown down ... Snipers seem particularly bad also and account for a good many ... No hospital arrangements except dressing stations and those not safe from fire and shells and bullets ... we heard the authorities were preparing for 22 000 casualties so are not surprised that there are thousands already.

'So many septic wounds, so many limbs likely to be lost,' she wrote. 'I have abandoned collar and cape for the time being, as I cannot cope with too much ironing and a collar only lasts 10 minutes in the heat of Mudros Bay.'

After Gallipoli was evacuated, Sister Kitchen was sent to a hospital behind the lines in France. Here, the story was little different from the hospital ship – Australian casualties were great and the wounded came in to her hospital direct from the battlefield.

At the beginning, Australian nurses were under the authority of the British Medical Corps, but Matron Jane Bell (who was later to be awarded the Royal Red Cross) believed their identity as Australians should be preserved. Except for her period of service in World War I, Jane Bell was matron of the Royal Melbourne Hospital from 1910 to 1934. This pioneering woman worked to found the Nurses' Board and the Royal Victorian College of Nursing, and helped to form the Royal Australian Nursing Federation. She had total belief in the ability of women at a time when such belief was not universal and, tactfully yet fiercely, she demanded nursing education and acceptance by the public of the high quality and dedication of trained nurses.

She completed her training at the Royal Prince Alfred Hospital, Sydney, in 1898 then became Night Superintendent there before taking up appointments as Matron of Bundaberg Hospital and Brisbane General. After doing her obstetrical training in London at Queen Charlotte's Hospital, she became Lady Superintendent of the Royal Infirmary, London. From there she returned to become Lady Superintendent of the Royal Melbourne. This hospital was the first in Australia to establish the office of Sister Tutor, the first preliminary training school, the first diet kitchen and diabetic department. As early as 1928, Jane Bell developed a proposal for post-graduate education for trained nurses at university level which was accepted by Melbourne University.

Jane Bell was the statesman of the nursing profession in Australia. Her intelligence, quality of leadership and character were the catalysts that brought about the professional acceptance of the trained nurse in this country.

The conditions of service she encountered in Egypt, as Matron of AGH No. 1, were astonishing, even for that time.

'All members of the AANS are under command of the officer commanding the unit to which they are attached.

'1 Matrons have no independent command.

'2 Matrons will be the medium of all communications of an official nature to and from nurses.'

Jane Bell considered that her status as matron and the compass of duties was decreased by these regulations and suggested that matrons should have greater authority over the domestic and nursing staff in hospitals.

By the time the Australian Medical Corps had reluctantly relinquished their authority over the nurses, Jane Bell had returned to her duties as matron at the Royal Melbourne Hospital and Matron Evelyn Conyers had taken on the negotiations. The AANS would continue to work in conjunction with the British Nursing Service and it was because of the harmonious relationship between Evelyn Conyers and Maud (later Dame Maud) McCarthy, the British matron, that this sharing of responsibilities worked at all.

In 1915, Evelyn Conyers was appointed the first matron-in-chief and took up headquarters in the famous Horseferry Road, London, from where she directed the AANS. By now she had experienced the war her sisters were to live through. She later wrote: 'I remember one day in Egypt when I was driving in an ambulance with both flaps up to create a current of air. In spite of that, the thermometer hanging in the ambulance registered 117 degrees. It was the first time in Egypt's history, I think, that white women had worked through the heat of the day. But there was no time for nurses to take the usual siesta between noon and 4.00 p.m.'

In 1916, she accompanied Nos 1 and 2 AGHs from Egypt to France. No. 1 went to Rouen, No. 2 to Wimeraux. Altogether, there were nine units in France three miles behind the firing line, under constant threat of shelling and danger from air raids, being frequently bombed.

'In France, when she and Dame Maud McCarthy were making a round of inspection of the casualty clearing stations, they came one night to a station whose matron begged them not to remain. It was too dangerous, she said. The enemy was in the habit of bombing them nightly at 9 o'clock. The previous night 10 German casualties and as many of their own hospital orderlies had been killed. The matron had ordered the nurses out into the fields.

'Miss Conyers and Dame McCarthy stayed, and that night three times –

at 9 p.m., midnight and 4 a.m. – enemy planes bombed them.

'They sat out in the dark fields with tin hats and gas masks on. Bombs were falling nearby, and anti-aircraft shells were whistling over their heads and making them duck, though they knew them to be in their defence.

'Miss Conyers had only one night like that. But can you imagine girls working all day, harder and in more terrible surroundings than they had ever imagined, and then waiting every night for the bombing to begin? Often their clothes, hanging in the bell tents that were their bedrooms, were riddled with flying fragments from exploding bombs.

'Nurses were wounded at these casualty clearing stations . . .

'To the nerve-wracking knowledge of personal danger, and the insistent demands upon their physical strength, was added the horror of the wounded pouring in. Sometimes in one room of a casualty clearing station 10 operations would be going on, while 50 men lay waiting at the door for their turn.

'After an attack the members of a surgical team would work for 24 hours on end, stopping only for food.'

Among some remarkable women who graced this Service were Matron E. Gould, who had charge of No. 2 AGH and Mena House, Egypt, in World War I. She had first served in the Boer War. She enlisted in Queensland as Senior Sister of the 1st Division troops and 'made several voyages facing submarines while transporting troops'.

Principal Matron Jessie McHardy White MBE, RRC, Order of St Sava (Serbia), in 1917 took a contingent of nurses to Salonika at the request of the British Medical Corps to relieve the Canadian nurses, and here encountered the armies of frost-bitten feet and fingerless hands in that ice-bound winter.

There was no precedent for these women. No one of their kind had been to war before. 'No history of war for us,' wrote Grace Douglas MID (twice), ARRC. 'We really did not know what war was.' But she learned, all too soon. 'What I have learned was how much could be done under the least favourable conditions, in auxiliaries, hospitals and camps, right on the border line of the Front.'

At Heliopolis, at the great Palace Hotel, she only noted the marble and splendour in passing as she wrote of the wounded coming in from the battles of Gallipoli. 'It was pathetic to see the nurses watching anxiously from the marble and alabaster balconies of the elaborate palace, feverishly scanning the faces of those brought in, afraid to see their own loved ones there, husbands, or brothers or sweethearts.'

As sister-in-charge of the theatre, she saw the men carried in after the evacuation of Gallipoli. There were not enough orderlies. 'Young troops were recruited from the desert.' The wounded came more or less direct from the battlefield.

'The trains ran from the ship's side into the grounds of the hospital and at those times we worked at high pressure in the hot theatre from the time the train came in until the early hours. We were to improvise continually because organisation of supplies was not complete. We became adept at "making do".'

As for Rouen in France: 'We thought we knew what work was in Egypt; here it was doubly hard. Sometimes, as many as 300 men would come in at one time.' She served in hospitals in Amiens near Villers Bretonneux and at a Casualty Clearing Station at Ypres. 'We died in hell, they called it Passchendaele,' the soldiers said of that place 60 years later.

Some women died young, their health undermined as a result of the demands made on them and their generous response. Mary McKenzie Finlay, from a sheep property at Kilmore (Vic.) was such a one, living only four years after her return from France in 1919, aged 53. She had sailed to war on 20 October 1914 with the AANS and, as well as nursing in Egypt, was Matron of No. 1 AGH at Rouen from 1916 to 1918. Rouen was in the midst of the battlefields, its marvellous cathedral sheltering the wounded. 'In our first winter, 1916–17, which turned out to be the worst winter in France for over a hundred years, we had no stoves to keep patients or staff warm and water was short.' Ice covered the window-panes in the huts that served as wards, and sisters worked muffled in scarves, greatcoats and boots.

Matron Finlay was awarded the RRC (1st class) in recognition of her work in Rouen that fearful year. In February 1918 she left for England to become Matron of No. 2 Australian Auxiliary Hospital at Southall, which had been established for the treatment of limbless soldiers, a cruel task for nurses in the days before antibiotics, common pain-killers and modern drugs, surgical aids and procedures.

She arrived home exhausted and was discharged on 26 July 1919, five hard years after sailing away, 15 years after enlisting in the AANS. As Honorary Secretary of the Victorian Trained Nurses' Association and its Council, she worked for the improvement of her profession and the maintenance of high standards of nursing training and practice. Like a number of these women, she wrote well on the subject, and her essay on surgical nursing had been awarded the prize at the Exhibition of Australian

Women's Work held in Melbourne on 23 October 1907. Had she not been exhausted by her war years, Mary McKenzie Finlay might have given much more to her young country.

Some were wounded in battle – Sister Rachel Pratt by a piece of shrapnel in her neck while serving at No. 1 Casualty Clearing Station near Bailleul, and Sister Eileen King with a fragment of shell in her leg. Louisa Bicknell died of septic poisoning in No. 1 AGH in 1915. Sister Rachel Pratt was awarded the Military Medal, ordinarily reserved for men only, for bravery under fire; she had remained at her post as the enemy approached, when she was wounded, and she was later removed to England. Altogether, 13 nurses gave their lives in this war, ten of them Victorians.

Grace Wilson, Matron of No. 3 AGH, was five times mentioned in despatches, was awarded the RRC and the Florence Nightingale Medal and, in 1919, the CBE. On Lemnos Island, she nursed the wounded from Gallipoli and was there when the peninsula was evacuated. Europe followed.

'Teams were organised to go up the line to the Casualty Clearing Stations and I went up in charge of No. 3 Station. My memories are of darkness. We were continually under fire here during any big push and were forbidden to show any lights. When moving from hut to hut, we had to keep our torches turned to the ground. We always seemed to be groping about. There were shortages. Hardly saw sugar, and envelopes were used two and three times over.

'I remember being very impressed with the way the cook served our dinner just as usual, shortly after his cookhouse had been blown to glory. This Clearing Station was first established out of Ypres, but we moved with the line as it advanced or retreated.'*

Like other women, whose diaries and letters describe those fearful years so vividly, Grace Douglas noted the interest that men at war take in women doing everyday things.

'Men, or boys as many of them were, were always dropping in to chat to us. They would watch us as we sewed or worked. It seemed to them ... something normal in an abnormal world. One day, two grubby little privates, very young and speechless with shyness, were persuaded to stay to dinner with us. One of the boys came from Bathurst and one of my sisters, a tiny little thing, was also from NSW.

'I told her to say she came from Bathurst. She sat next to him and in next to no time they were chatting away, nineteen to the dozen. She gave

---

*From reminiscences in the Melbourne *Herald* (undated).

both boys a clean change of clothes from the Red Cross cupboard. Several weeks later, a letter came to the station addressed to "The very little sister in Ward – ". It was just overflowing with gratitude.

'The airmen, whose flying life was estimated to be five weeks in forward zones, came often and we made the costumes for their theatricals. Those boys would sit for hours and just watch us sew.

'We had to get to know one another very quickly for there was always so little time before they would be moved up the line again. At Poperinghe we were continually under fire.'

Matron Gertrude Davis RRC, another who was mentioned in despatches, nursed men from Gallipoli in tents on Lemnos Island. 'First the cold and storms, then the heat and swarms of flies . . .' During the Australian attack on Lone Pine, she was receiving the wounded nearby at Mudros and she wrote: 'The accommodation was primitive for all patients and workers, tents and marquees being the covering. There were no amenities. The weather was cold; harsh winds and blizzards had to be endured . . . a scarcity of medical equipment and no comforts for the wounded men. Food was not only scarce, but unsuitable for the sick. Swarms of flies complicated all problems. Tents were blown down frequently.'

By 1916 she was in India and in 1918 she was the second Australian nurse to be awarded the rare Kaiser-i-Hind, the highest distinction bestowed by India for service. In those years, she nursed epidemics of cholera and smallpox at Doolali, Poona and Bangalore, and attended to victims of a bushfire in southern Persia.

One of the Australian members of the Queen Alexandra Imperial Military Nursing Service (Australia), which many Australian nurses joined in that first world war, was Matron Mary McLean Loughran. She had the rare honour of having her portrait placed beside that of a French *poilu* in the Portraits of the Allies in Luxembourg; she was awarded both First and Second Class Royal Red Crosses, was mentioned in despatches three times and awarded the Mons Medal, having nursed behind the lines in that deadly battle.

Her MIDs read: '. . . was mentioned in Despatches by General Sir Douglas Haig . . . for her gallant and distinguished service in the field.' She enjoyed being decorated at Buckingham Palace, but as for the rest, 'It was like hell'.

At the beginning of 1915, Mary Loughran embarked for France with an Australian government medical team of 20 doctors and 20 nurses.

There, they 'collected wounded from the front line'. On one occasion, after loading wounded on a train, the front carriages were hit by a bomb which killed many of the wounded as well as medical attendants. 'It was terrible. The bomb wrecked the railway line and we were marooned there for a week. We had on board 300 patients, two trained sisters, 24 male orderlies and two doctors. The carriages were converted cattle trucks with stretchers for the seriously wounded, but walking wounded had to sleep where they could. One doctor received a shrapnel wound in the leg, one sister was sent on leave and the other fainted. I was left to carry on ... it was a shambles ...

'In France, we received a lot of poor fellows who had been gassed. I can still hear them calling out for their mothers and sisters, while we tried desperately to ease their lungs.'

Many nurses in this war were called upon to do remarkable things under stress. Some, such as Sister Nellie Isaacs, served in places with names straight out of Rudyard Kipling's novels: Bangalore, Secunderabad, Kirkee and Poona. She was also in Salonika. Sister G. Ross was Matron at Double Amputation Hospital, Southall, England, and her final appointment was to Special Hospital at Watford, as Matron.

In June 1915 the army eventually agreed to accept male masseurs, although they had originally refused them, even when Red Cross had offered to cover all costs of sending two masseurs to Egypt to help hasten the recovery of men wounded on Gallipoli.

By August, when the first physiotherapists left for service in Australian hospitals in Egypt and England, 12 women had been chosen, along with six men. The women were to have the title of staff nurse, the men staff sergeant. In 1915, an Army Massage Reserve was formed in Australia. Ten more therapists were sent off in October that year and one to each hospital ship, the total overseas for that war. Their brief was '... to prevent muscular atrophy after nerve injury, promote nutrition in the tissue of amputated stumps, and prevent atrophy in stiff limbs and contractures of muscle or tendons after bullet wounds.' Altogether, 175 of their members were distributed in army hospitals around Australia. Prior to this war, men and women trained in physiotherapy were accredited by examination by an influential body of high standing, the Australian Massage Association. Most had studied at Sydney University and other university medical schools. In 1919 an army order was promulgated to the effect that the massage service was to form part of the AAMC.

Nurse Mary O'Rourke embarked for India in 1917 and served on the

North West Frontier for six months before joining the Rawal Pindi Ambulance Train, then the hospital ship *Elora*, sailing between India and France. She nursed in France until 1920, when she came to Australia.

Among those who paid all their personal expenses and contributed their nursing on a voluntary basis was Sister A. E. Cassidy. She had trained at St Vincent's Hospital in Sydney, beginning in 1889, and paid her own passage to England, sailing on 6 October 1914. She joined Mrs Doughty Wylie's Imperial Staff in Paris and was sent to Pas-de-Calais, where she spent the war working under the French Red Cross.

Sister A. V. C. Reay travelled to London in 1914 at the outbreak of war and went immediately to the War Office, requesting that she be attached to an Australian Unit. The following week she was in France with the Australian Voluntary Hospital behind the lines where the battle of Mons was being fought. 'Equipment was insufficient, also supplies. The beds were camp beds, nursing was inconvenient and difficult. Food was in short supply, staff insufficient. Wounded were being received from the Mons front, and as a result of the pressure at the front line, a serious condition arose, when the hospital had to be evacuated. The people of the district also fled ... The evacuation of the wounded was right in the line of the retreat.

'There were four days and nights with a minimum of sleep; no water for washing was available. Staff had no possessions, having had to leave everything behind. Finally, the evacuated hospital wounded and staff reached Etaples.'

The Clearing Stations she worked in were constantly and hastily moved from the path of battle. She was awarded the RRC and was mentioned in despatches in 1916.

Matron Ida O'Dwyer RRC was another who was recognised for her outstanding work in Casualty Clearing Stations. 'She was trusted entirely by the surgical teams and accepted great responsibility. She learned to perceive the condition of dangerously ill troops arriving in convoys, and decide the case for immediate surgical attention. In this discernment of the dangerous condition of the troops, she became highly skilled. She possessed stability and endurance.

'Co-operation between all personnel in a Casualty Clearing Station was of a high standard. Duties were shared by all as pressure increased. In every way, nurses, orderlies and stretcher-bearers, all members of the team, proved their will to function, whatever their duties. Sisters were not sent to Casualty Clearing Stations until 1915, and the contribution of the

Sisters was so acceptable in a field that was traditionally accepted as a male area, that they were never again overlooked.'

Another nurse, Lily McKenzie, was the only Australian nurse to serve in the primitive conditions of a Casualty Clearing Station on the Italian front where Australian soldiers were attempting a breakthrough. They lived in dug-outs, nursed in the open and suffered shortages of food, equipment and medicines.

Sister Valerie Woinarski RRC described the British Casualty Station at Vimy Ridge as: 'A tin shed ... erected, camouflaged, and furnished with rows of wooden trestles, upon which were placed stretchers of wounded men awaiting surgical treatment, or rest and nursing before joining a convoy to a base hospital'. In the latter part of the war, Sister Woinarski nursed Spanish influenza patients in Fiskerchen, near the German area. Many patients died in this epidemic which swept the world, including Australia.

Sister Beatrice Mawson, after nursing the wounded from Gallipoli, made 23 journeys on hospital ships from France to England. This Le Havre to Southampton run was dangerous. On one trip, seven ships, including the vessel she was on, left Le Havre one night; of the seven, her ship was the only one to arrive safely. On another voyage between Malta and Alexandria in the Mediterranean, her ship was held up by a German submarine, and on three occasions the enemy fired explosive shells across the vessel's bows and over the wireless apparatus.

'The chief officer of the British boat immediately rowed over to the submarine to inform the commander that this was a hospital ship, and the nationality of those on board. The commander demanded a personal examination of the ship's papers, then permitted the ship to go on her way unharmed after four hours.

'On another occasion, when conveying a boat-load of wounded, 150 Germans were carried with our men, and the fine spirit of chivalry shown by the British Tommies to the enemy was really touching. The Tommies showed ... camaraderie by sharing ... cigarettes and matches, and even lighting the fags for the Germans.'

In 1917, she set off for Australia in the troop-ship *Mongolia*. One morning, as she was playing deck quoits, 'there was a terrific explosion'. She was thrown on her face down the companion-way. The vessel had struck a mine. 'Steam and smoke were issuing in noisy, forbidding clouds, and debris flying about in all directions. Almost immediately the vessel began to sink. The 400 passengers and crew were got off into lifeboats and, within 16 minutes, the *Mongolia* was out of sight with the exception of four feet of mast above the water. At the time, a monsoonal storm was raging and the men rowed for their lives.' After four hours of anxious battling, they sighted the coast of India, 40 miles south of Bombay.

When the mine hit the ship, many were injured and surgical treatment was improvised for several of them. One winchman, who had been scalded, had his burns dressed with torn-off strips of the women's clothing soaked in crude oil. A soldier with a fractured leg was provided with splints made from one of the spars, and again the women gave some of the scanty clothing they wore to pad the splints and bandage the fracture.

The survivors had only a few ship's biscuits and some bananas and coconuts that grew on the promontory, and fresh water from a mountain stream. It was 48 hours before they were picked up by a mine-sweeper and taken to Bombay. 'The appearance of the passengers was odd in the extreme,' Sister Mawson wrote. She wore improvised shoes made from pieces of sail, as well as tattered and stained clothing.

During the final battles of the war, when Australian troops turned back the advancing German army, but suffered crippling casualties in the process, Sister Ella Redman described the Casualty Clearing Station where the wounded and dying were carried or dragged themselves for attention. 'Left 3rd AG Hospital on 22/3/1918 with five other Australian Sisters, met seven other Sisters at station, thirteen in all including Matron, forming the 38th CCS ... Arrived Mericourt about 4.30 p.m. ... on duty by 6 p.m.

'I was put in the Dressing Station with another Sister and Medical Officer. The wounded were just pouring in, abdominal, chest and almost every other kind of wound men walked in with. In a good number of cases the men collapsed and fainted as soon as they got inside. Every wound was dressed.

'The rush was so great that the Colonel gave us permission to mark up the cards as the men were dressed, except in the cases where the chest, abdominal or severe haemorrhage was involved, then the medical man sent as many as possible to the pre-Op. Ward for operation. We had brandy which we gave freely to the men and hot drinks of tea. All that could walk went outside where they had food given to them.

'After we had been there about 36 hours food gave out, splints were finished and we had very little dressings. In many cases of broken limbs, and in some cases where the limbs were just hanging by muscle, all we could do was to bandage as firmly as possible, give an injection of morphia and turn the case into the paddock with a couple of blankets over the patient.

'The men were splendid, not one of them complained ... In many cases, as soon as they were dressed they started to walk, hoping that some of the transport or an ambulance would pick them up. We had very little accommodation, six marquees and two huts in all, from 700 to 1000 stretcher cases in the paddock.

'On the evening of the 23rd between 5 and 6 p.m. soldiers, guns and transport of every kind started to pass our CCS, retreating from the front lines. All the soldiers looked tired out, even the horses looked done. Mingled with the Army were civilians, in many cases the very old folk and children in carts, all absolutely panic-stricken, flying for their lives, the firing and bombardment was terrific.

'About 2 a.m. the Colonel said he could not take in any more wounded as we had over 1000 stretcher cases and very little dressing left, and we could not get a train or any transport to take away our wounded. We had no food and very little water and the enemy were on the railway ... five miles away. It was terrible to see the distress of the patients; their one cry was would they get away before the Huns took them prisoners ...

'On the morning of the 24th, about 4.30 a.m., the Colonel told us to get a small hand case and be in the ambulance in a quarter of an hour's time to go to Abbeville, that they hoped to get a train in shortly and get all the patients away, if not, they were going to stay with them.'

From Abbeville they travelled by train to Amiens, then by ambulance to Corbie. 'We put our beds down and one of the girls went on duty. I went to bed and was called at 3 a.m. ... the wounded were coming in fast. Some of the cases had a pad tied over their wounds with ties, putties, handkerchiefs. There was no Field Dressing Station in front of us, every man had to have an injection of ATS and, in many cases, morphia was injected also ... a severe abdominal case was carried in by four of his pals a distance of ten miles ... hopeless. We packed him with hot water bags, injected morphia; he died shortly after being admitted. The Hospital this time was pitched near the ruins of some old mill. We had our dressing station in a large barn.

'We ... were told not to unpack anything but our beds as we might go any time ...

'At 5 p.m. on the 26th the Ambulance train came and took all our cases away and we were told to get ready to leave for Abbeville at very short notice. Almost immediately two Ambulances came along to take us away.

We were told ... by some wounded that just came in that the Germans were coming over the ridge just two miles behind us, and that all the bridges were to be blown up immediately. As we came through Corbie the village was deserted by all the civilians, only soldiers, guns and ammunition to be seen. All the bridges we crossed were ready to be blown up at any moment. One Tommy rushed to our car and gave us a little canary in a cage.

'As we flew along towards Amiens we could see huge explosions and fires, did not go through Amiens – just the outlying parts, seemed quite deserted. About 8.45 p.m. we could see the aeroplanes over Amiens and the explosions in the air.'

There had been resistance by medical officers in the beginning of the war to the use of nurses anywhere other than in base hospitals. At war's end, Major J. T. Tait, Acting Registrar at No. 1 AGH said of this: 'The outstanding feature of their work through all vicissitudes of administration was that ... they made it plain that they were there to nurse and care for the sick men, and that duty they were going to do, in spite, if necessary, of rules and regulations and military procedure.

'It may be said of nurses, as of all good women, "For surely she giveth her mind to little things and bringeth order out of chaos." Long generations of women stand behind her, many Marthas.'

# CHAPTER 3

# *All Men are Brothers*

'All men are brothers!' was the rallying cry of Henri Dunant to the women of Castiglione in the midst of the battle of Solferino, where the Red Cross had its origins.

When Jean Henri Dunant proposed the formation in all countries of voluntary relief societies 'for the prevention and alleviation of suffering in times of war and peace – without any distinction of race or creed', he was not to know that countries that had not previously suffered from war would take up his challenge, as did Australia in 1915.

Dunant, a Swiss, had been an eyewitness of the battle of Solferino in June 1859, where there were almost 40 000 casualties. He organised aid for both sides, the Austrians and the French. Until this time, camp followers had cared for the wounded, and men taken prisoner had no protection, nor had their loved ones any means of learning their fate.

For his work as founder of the Red Cross, Dunant was awarded the first Nobel Peace Prize, in 1901. From the time he began his great work, which culminated in the first Geneva Conference in 1863, Dunant's child of the heart, the Red Cross, became the best known organisation for helping mankind in war, or peace.

A Red Cross branch, formed in New South Wales before World War I, began under the leadership of Mrs Langer Owen and the patronage of Lady Helen Munro-Ferguson, wife of the Governor-General, who had been closely associated with the British society in England. This branch promoted classes for first aid and nursing. Two days after the declaration of war, Lady Helen made an appeal through the Australian press for support, and by 13 August, nine days after the outbreak, she presided over a gathering at Government House (then in Melbourne), and appointed a central council to direct the affairs of the British Red Cross Society, Australian Branch. The first Annual General Meeting was held at Government House on 25 August 1914. By the end of the year, a permanent secretary, Miss Philadelphia Robertson, was appointed. She remained in that position until 1938.

At first, the Australian army saw no role for a voluntary organisation in an auxiliary capacity – until July 1915, when the invalid transport *Kyarra* returned with wounded and invalid soldiers from Gallipoli. The reception given these men brought forth great criticism of the army from both the press and civilians. There was no organisation for the arrival of such men: transport, food, allotment of moneys, all was lacking. One man, reported the Melbourne *Argus*, was to travel to his home in Melbourne and was given 1s 0d meal money for the journey from Sydney! Worse, so bungled was the disembarkation that prisoners – Australians being sent home for criminal offences and other problems such as venereal disease – were brought ashore first and the crowd, thinking they were the heroes, gave them a heroes' welcome. Later, when the real heroes came down the gangplank, they were ignored by the bewildered crowd. When the truth was known, there was rage and dismay.

By 1916 the newspapers were able to write pages of praise for Henri Dunant's great organisation. 'The arrival of a hospital ship at Melbourne always means a great deal of extra bustle and stir at the various departments of the Red Cross Society. Their Motor Corps, Rest Home at Wirth's Park, central depot at Federal Government House and the Red Cross Kitchen in the Domain each have important work to do for the returning invalids. The Motor Corps sets in motion a fleet of beflagged cars whose owners meet the ship on its arrival and drive the home-comers in procession through the city. On almost every ship there are men en route for other States and the Motor Corps, realising the benefit of a trip into the country for the homesick men, takes them on motor runs amongst the hills where the local Red Cross branches prepare, at a few hours notice, a picnic meal.

'Meanwhile, the Rest Home at Wirth's Park is in a whirl of preparation. Beds are made up and Voluntary Aid girls bustle about setting up the long tables for the extra diners. The central depot is ready for anything on these occasions. Cigarettes, fruit and a liberal supply of the daily newspapers are packed into a Red Cross car which starts off bright and early, so that a representative may be on the pier when the ship draws in. The first request of a home-coming man is for a newspaper, the second for a cigarette.

'The depot phone rings with ... requests for extra beds, blankets and pillows for the Rest Home, comforts are wanted for the men's onward train journey to their homes, or for the sea voyage to Tasmania, Queensland and New South Wales, and bales and cases are rapidly packed and despatched.

'Meanwhile, at the Red Cross Kitchen, parties of ladies are turning out supplies of scones, cakes, sandwiches, jellies etc. which provide a pleasant change of diet on the hospital ship during the voyage around the coast.'

All this was a far cry from the sad experience of those first returning men.

Thereafter, the army could scarcely deny the need for this organisation. In September 1916 they capitulated and agreed to give honorary military rank to Red Cross field personnel who were, in the main, men. But the troops of the Red Cross have always been women. Sewing, knitting, packing, labelling and transporting comforts from every state in Australia, the Red Cross was soon accepted as being able to provide whatever was needed for the care of sick, injured or POWs, with speed and compassion. It could truthfully be said that this service, initiated from the ballroom at Government House in Melbourne, laid the foundations for the present-day operating principles of the Red Cross.

In 1915, a Wounded and Missing Enquiry Bureau was established by Miss Vera Deakin, daughter of the second Prime Minister of Australia. (Later, as Lady White, it was said of her that she had a greater influence than any other single person on the development of the Australian Red Cross.) The first centre was in Cairo; other centres were called for, and by 1916 Vera Deakin and Winifred Johnstone were sent to open one in London and to visit hospitals so that information could be sent back to anxious families. Their habit of taking gifts – cigarettes, fruit, books and playing cards – to the men began the Hospital Visiting Service, which is today a feature of Red Cross in Australia.

Convalescent homes were set up for men repatriated on health grounds, the most notable being on the site of Wirth's Circus in St Kilda Road (now the Melbourne Arts Centre). This also became a training centre for Red Cross Voluntary Aid Detachments.

Early in the war it was found that discharged servicemen needed help, and an Amelioration Committee was formed in 1915. (Today this is called welfare.) In 1917 they pioneered rehabilitation training and, in October that year, established a Farm Training Scheme in the Murrumbidgee area. Also in 1917 they sent 28 blinded ex-servicemen to St Dunstans, the famous blind training academy in England, at a cost of £3 per week. In 1918 they provided occupational therapy.

All this new work, so innovative for the time, cost money, and that was what Red Cross was good at collecting. The Australian public contributed £12 million to the Red Cross during World War I. They were indefatigable. Mrs Eleanor McKinnon in New South Wales encouraged the involvement of children in the case of families of sick or wounded, thus paving the way (with a Canadian Red Cross officer) for the worldwide Junior Red Cross movement, which now numbers some 87 million members in 22 countries.

In 1917 the musical *Zig-Zag* was all the rage in New York and everyone was singing its hit song that took America into the war.

> *Over there, over there*
> *Send the word, send the word over there*
> *That the yanks are coming*
> *The yanks are coming*
> *There's a drum drum drumming in the air* ...

'We were all singing it,' Douska Kahan remembered in 1981, when she was 97 years old. 'I was a young Australian girl over there with my parents. My brother, Harry, had been at the war since 1914. He'd stayed in Australia when my parents set off to the States on business. I decided I would go to France and see him.' And she did. She joined up as a Red Cross nurse, 'rather like the VAD' and left for France with a TB unit.

'We went to the Maginot Line. Hindenburg's men had gone. We were warned not to touch anything as things might be mined. There was part of a man's body in a tree, bits of his clothing where he had been blown. It was a shock for a girl born in Bairnsdale, Victoria, Australia. Then we were up the line. In tents. Undressed on our stretchers as mud *and* rats on the ground.'

Douska spoke French, so she was sent to houses asking for fresh food and milk for the patients. She met the trains coming from the front lines and took food to the men. Then, Paris. 'Harry had sent me a copy of his colour patch, the blue and white of the 28th Battalion. I watched men go by on the streets of Paris and then one day I saw it – three Australian men with blue and white colours on their sleeves. I ran to them. "Do you know my brother Harry?" Yes, they did. He had told them when they got to Paris that if they saw "a little girl in American Red Cross nursing uniform speaking Australian" it was his sister Douska.'

The American nurses were surprised at her behaviour. 'They said, "Fancy running across the street calling to men! What will people think?" I said, "I don't care." I was determined to speak to those Australians.

None of us had a pencil, so one of the Australians lit a match and with the burnt end I wrote my name to prove I'd met his friends.' When Harry got leave he stayed with Douska in her Paris flat. 'The greatest days of the war for me!'

# CHAPTER 4

# Socks, Socks and More Socks

The Australian Army was 10 000 miles from home. It provided the men with no comforts, no tobacco, preventative medicines or extra clothing. In the mud and cold of the trenches socks could not be washed – or dried – and the army provided only three pairs per man on enlistment. To fill the gap, many groups of women – and some men – in Australia worked for the Australian Comforts Fund.

Each state had its division of the ACF. In NSW the division was named The Citizens' War Chest Fund. 'Comforts for the Soldiers' was their unofficial motto as they kept comforts of all kinds flowing to the soldiers in all battle zones. When the army ran short, or exceptional strain occurred, the War Chest distributors sped in.

In the winter of 1916, the troops ran short of warm socks, and General Birdwood, unable to receive any assurance of a further supply from the military authorities, appealed to the Australian Comforts Fund. In an incredibly short time 80 000 hand-knitted pairs were supplied. Again, intense cold and inclement weather made it imperative that the men should have a permanent supply of hot drinks in the trenches. The Comforts Fund came to the rescue with 20 000 Tommy Cookers (small cans packed with sand and petrol). During this trying period, these furnished the only warmth that the men obtained in the front-line trenches. A perfect 'Hallelujah Chorus' was the soldiers' tribute to both socks and Tommy Cookers.

Foreseeing the probability of another winter, 1917, being spent in France, the War Chest and the other state divisions of the ACF made an appeal for socks. In one appeal, the War Chest alone obtained 125 636 pairs. Many women knitted one pair a day – and, remember, wool was sold in skeins and had to be rolled into balls before knitting could begin. Scarcely a woman over 50 today has not asked (or been asked by) someone to hold her arms out for a 'wool rolling'.

In order to secure the utmost effectiveness without overlapping, the various funds had special duties allotted to them. The Australian Comforts Fund was given the zone in immediate contact with the fighting men. Next to it, the YMCA had its own special zone, and the Red Cross looked after the needs of the sick and wounded of the zone at the rear.

The War Chest concern was thus officially with the fighting man nearest the actual line of battle; its duty and privilege was to do all possible to keep him well physically, and to provide him with comforts.

All this organisation involved continuous expenditure, yet the only source of income was the liberal donations of the public – and the works of women. Among the thousands of volunteer workers there were many men, but their numbers were swamped by the women anxious to do something, anything.

There were 226 separate groups working autonomously in areas as far apart as Pymble and Tibooburra, Booligal and Armidale, and sending the results of their labour to the War Chest in Sydney. And this figure does not include sewing and knitting parties, nor the large number of women working alone.

The War Chest Depot at 68 Elizabeth Street, Sydney, was inaugurated at the outset of the war in order to assist the military authorities by providing clothing for the men in camp before the regulation ordnance issues were completed. When that part of its work was accomplished, it was decided to forward clothing and comforts to the men on active service, and in order to ensure a satisfactory distribution, volunteer Commissioners were appointed for that purpose.

The Depot was not so much a sewing room as a distributing and receiving agency for country and suburban branches and work parties. Flannel was cut into shirts and blankets into cap-mufflers all day long by a party of trained cutters, then made into parcels by other workers and sent out to be made up. When the goods were returned, each parcel was carefully checked, each garment and sock overhauled, a few put aside for alteration, and the others sorted and tightly tied in bundles. These were then packed with naphthalene in waterproof, paper-lined cases and shipped to the men on active service in France, Egypt and wherever Australian troops may have been.

The Sock Department formed an important part of the depot. During the quarter ended 17 August 1917, during which there was a special sock appeal, 150 000 pairs were received and sent forward. 'The work is done not for any special Unit or individual men, but for those Australians whom the Commissioners deemed most in need when the comforts arrive at the front.'

The colonel's lady and Judy O'Grady were all involved; some helpers were titled ladies, some were factory workers. Some worked for battalion comforts, some were just knitters, happy to put their name on a slip of paper in the socks they turned out at the rate of a pair a day.

The Soldiers' Sock Fund, Sydney, was formed at the beginning of the war. Its purpose? To help the public realise how important it was to keep our men's feet in good condition, by sending only well-knitted and well-finished socks to them. 'This was accomplished by constant teaching at lecturettes, and seeing that no socks left the Depot until they were made practically perfect. The SSF sent away 20 986 pairs a year and has received numbers of letters from soldiers in the various fighting zones, saying how much good socks were appreciated,' said the President, Martha Jopp. And the Queen Mary's Needlework Guild collected 1200 pairs of socks every month for sailors and soldiers: 'Her Majesty has sent a most gracious message to the knitters of the 3800 pairs of socks sent to the Palace.'

The Sydney Women's Band Fund was lectured at Government House on 'the value of martial music as an incentive to battle'. Soon, on their behalf, Lady Edeline Strickland was able to accept a whole set of band instruments donated by the French residents of Sydney for the 1st Battalion of the AIF.

The women quickly raised funds for another set for the 2nd Battalion. As well as full band sets they sent off mouth-organs, concertinas, sheet music, a fife and drum band set for the Royal Australian Navy and gramophones and records to the Expeditionary Force at Rabaul.

The War Chest was even involved in recruiting campaigns, and members travelled through the countryside speaking, issuing literature and posters where volunteers were lagging.

At the other end of the spectrum was the War Chest Thimble Fund. Mrs Ninian Thomson donated 13 000 white ivorine thimbles, engraved in blue with the words 'War Chest Fund', for sale as souvenirs.

The 226 groups covered many walks of life, many disparate interests. The Oakhampton Knitting Class was formed on 17 May 1915, and had for its object 'the welfare of boys who enlist from Oakhampton', each boy being presented with a parcel of knitted comforts prior to his departure for the front. After his arrival at his destination abroad, a pair of socks or other article was forwarded to him through the post each month. In addition, the class sent special parcels for Christmas, containing knitted comforts, tobacco and sweets.

The Women's Reform League from Maitland sent a 'large parcel' of socks. The Australian Nurses' Gift Fund of Oakhampton sent boxes of comforts to hospitals in Egypt, England, France and Belgium as well as gifts to nurses. Early in June 1916, the committee reported that '... though the class is only a small one, yet during the year the following articles have been made and sent away: 43 night-gowns, 20 aprons, 10 pairs bloomers, 32 suits pyjamas, innumerable collars, washers, bandages, bed sox and knitted stockings.' If we reflect on Sister Kitchen's diary entries, we can readily understand how welcome these articles of clothing must have been.

Every Tommy's Sisters' Circle of War Workers (English women in Australia) worked at Quirindi and sent tins of toffee 'for men in the trenches' among the comforts for the troops. In six months the South Gundurimba Branch of the War Chest sent away 170 shirts, 129 socks, 90 caps, 70 mufflers, 11 pairs mitts, 170 handkerchiefs and 12 air cushions, as well as tins of preserved fruits, vegetables, condensed milk, chocolate and milk, jam, cheese, Bovril, tobacco, cigarettes, ginger and soap. The Tanned Sheepskin Committee made 110 734 sheepskin vests for use by troops in the trenches.

There was even a Babies' Kit Society, which dispatched 125 000 'layettes to little ones in need' in Belgium, France, Russia and Corsica (for Serbian refugees), to Holland for refugees and to British soldiers' and sailors' families. Women and girls and pupils from 150 schools made and knitted the garments. The French-Australian League of Help sent full kits of baby needs to French mothers.

The Blue Gum Women provided cakes and tea for workers at the hospital at French's Forest. The Sydney University Women's Patriotic Society met every morning in Manning House for one hour. Providing sweets for sale at patriotic fetes was one of their activities – mostly for university functions – and their honorary secretary, Olive Crane, reported in 1917: 'Although the time that the women students can give to patriotic work is limited, the following articles have so far been finished during this year: 226 pairs of socks, 142 handkerchiefs, 89 baby shawls, 20 baby petticoats, 9 baby nightdresses, 84 pillow-slips, 470 rolled bandages, 30 cap mufflers.'

Money was raised. The Commercial Travellers' Patriotic Carnival held on 24 May 1915 raised £10 000 at Lismore, which was added to the eggs and other farm produce sent to the central fund by the local women; the Joan of Arc Committee performed a play annually to raise funds to 'help mothers, widows, daughters of dead soldiers'. The old Gold and Silver War Fund collected 'old and broken gold and silver articles to be melted down for sale'. Madame Melba gave a concert for the 'Relief of Polish Victims of the War'.

A Soldiers' Club was opened on 29 March 1915 at 426 George Street; 1000 men a day poured in. 'Those on leave from camp rush in, deposit their kit in the cloakroom, book a bed, have a hot bath, light refreshments, and then set out to their different businesses or pleasures. The soldiers, still weak from the strenuous campaign, pass many hours with their comrades. The Trustees have had the pleasure of watching many of these, highly-strung and over-wrought, gradually regaining health and control, and settling down to civil life again.

'The Club gives special care to the country soldiers and to soldiers from the other States.

'The Special Saturday and Sunday Teas carried out by the Club Patriotic Circles of Girl Voluntary Workers have home-like features.'

Individuals also provided retreats. 'The Soldiers' Comfort Depot, 325 Castlereagh Street, organised by Mrs James Shaw and her daughters, has formed a "home from home" . . . During the first 15 months of the war, Mrs Shaw entertained parties of soldiers at her home, Kingsburgh, Strathfield, each weekend whilst also ministering to the comforts of numerous soldiers on picket duty in the city. This necessitated providing supper for as many as 180 men, and when these were increased to 500, the city depot was opened.

'The depot was supported by Mrs Shaw and her daughters, without dependence on any fund.'

Soldiers' entertainments were arranged by a group led by Mrs Earp, wife of the Hon G. Earp, MLC. By 1917 they had sent 541 concert parties to camps and hospitals as well as sending out lectures and cinema shows.

The Battalion Comforts Fund of the War Chest of NSW cared for 60 army battalions, hospitals and batteries, including the Army Vets Corps, Australian Flying Corps and several light horse squadrons.

When the 19th Battalion left Australia for Gallipoli, they took with them cases of comforts, which were welcome during the initial camping in Egypt. On Gallipoli there was difficulty getting the cases up to the trenches occupied by the 19th Battalion, and for some time the cases lay on the beach, while the men, in their spare moments, could only count them through their binoculars! Volunteers were called for, and two cases were got up. The contents did not go very far, so a bush was made into a Christmas tree and lots were drawn for the prizes – who would make the dash to the beach to rescue the other case. At Lemnos, immediately after the evacuation of Gallipoli, 70 cases of tobacco, clothing, and Xmas billies were distributed among the near-naked men.

In Egypt, the officer who had to prepare the camp at Tel-el-Kebir for the battalions had nothing to use as a shelter for the food and papers, till a few empty Comforts Fund cases were knocked together as a temporary measure. For many months in Egypt, comforts were regularly supplied to the men and when they arrived in France in March 1916, about 20 cases were delivered to them. After the battle of Pozières, where 'more Australians fell dead than any place on earth', the remnants of the battalion had a few weeks' rest, and many more cases containing flannel shirts, pants, socks, cakes, medical comforts, fruit, tobacco and sweets were given out.

Later in the war, the War Chest Commissioners asked all Comforts Funds to pool their shirts and socks, as it was almost impossible to sort the cases at the base and transport them to the different battalions, and this was agreed to.

An idea of the difficulties facing the War Chest Comforts Fund Commissioners, when so many separate crates of goods arrived at the battlefront, can be given by quoting one group alone. 'Since its inauguration in 1915, the 19th Battalion Comforts Fund had sent by 1917 to the front many cases of food, medical comforts, tobacco, soap, private parcels, registered letters, Xmas billies and boxes; also 5388 flannel shirts, 502 silk shirts, 2578 handkerchiefs, 698 warm waistcoats, 5673 sandbags, 7216 pairs socks, 1716 pants, 235 mittens, 340 fly veils, 1669 balaclavas, 83 mufflers, 432 sheepskin vests, 449 muslin vests, besides many other comforts.'

The logistics of delivering similar crates from bodies working for other battalions to the right groups, all in the middle of one battle or another, were formidable.

Linked with this remarkably well-organised War Chest was the Australian Women's Service Corps. Although it was the ambition of the members to use their energies, patriotism, and special training in working nearer the front, it is for their efforts on behalf of the Returned Soldiers at French's Forest that they are best known. Several times their services were offered in England or France. But the French's Forest work was near at hand.

Six women visited the Forest and, impressed with the possibilities of helping the soldiers there, they persuaded about 100 of their women to take the work in hand. They divided into working parties of about 20 each, and for some weeks they went from block to block, clearing brushwood, felling timber and making ready for ploughing. Wielding mattocks, carrying stone, and even building the stone foundations of a large shed for one of the settlers, fell to their lot.

The Service Corps workers now attached themselves to a particular block and worked at it till the task was completed. They got the farms cleared and converted into paying homesteads for the soldiers, working regularly week after week towards this end.

All these varied groups of women continued through the war. Was it patriotism which drove them on? Righteousness in the cause? Boredom? Heartbreak? Or the excitement of 'doing something', no matter how small or ordinary, bobbing around on the eddies at the furthermost distance from the eye of the storm? At this distance in time they may appear to be quaint, their deep, unquestioning belief in loyalty to a country and a cause to be simplistic, but they were women of their era and, as such, they deserve our admiration. Each worked in the way each knew best, taking part in the great events, even at this remove. It was the first time our women had attempted anything like this volume, and variety, and lengthy effort.

# CHAPTER 5

# A Great and Glorious Sisterhood

*Could I e'er cease to hold you in remembrance,*
*To think of you with tender, sad regret,*
*I should not be myself, but some poor changeling –*
*Did I forget.*

The despatch of the first contingent of troops to World War I was attended by considerable enthusiasm. They were regaled with comforts and feted while in camp, and on marching through the streets of their home cities, immediately prior to embarkation, the men were farewelled in the most happy fashion. When, however, the recruits for the second contingent began to assemble, there was an almost entire absence of public interest. One soldier remarked, 'We don't seem to pan out one pennyweight to the ton among the people'. Scarcely anybody visited the camp and the soldiers were left with little more than the comparatively hard military fare (military pay did not permit of luxuries) and practically without entertainment.

In South Australia a small coterie of Adelaide ladies, who had worked for the comfort of the soldiers from the beginning, observing the state of affairs, determined to use every effort to rectify the omission. They were led by Mrs Seager, who 'sprang from soldier stock' and yearned exceedingly to help the 'boys'. A letter, dated 3 November 1914, was written to the Adelaide *Register* and signed by 'The Girl in White'.

'In company with a member of the Military Force I visited the Military Camp at Morphettville on Sunday... Imagine my surprise when I found the camp practically deserted. The First Contingent were overwhelmed with attention and gifts, but the second force do not seem to receive the slightest notice. Surely the generosity of the Adelaide public has not been exhausted?'

In a way it had, or at least the novelty of the situation had gone. The fickle public feed on diversity – or challenge. 'The Girl in White' offered them both.

'Could not some of Adelaide's charming young ladies give up some of their frivolity and exert themselves to provide small comforts for the lads? I can safely assure them that their efforts will not lack appreciation . . .'

The Editor of the newspaper, William (later Sir William) Sowden, added a stirring leader to the same edition. 'Our boys must not be allowed to believe for even one solitary hour that they are forgotten or neglected by the people for whom they have shown their willingness to make the supreme sacrifice . . . Who will form the first Cheer-Up Our Boys Society?'

On the following day a letter written by Mrs A. Seager, and signed 'The Woman in Black,' appeared in the *Register*. 'No longer are the tents piled high with delicacies and comforts. Even the once ubiquitous "Balaclava" has vanished. One incident struck me as pathetic in its resourceful cheeriness. A tent of gallant lads, with evidently strong yearning for a band, made the best of things with an upturned bucket, two mouth organs, and a tin whistle. Several tents seemed to be the joint and proud possessors of a single set of boxing gloves. But there is never a complaint about anything, or a murmur against the monotony of a menu characterised chiefly, as far as I could see, by bread and jam. The *Register*'s suggestion of a "Cheer-Up Our Boys Society" is an excellent one, and I will be very pleased indeed to become a member.'

This appealing letter was accompanied in the same 5 November issue by a further enthusiastic leader. Mrs Stella Baker, President, and Mrs A. Seager (Hon. Secretary) wrote in the same newspaper: 'We are pleased to announce that the *Register*'s suggestion of a "Cheer-Up Our Boys Society" has resulted in the formation of such a body.'

The Cheer-Up Society was not allowed to grow without opposition. Letters to the press by Colonel Blimps (signed with such sobriquets as 'Cynicus' and 'Doubtful') expressed strong disapproval of what they felt was 'unnecessary coddling' of the soldiers, letters from men who had themselves never seen a war as terrible as the one to which these boys were going.

Their complaints were immediately and, for the duration of the war, totally negated by the tens of thousands of servicemen who came to look on the Cheer-Ups as their salvation.

The Cheer-Up Society first met on 5 November 1914 and swung into operation on 9 November, less than a week after inauguration, 'to make the path of the soldier before he left Australia as bright and easy as possible'. Although the little band of women who formed the nucleus of the Society set out with a fixed determination to 'see the job right through', it is doubtful if they had the remotest conception that it would be almost a six-year job, calling incessantly for the most magnificent spirit and endurance.

On 10 November the first Cheer-Up Concert was held. 'It went right royally. When the men asked for more, they got it. The men were lavishly entertained to supper with hampers supplied by the women.'

'How did they do it?' was the enquiry of many hundreds of people when the Society immediately and successfully undertook the enormous task of providing on 15 November at Montefiore Hill, Adelaide, a farewell luncheon to the 2nd Reinforcements, comprising 1053 officers and men. By dint of clever propaganda arranged by Mrs Seager, and assisted greatly by the *Register*, the public provided the cash or supplies within a few days, but there was still tremendous work to be done by the Cheer-Ups, who accomplished their first great task amid general approbation. 'It was shortly after noon that the troops began to assemble at Montefiore and were provided with lunch by the Cheer-Up Our Boys Society,' reported the *Register*. 'More than 150 girls waited on the men. The Medical, Light Horse and Infantry officers were presented with a gift and all men were handed a pipe.'

For a time, the general work of the Cheer-Up Society consisted of providing concerts and refreshments at camp on Thursday evenings and Sunday afternoons. Of these gatherings, an enthusiastic member of the Cheer-Ups has written: 'Shall we ever forget the first Cheer-Up room in the Royal Exchange ... Don't you remember those cheery flutters to the camp, and how the boys ... cheered lustily as you hove in sight, laden with baskets ... of good things ...

'And those impromptu concerts which followed. Weren't they "some"? Did the choruses make the old YMCA tent flap and stir up the dust a treat – too right? And wouldn't the boys – 3000 of them did once – assemble as you left, and roar "good-nights" and cheer up and sing "The Soldier's Farewell" to you?

'Girls, those soldiers were proud of you; they honoured and loved you ... And wasn't it an honour to have ministered to those boys who afterwards scaled Gallipoli's dread heights, rushing to death as if it were a football match?'

Mrs Seager's office in the Royal Exchange Buildings, King William Street, were made the first headquarters of the Society. Here, with her little band of friends and helpers, she laid the foundations of one of the largest and most valued institutions called into existence for the practical assistance of sailors and soldiers. The appeals through the press and private solicitations soon brought responses in money and kind. It is interesting to note in the records what a variety of articles were received from all over the state. For instance, one paragraph of acknowledgement lists: biscuits, cake, fruit, woollen goods, pyjamas, books, boxing gloves, money, writing paper, sweets, plum puddings, a lamb, ox tongues, caps, eggs, pigs' trotters, honey, pipes, cigarettes, tobacco, belts, fowls, ham, mittens, cards, tin whistles, chess and draughts, a gramophone, and cheese.

Mrs Seager's apartments were a busy hive from early morning till late at night. They comprised two rooms which were reached by stairs, and sometimes by lift when the latter happened to be working. Very soon people began to stagger up those stairs with gifts for the boys. The Cheer-Up headquarters would fill up with goods that even flowed onto the balcony. Mrs Seager's famous blue hat could be glimpsed occasionally between chinks in piles of parcels as she sat at her table directing the work. 'Bright-faced helpers' were there to unpack and classify the good things and ready them for the camps.

The soldiers came from every part of the state; many were quite friendless. The fact that the Cheer-Ups were mostly young, winsome girls, full of the sweetness and freshness of youth, added to the attractiveness of the visit. Discipline was a natural quality with those girls; Mrs Seager, with her intuitive insight into character, selected only helpers who were reliable 'from every viewpoint'. The result was that the girls moved among the soldiers with the utmost freedom, and 'the roughest men paid them the most studied respect'.

'The moral effect was most marked, as it brought these men into touch with the highest type of womanhood, and taught them in many instances to view the other sex from a different and unaccustomed angle. Many a soldier gave verbal testimony of the restraining influence of those bonny girls, which caused them to "go straight" where otherwise they would have gone crooked.

'Although no actual favouritism was allowed generally, it was the invariable custom to find the lonely and friendless soldiers and show them particular attention . . .'

Towards the end of November 1914, Oaklands Military Camp was opened and the work doubled for the Cheer-Ups. They decided to provide Christmas dinner for every man in camp. And this was only the beginning.

Money and supplies had to be coaxed from the public, then arrangements for serving meals at the camps had to be made. As many as 3000 soldiers would be fed and entertained on a single afternoon or evening. The food for each occasion had to be packed for carrying eight miles, then unpacked and distributed to the soldiers.

For Christmas dinners the men arranged themselves in groups according to their companies of infantry and light horse. 'The large infantry store tent had been requisitioned as a commissariat department ... It was all like a big picnic of boys and girls, and I doubt not that all of them caught the spirit of the hour ... Hosts of delightful turkeys, the unending lines of meat and hams ... even an apparently inexhaustible supply of Peter's ice-cream. And the historic queen of all Christmas gatherings, the immortal plum pudding! There they were, like enslaved cannon-balls, gladdening all eyes ...'

Mrs Seager once said: 'We cannot go to the front, and there face with them the horrors of the campaign, but we can and will do everything in our power, while they are still near us, to make life brighter for the gallant men who may never more return to South Australia.'

Monster concerts were held to raise funds for their work, for the food and gifts for the soldiers, that is; all the women's labour was voluntary. Stories written by some of them for a booklet published in June 1920 tell a little of the life they led, for life it was. They gave almost their whole week to this work, which meant hard and exhausting 'going' from weekend to weekend. Ladies of leisure found themselves side by side with their sisters employed in offices, who would rush from their daily duties to take up the Cheer-Up burden, often until midnight. Social distinctions went by the board. 'A great and glorious sisterhood was born with the Cheer-Up Society, and it lived and flourished throughout the dreary length of the war.'

Handkerchiefs, pillows, even the instruments for a military band, were supplied to the men. They gave cups of tea and home-made cakes to recruits waiting daily 'to breast the tape' – be examined medically. Twice a week they visited the camps, carting huge hampers with them.

There were few places other than hotels for soldiers on leave to go to, particularly boys from the country. So the Society put up a big tent near the Adelaide Railway Station under the banner 'The Cheer-Up Tent for Sailors and Soldiers'. Here they served food, meals for a nominal sum of sixpence, as well as providing bright entertainment.

The women had their own badge of a flag, wattle and trumpet surrounded by the words 'Cheer-Up Our Boys Society, Adelaide', and troops recognised them in the street, even when they were not wearing their 'uniform' white.

Contingent after contingent of the AIF was enlisted and Mrs Seager, 'the little mother' as she quickly became known, with her helpers worked on in sunshine and rain, dust or slush. The 'boys' trooped in to their concerts and tucked into the best of food. The opening of the Cheer-Ups' Tent on Friday, 5 March 1915, in sparkling sunshine, was attended by tremendous enthusiasm and general success. The Society's booklet describes how 'It was made the occasion to welcome back . . . the members of the South Australian quota of the Commonwealth marines who performed so gallantly in the capture of German New Guinea. The blue jackets marched through the streets (one carrying as a trophy a German flag which was captured at the main wireless station of the enemy) amid the admiring applause of thousands of spectators and then marched into the Cheer-Up Tent . . .

'This was the first formal public welcome home ceremony in Australia to any of "our heroes" who participated in the war.'

When the Minister for Defence, the Hon. Senator Pearce, officially opened the tent later that day, 'He thanked the Cheer-Up Society on behalf of the sailors and soldiers. Many of the men would, before long, be among the grim scenes of war, and it might be that the last thoughts of some of them would be of the love, sympathy, and affection that had been extended to them in this tent where they had been made as welcome as in their own homes.'

Visiting troops and troops being farewelled or welcomed were not charged for meals. The first visiting troop was a detachment of Western Australians journeying through to Broadmeadows Camp, Victoria. These soldiers were delighted with the hospitality shown them at the Tent 'and testified thereto by farewelling the girls with a series of weird, wild-west whoops' which made the crockery rattle.

Any cooking had to be carried out for the most part in the open air adjacent to the tent. The Cheer-Ups perspired or froze, according to the weather, with perfect cheerfulness. A soldier writing from the front remembered Mrs Mary Wallington JP, carrying hot soup from the coppers to the tent on a cold, windy, rainy day, and keeping the rain off the soup with an umbrella. 'How many acts of kindness have you performed for soldiers, soldiers' wives, widows, children and orphans since that day, Mrs Mary Wallington?' he asked.

With the opening of the Cheer-Up Tent, the visits to the camp became less frequent. The tent proved to be of such immense benefit to the soldiers, and so much money and energy were required to keep it going, that the women decided to concentrate on the city effort.

And then the moment came, that second, when Australian women, for the first time, knew war. News was received of the landing on Gallipoli. The first casualty lists were posted.

The Cheer-Ups, like thousands of other wives, mothers, sisters and sweethearts, were seized with apprehension because most had a loved one who was likely to have taken part in the great battle. They went about their work with cheerful faces, because it had early been established as an unwritten Cheer-Up law, that no matter what happened, all would, for the sake of the boys, 'pack up their troubles in their old kit bag, and smile, SMILE, SMILE!' Their boast was that this rule was never departed from (except in very isolated instances), although many a time the smiling face hid a wounded and aching heart.

Their President, Mrs Baker, had word her husband had been seriously wounded. How serious? One never knew. One worked on.

They had little time to weep. On 8 May 1915, the 27th Infantry Battalion was to be farewelled. Coming so soon after the news of the landing, the event brought forth the now more excited populace. The tent was not big enough to hold so many men, so the whole battalion – 1700 men – marched into the Exhibition Building amid 'a rapturous welcome from the Cheer-Up ladies'. Bands played, the galleries were thronged with the relatives of soldiers, food was never more plentiful – even to red, white and blue jellies.

The Governor spoke: 'You are going to tread in the footsteps of men who, as we have read in the past few days, have covered themselves and Australia with honour and glory.'

And then, at this largest public farewell to soldiers in Australia to date, Mr Sowden of the *Register*, now President of the Society, proposed the toast which, in some form, is perhaps as old as humanity, but which had been freshened and rendered more keenly poignant to Australians since 25 April 1915: 'I am going to ask you to perform the most solemn task that can be set to any mortal man. I am going to propose to you a toast which is hallowed by every sacred thought which can be imagined. I am going to ask you to drink to "Our Heroic Dead".'

> *They are gone we loved so well –*
> *God accept them, Christ receive them.*

The whole company stood and the solemn notes of 'The Last Post' resounded through the hall. 'The toast was drunk in silence, and repressed feelings found vent in a long-drawn sigh, which went whispering sadly through the building.'

With the slow despatch of the time of casualty lists, no one in that hall yet knew how their own 'boy' had fared. Whether he was alive or dead, wounded or well. Only through thinking on this can we hope to understand the strange dichotomy of the times. When war comes, men must go and, ultimately, they must die, or return maimed. Could a community remain sane if they dwelt on the stupidity, the inevitable obscenity of war? We will never know, because with the outbreak of war, an outbreak of fervour for the homeland and hatred for the enemy explodes.

It is easy for us, at this remove, to smile at letters from an earlier age, but one cannot doubt the effect these pretty, bright, cheery girls had on men who had known them. *Egypt, 2 April 1915*: 'The 9th Regiment is quite settled at Mena camp; on the East are the Pyramids and the silent Sphinx. I thought as I stood on the historic site of the Temple of the Sphinx, that it would simply be heavenly if some magical force would waft over the bonny girls of the "Cheer-Up" Society for just one moonlight evening by the mighty Pyramids. There are might, mystery, and majesty in the Sphinx and the Pyramids. It needs our dear Australian girls to add beauty to the scene. The age of chivalry has not passed. I believe that today many (in fact, all) of the boys will fight better because they know that they have got such treasures to fight for. I do not think that one man of the 9th will be sent back for disease or drunkenness. They are trying to play the game, and I earnestly pray that the mothers of the good fellows will have reason to be proud of their boys. Cairo is the wickedest city on earth, but we are trying to keep them straight. Good-bye. God bless the dear girls of the C.U.S. May they not be weary of well-doing. Their influence is greater than they think.'

We have no reason to doubt the final line. The figures for venereal disease among troops in Egypt were high. Perhaps the memory of those white-clad girls remained in many a man's eye and protected him from the ravage for which there was no sure cure.

Eventually the Society had to move to Bentham Street to larger quarters, the Cheer-Up Hut. Eighty suburban and country branches were formed. This brought in money and hampers of food and to some degree relieved Mrs Seager of her constant search for funds as Secretary-Organiser, General of the Commissariat and Deputy Storekeeper-Quartermaster.

As well as raising funds for the by now vast numbers of men enlisting,

Mrs Seager planned a day when the civilian population would wear a violet 'in memory of boys who gallantly gave up a precious life for love of country'. The first such day was held on 2 July 1915 and bunches of violets and commemorative buttons were sold. Up country, at the Burra, one spray of violets was sold for £384. (The Burra, on occasions, provided the whole of the food for functions at the Cheer-Up Hut.)

The women were indefatigable. Boys wrote and asked for items and, whatever they were, the women procured them. They sent trench periscopes. They sent tobacco, cigarettes, writing materials, bugles to all battalions they were in contact with. No mail boat left Australia without some articles of comfort and cheer on board from the Society for their soldiers.

When the time came for the girls to meet the first of the returning wounded, Mrs Seager said: 'It is up to us to show the boys that we can display a brave front, no matter what occurs. It will be hard enough for the poor dears to bear their troubles without our augmenting them by showing any weakness.' Sometimes that was not easy when the wounded men walked, limped or were wheeled and carried into the Cheer-Up Hut.

Among the officers who had originally helped the Cheer-Up women with their first visits to military camps, some were wounded, some were killed. When Lieutenant-Colonel Miell was killed in action, the ladies were despondent until his widow came to the Hut as usual with her big smile. 'Many other women are being similarly affected every day,' she said. Then the real blow fell. Mrs Seager's son, the youngest of her three sons at Gallipoli, was killed. She carried on. 'It is only my duty,' she said.

These women did not go unscathed in the public arena. There were comments, slanderous statements, smutty remarks, both written and spoken. Mr Sowden, when opening yet another new Hut on 16 September 1915, referred to this. He had personally investigated every charge against the Cheer-Up Society ladies which had been brought to his notice. In two cases only was he able to trace the stories to a tangible source, and in these he found that the aspersions, originating in jealousy, had been magnified into 'baseless, infamous lies'. He told his audience that the Cheer-Up women and girls represented all the respectable and honourable classes of society, and were some of the finest and kindest women in the world (Cheers) including mothers of soldiers who were fighting at the front, wives, daughters and the sweethearts of their honoured warriors.

He closed his speech with a warning that if, from that time onward, similar charges were made, legal remedies would be taken, without the slightest reservation.

A returned wounded soldier, Pte Harris, later expressed contempt for the persons who had slandered the Society's members. 'If any of the wounded soldiers hear anything against the ladies of the Cheer-Up Society,' he continued, 'thank God most of us have one arm left with which to protect the women.'

These attacks on the Society had the fortunate effect of bringing it into the 'limelight', where its splendid work became more evident to the public. Each attack thus brought needed support in the form of money, goods and sympathy, for the large numbers of soldiers visiting the Society's rooms imposed a severe strain on finances.

The number of men the ladies farewelled was truly stupendous. On 16 October 1915, they fed and sang to 2300 reinforcements. For several days the women performed tremendous drudgery, gathering goods, cooking, washing and cleaning the Hut then decorating it, and they were all at the Hut, at their posts, dressed in their white dresses to welcome the soldiers and wait on them.

Their example brought in many gifts for the soldiers, including a 'splendidly appointed' motor ambulance donated by an outback sheep station. The country areas rallied round and the little town of Burra was so splendid with its donations that the main hall of yet another and bigger Hut was christened Burra Hall. (They had collected £1300 to help build the Hut, almost half the required amount.) On the day this was opened, 70 girls from the Burra Cheer-Up Branch rode on 'magnificent' horses through the main streets of Adelaide, 'enticing shillings from the public pocket'. By the end of 1915, the town had raised £13 968 for patriotic funds.

On 12 November 1915 the Cheer-Ups farewelled a band of nurses leaving for the front, and presented them with a cheque for the purchase of comforts for the voyage. Only five days later, a farewell was tendered on behalf of the Peterborough Branch of the Cheer-Up Society to the 12th and 13th Reinforcements of the 9th Light Horse Regiment, in which that town was particularly interested. 'My chief recollection of that evening was the lively singing – except for that song which was so popular at the time, and was always rendered with great feeling: "Keep the home fires burning . . . till the boys come home".

'Yes, in many cases the home fires were burning brightly when the boys came back: but, alas! in too many others they burnt out prematurely, and nothing but the sad ashes of memory remained.'

Whenever the larder became dangerously depleted, some generous donor always showed up with the necessary relief. At the end of November 1915, a Mr Wade sent 80 fat sheep down from his station and the meat problem was solved for a time. Country hampers were also of the greatest help at periods when there was a lull in revenue returns. The average monthly meat bill (excluding gifts from country branches and elsewhere) was then £300 and the total expenses were about £500 a month. Without the regular hampers from the country branches, the total would have been nearer to £700 per month.

Home-made jams and preserved fruits, dairy butter, bacon, chickens galore, pickles, sauces, brawn, fish and many other products of this bountiful land were donated. 'Gosh, this is Mount Pleasant butter!' once exclaimed a soldier, as he attacked a rich yellow pound. 'I can tell the taste of it, and I know the cow it came from!'

About 10 000 meals monthly were being served in the Hut, apart from the farewells and similar functions. The exhausting day-by-day regularity, together with the frequently interspersed farewells and other large functions, rendered the task at times gargantuan. Often a large gathering would terminate at eight o'clock, but it was another three hours before the Cheer-Ups could finish washing and drying the dishes. A farewell to one thousand men would involve the use of at least 3000 pieces of crockery, and 4000 pieces of cutlery and spoons! It was common for girls to be on duty for 13 hours continuously, and they stuck it for years, smilingly and uncomplainingly; they were proud to do it. Troop trains from Melbourne arrived between midnight and daylight, but the girls were always there.

Early in 1916, the South Australian Returned Soldiers' Association held its first meeting in the Cheer-Up Hut. Mr Sowden was elected President and Mrs Seager one of the Vice-Presidents, until fit returned men could succeed them.

By June 1916, Mrs Seager was the butt of public criticism – but mostly because she was a woman. She had been appointed a salaried officer of the Society. She averaged about 12 hours a day in that Hut, and was there every Sunday, too; and her salary was hardly commensurate with that which would be paid to a man in similar circumstances. For every £100 received, £95 10s 0d was devoted to the interests of the boys, and the remainder (about 4½ per cent) was her salary. That was much below the ordinary rate of commission.

Mrs Seager had been forced to relinquish a lucrative business in order to continue her self-sacrificing work for the soldiers. Recognising that her genius for organisation, her tact and diplomatic skill, were essential for the successful carrying out of this vast scheme, the Board of Management decided to pay her a nominal salary; from a business viewpoint, the position of Manager of the Society, with more than 80 branches, was really worth considerably more.

She personally welcomed thousands of lonely men to the Hut – Cook Islanders, New Zealanders, sailors, Frenchmen on a convalescent journey. It was the splendid vision of this woman that made the Society great. She had no humbug about her.

The 1916 Christmas saw surprise expeditions to military camps (as well as the sumptuous spread at the Hut). Everyone, including the guard and men in the 'clink', was entertained. By 16 January 1917, more than 25 000 men had passed through the Society's hands. Few groups from so small a population could have done more.

One day, 400 men had just been fed in the Hut when word came that another 600 were arriving from a ship. They were all cooked for and waited on. Another day, between 2.30 and 7.00 p.m., 3500 hot meals were served – all at sixpence a meal. The building was constantly filled with wounded soldiers to feed. Nine hundred soldiers on their way home to the eastern states by hospital ship were entertained one afternoon: 'All of these poor fellows were more or less wounded or ill.' (The Hut had erected a chair on a hoist to lift men who could not negotiate the stairs.) Another day, soldiers from a hospital ship ate 130 lbs of sausages, 50 lbs of bacon, 50 legs of mutton and 40 gallons of milk, as well as cake and fruit. Each week, 5000 meals were provided, totalling approximately one million during the war. On Anzac Day 1918, all soldiers who took part in the march were fed with ham, chicken, plum pudding, cakes and fresh fruit sent down by country Cheer-Ups.

Funds were always stretched beyond the limit, but the quality never flagged. The helpers received no pay and had to supply their own uniforms, but were regimented as if they were 'on service', as indeed they were. They were drilled, had to sign on and off, and their uniforms were inspected by Mrs Seager. There was no such institution in any of the other states.

As the years went by, each with its farewells to the boys, and the receptions and the welcome homes for the wounded, the walls of the Hut were covered with memorial panels erected by relatives of the dead, officers and ranks being side by side as that unforgivable toll rose. Finally, 500 portraits of 'heroic sons' of South Australia, plus 1500 pictures of various companies and units who had been farewelled or welcomed in the Hut and hundreds and hundreds of names of dead boys were inscribed on tablets in the building.

And then came Armistice Day. The returned wounded soldiers and sailors assembled in crowds at the Cheer-Up Hut all day long. Meals were in progress from breakfast time until the supper hour, and the 'ever open door' welcomed the men to a proudly bestowed hospitality and service. The girls had a long and arduous day, and the heat was trying, but while there were heroes to serve, no one considered physical weariness. That war had taken its toll of strength was seen by the crippled forms and delicate faces, but the universal brightness of all the men – some still hospital cases – was a happy omen. The orchestra of girls played throughout the day – some of them had played regularly for the four years of war.

On Sunday, 25 November, 100 Anzacs on furlough from the front arrived. Three hundred Cheer-Ups formed a guard of honour for the motor cars of Anzacs to pass through. Across the incomplete Anzac Arch, decorated with flags and flowers, was written the inscription, 'Thank you, Anzacs, from the Cheer-Ups'. It was a wildly exciting and historic scene as these men returned to their homes after long years away.

War's end did not close the Hut, nor did it dampen Mrs Seager's and the women's enthusiastic service, although their energy was severely taxed by the arrival of soldiers from transport after transport.

Often there was little warning. A wireless message was received one day that 700 invalids from abroad would arrive in a few hours. The weather was insufferably warm. Said Mrs Seager: 'Now, I wonder what those poor boys would like? I have it, milk – iced milk!' And when those soldiers came into the Hut, hot, weary and many rather weak, they found the cold, fresh milk awaiting them. 'This is our first taste of Australia for four years, and by gosh it tastes good!' said one. One can imagine what the Hut meant to these men, as it did to thousands of others, after their long voyage around the Cape, and the monotony of transport fare. 'Our first taste of Australia for four years!' It was feared that the intense strain of these last months would be too much for many of the women; but, having seen the boys off to the fight, the 'sisters' were determined to be there to welcome them back in victory.

The Hut was formally closed on Christmas night, 1919, but with the proviso that it would be re-opened, should any stray transports put in at Adelaide.

Sixty-five thousand soldiers had been entertained during the final six months, and the expenses were as high as £1600 a month. On the last day there was a splendid Christmas dinner for all soldiers, and in the evening a farewell social and concert were held. The Premier (the Hon. A. H. Peake) arrived in the afternoon to express the thanks of the Government to the Society for its colossal work so faithfully performed. The Defence Department recorded deep appreciation: '... for the magnificent services rendered ... by this splendid body of lady workers in the interest of our fighting men, both of this and other States. It would be a difficult matter to express in fitting terms what we all owe to the sacrifice and unflagging efforts of the ladies ... We will never forget their goodness.'

The Cheer-Ups did not forget either. 'One loves to dwell on those days in the earliest military camps. A sweet essence seems to linger in the corridors of memory as along them re-appear the scenes of training of those gallant men who first made Australia a proud name among the nations. The laughter and wit and surging vitality of those debonair Aussie boys! Can one ever forget them?

'It was at Morphettville that a young trooper who had not quite completed his riding lessons rode past the Cheer-Ups with the air and seat of a commander of cavalry. Something startled the horse, which plunged a trifle, and the soldier suddenly vacated the saddle, curved gracefully in the air, and arrived on Australia on the summit of his hat. "Oh, he's killed – he's killed!" said somebody; and so he ought to have been by all the laws of accidents. But he sat up, removed his hat, and taking half a cigarette from behind the hatband, calmly lit it. "That just reminded me I had a fag in me 'at," he remarked.'

The Hut was specially opened a number of times after Christmas, 1919, to welcome home the 'bride ships', with soldiers and their English wives and babies. Once Mrs Seager received a wireless from a transport approaching the state, stating that there were numerous soldiers' babies aboard, but no babies' food. When the transport arrived, a large supply of babies' food was waiting on the wharf 'with love from the Cheer-Ups'.

It was a service by one of the finest and most representative associations of good women ever known in this country – or any other – led by a woman the like of which few countries see. In the most restricted of ages, Mrs Seager went against all propriety of the time by admitting to and putting into action her belief that nothing cheers a soldier so much as the sight of a pretty, laughing girl. She founded and managed an organisation on a scale which few hotel managers of international standard could successfully run. That 'great and glorious sisterhood' that she created with the Cheer-Ups was something that has rarely since been emulated.

> *And it isn't always heaven when they wash up all the while,*
> *But the Cheer-Ups do it smiling, for they're soldiers' girls and wives.*
> *And it's smile, and keep on smiling though their hearts be fit to break,*
> *There are some would not be smiling if they knew what Fate could tell,*
> *Of a soldier who will never, in this world again awake –*
> *Of a lad who trod to heaven by the blackest roads of hell.*
> *There are some whose smile is weary, but there's pride behind the pain;*
> *Like the lads who went out laughing, they will grit their teeth and smile!*
>
> *Tho' the sacrifice be heavy, we would make it o'er again,*
> *For your honour lives for ever, and our life is but a while.*
> *So it's scrubbing floors, and scouring, and not heeding what is said.*

# CHAPTER 6

# *The Yearning Heart*

*Keep the home fires burning,*
*Tho' your hearts are yearning*
*Tho' the lads are far away*
*They dream of home.*
*There's a silver lining*
*Through the dark clouds shining,*
*Turn the dark clouds inside out*
*Till the boys come home!*

The more destructive the war became, the more people were fascinated by it. Hundreds of charitable organisations were set up to raise funds for anything and everything – £13 802 301 was raised by 'Patriotic' funds ranging from the Sandbag Fund to Xmas Billy loans and Cheer Fund, War Horses, Belgian Nuns, Belgian Canal Boats and Tobacco for Troops Fund. The 'gifts' ranged from aeroplanes to motor transport to the 'comforters' women knitted along with woollen arm-stump socks. War fever had reached its highest pitch.

Muriel Mills wrote on 16 August 1915 to her brother Roly on Gallipoli: 'My own dear old brother, I do hope you are still quite safe. A lot of the boys have come home and, poor fellows, they are such wrecks. Did I tell you what a great day Australia Day was here? It will always live in the memory of Australians. I think there was the biggest crowd that ever was in Melbourne before, and the wounded soldiers – well, the people fairly threw the money at them. It was great.'

This excitement conrasted sadly with the experience of the young boy 'over there'. Later, in France, young Roly saw how 'at every village we passed, the people were out waving handkerchiefs to their lads, welcoming them home on furlough. It made me realise I am away from home ... When we got to London wounded and saw all the English Tommies meeting their mothers, sisters, brothers and friends, we Australians realised a little more that we are far from home.'

Although the South Australian Trooper H. H. Moule, of 3rd Light

Horse, was obviously delegated to write a thank you letter for gifts received, he gives a spontaneous picture of the excitement when a parcel from 'home' arrived. He writes from 'somewhere in Palestine', June 1917: 'Dear Miss Fenton, Our advance over the desert was hard and wearisome with very little water, but now we rest on hard ground and can look back on the glittering sand that so tired us. A good many of us would not say "no" to a spot of leave in Australia! I have been a soldier since 1914.

'I wish to thank the ladies of our Trench Comfort Fund on behalf of the boys and myself. Although we are doing our bit, everyone of us recognise that our womenfolk are doing theirs grandly, in fact more than we ourselves, as we do see the excitement and serious things of this war face to face, you never do. Everyone is more or less disgruntled and tired of everything, then – word comes through that parcels or cases of gifts have arrived at the Rail-Head. A limber of camels is at once despatched and the Treasure carted out to the Regiment; in the meantime everyone is asking "Is it true a consignment of gifts is coming out?" A reply in the affirmative soon brings a smile to their faces and we are again reminded of our friends far across the sea – the 3rd L.H. Comforts Fund – then they arrive, are divided out, and a right royal feeling it is to insert the tin-opener into a new tin of *Australian* fruit. Perhaps a Stunt is on tomorrow but suddenly everyone is in a good mood or, in other words, an army fights on its stomach and that's the way the women of Australia are making it very hard for Jacko in Egypt and the Hun in France!'

Lady knitters were slipping notes into the neat toes of woollen socks, and children at school were being encouraged to write to 'our brave soldiers'. From Diamond Creek (Vic.) a child wrote in July 1916:

'Dear Soldier,
  'How are you today? I think you might be lonely so this is to tell you that I am thinking of you. I am 8 years old. At school we sing a song about our brave soldiers and ask God to send them home to us again. Thank you for fighting for us. I pray for you each night. Good bye.
  'I remain, Your loving friend, Norman Bass.'

It was difficult to know what to send to men so far away. Australians had had no experience of war – *no one* had experience of a war such as this one. In their desperation, mothers packed everything they felt their boys might need. Higham Pepper, who was to die at Villers Bretonneux near the end of the war, wrote to his mother at Nar-Nar-Goon about parcels;

the most recent one had contained malt biscuits, a towel, sugar, sardines, dried apples, a pair of grey socks and a flannel washer [face-cloth]. 'Thanks very much for them. Still, what I said before about only sending socks and handkerchiefs, tobacco and perhaps a few cigarettes still holds good. I will say again, that is all I wish you to send. Fly nets are useless. Socks get a hard time here. This game is "rough on them".'

The men got tinned meat – bully beef – until they were sick of it, also sardines, sometimes dried fruit and sugar; by the time biscuits arrived, they had crumbled and softened. The number of parcels sent was enormous – we will never know to the nearest thousand. But what else was there for women to do in between waiting for *that* name to come up in the casualty lists. And so the women waited – for the telegram, the visit of the minister or the priest. 'Some women wouldn't open their doors to a clergyman during that first war,' my grandmother, Isabella Adam-Smith, told me. 'I had four boys away, and when I hadn't heard from your father for some months I used to stand at the side of the curtain peeping out the corner of the window so no one would see me watching the road. I was waiting for Mr Nancarrow, our minister; for days I expected him. He did come, and I saw him walk up the hill and look straight at our house. He couldn't see me behind the lace curtain. I must have closed my eyes for the next thing was I saw him go into Mrs Mason's place on the other side of the road. I sat down, plonk! on the settee, I was so drained out. Then I thought, poor Mrs Mason's Harry, that's who it must be, and it was. Mr Nancarrow came and knocked on my door after he told her and asked me to go to her. When the minister did come for me – three times he came – I knew each time which one of the boys it was.'

Such was the burden of their work in World War I that clergymen asked that the task of 'breaking the news' be lifted from them in World War II. 'Mr Nancarrow said that it interfered with his work among his parishioners; he would not visit people because the very sight of him coming up the road made women faint with fear of his knocking on her door.' (In World War II army telegrams and letters were used to inform next-of-kin of wounding or death.)

Not all women in the 1914–18 war had the comfort of a clergyman at that most awful moment. My other grandmother, Brigid Adams, living in an isolated part of the Gippsland hills (Vic.), merely received a card with her two sons' names filled in on the dotted lines and the word *missing*. Every six months or so a Catholic priest rode out to say Mass in a small hotel-shanty in the hills and at these gatherings she would go to the other women in the congregation and say 'Is your boy missing?' My mother has told me that grandmother never understood what it meant.

'The women are capable,' Gilbert White, Bishop of Willochra wrote in 1916, 'used to making the best of things and not daunted by difficulty. What an opportunity the war has brought to us. One almost shudders from fear that we should neglect to take advantage of it.' Maybe, but the 'best of things' had never before included the sacrifice of sons.

> *They are sand in Egypt*
> *The wind ruffles the meads in France*
> *And the flowers dance above Australian earth that feeds them;*
> *They lie mingled with the old dust that set up Asian empires.*
> *Australia, thou'rt written now into the chronicles*
> *Of these kingdoms forever.*\*

Even women without sons to give to the 'chronicles of these kingdoms' felt deeply for the young men. ' "They are some mothers' sons who answered the call", the Misses Williams say,' wrote Matron Alma Hancock on 3 February 1916 of the Misses E. and V. Williams who, during World War I, formed themselves into the 7th AGH Hospital Helpers at Keswick (SA). 'On so many occasions I have seen them carrying heavy baskets on extremely hot days down the dusty Bay Road to the hospital.

'The Helpers always come at the time they are wanted with just the things our men need. Many times they have helped us with extras when we have not known what to do. During all weathers they are consistent in their self-imposed duties.'

When war broke out in 1914 these two sisters 'commenced . . . war work by visiting the military camps twice weekly taking cakes and woollens – at our own expense – to boys who had neither friends nor relatives. At Christmas, 1914, we collected 1000 handkerchiefs and delivered them to the reinforcements of the 10th Infantry and 3rd Light Horse. We continued our camp work until 1915 when the boys began to come home sick and wounded.

'We then learnt from the Matron at 7 AGH Keswick that the hospital needed steady helpers who would not grow tired of the work; we at once organised a small band of six helpers including a President, Hon. Sec., and Hon. Treasurer. Three of our helpers found the work too strenuous and

---

\*'Australia's Dead', William Blocksedge.

dropped out, leaving my sister and I to do all the actual work, our Secretary still continuing in his role. [Many women, while doing the actual heavy work as well as most of the intellectual planning, were still impelled by their conditioning to employ a male office bearer.]

'For the first 6 months we had ourselves to carry the heavy loads of cake, fruit, jellies, etc., in all weathers. When some of our friends saw what we were doing they came to our aid with their motor cars and relieved us of much heavy strain. As well, at that time, we were doing work that was later undertaken by VADs. At our own expense we also sent garments to Belgian children, whole outfits for war babies, mufflers to the men of the fleet, parcels every other mail to the trenches; we assisted motor ambulances and orthopaedic associations for 4 years and took days on duty at the Red Cross Rest Room.

'Since we started our work in 1914 we have continued without a break, never taking a holiday and still working,' they wrote in 1925.

'We visited the hospital twice weekly . . . We commenced our hospital work with £12 8s 0d in cash but it did not go far and we decided it would be necessary to raise £20 per month to continue to provide delicacies for patients. We then started what we called our "route march", walking miles every month to collect a few pounds.

'Finding this would not give us the sum we needed, we organised and held concerts, continentals, etc., and kept going. We supplied each ward with dainties, taking them ourselves from bed to bed.

'During the epidemic of Meningitis and Pneumonia Influenza we kept on steadily . . . We had sometimes to tramp the whole city and some of the suburbs to procure bananas because some of the patients cared for no other fruit. Up to the close of 1919 we were wholly responsible for the funds, also for procuring the food. Since the beginning of 1920-22 we have been financed by the Red Cross Society.' And so, these great little ladies stuck to their task to the end.

One can learn much about women at home by reading the letters from their sons, brothers and husbands at the battle fronts. These carefully treasured letters unintentionally picture for us the man – or boy – and what he meant to his people back home.

Private Henry Higham Pepper left for the war in October 1915, aged 21. This bush boy from Gippsland, Victoria, wrote regularly to his parents, the Reverend Henry and Mrs Pepper, and his sisters Ivy and Elsie. From Broadmeadows (Vic.), just before his departure in October 1915, he wrote 'I allotted you 4s 0d a day. I draw 1s 0d and 1s 0d is deferred till the end of the war. We never expect to see it though. It is said some have not got theirs from the Boer War yet ... Now mother – *please remember* a large number of soldiers' letters go astray on their way home so *do not worry*. Please number your letters and I will number mine. Thank you for the Testament. I nearly cry every time I open it. You look very sad in the photo.'

On board the *Ulysses* on the way to Egypt he fills a page with names and regimental numbers. 'The fellows in our section are sending home the names and numbers of each of us so that friends or people can watch for them in the casualty lists.'

*Egypt:* 'Some chaps have had no word from home since they left. I do not feel far from home. The regular letters and papers have a lot to do with it.'

*France:* 'Old Fritz takes a bit of shifting. I will be glad to get back to "Civvy" clothes and never change them again.' In the fearful winter of 1916 he scrawls, 'my hands are so cold. I enjoyed the cocoa you sent and the best pair of socks I ever had. They come up to my knees, lovely and snug.'

*France 27 April 1916:* 'Lovely weather, just like spring in Australia. I must gather some buttercups and daisies and press them. The fruit trees are in bloom and everything reminds me of home. I went to communion last night. The Chaplain seems a decent bloke. He is High church though. Had 2 candles burning all the time. Had a nice bath in the drain last night, reminds me of Bessy Creek.'

*France 20 July 1916:* 'Got a parcel from Nar-Nar-Goon school, a tin of cocoa, tin of milk, tin of light Havelock tobacco, 6 packets Capstan cigarettes and 2 boxes of matches. It was very good of them and I'll write thanks. The photo you sent is good. Elsie must be a darling little kiddy and beef to the heel she looks. I would love to see the little nip. I long to see you all, but if it is willed otherwise, then, as you say, we will look forward to our meeting in the next world. If I'm spared to return I'll camp with Darkey [his dog] as the nearest approach to present conditions at their best.

'When I get home I want to forget this war and would like to go to a fresh place. I can then say I was not here. And if any galoot tries to tell me what I missed I'll run for my life. I was very sorry to hear about poor Jim. Billy Lewis who used to drive for O'Halloran has been killed too.'

Henry Pepper is himself in hospital in Bournemouth, wounded, by 9 June 1917, when he learns of his father's death. Since he, the only son, was away, he was consulted about the necessity to sell the farm: 'My dear old Mummie and Elsie, don't worry on my account over selling . . . it would be so much better for you . . . and [would] ease my mind a lot.' Bournemouth had been his mother's birthplace. 'One could spend months going round Bournemouth, mother. Perhaps it is possible for both of us to do it in happier times . . .'

By April 1918 he was back in battle again. The country boy, brought up in the Snowy Mountains, tells his mother and sisters that 'such a nice, clean little dog [came] into the tent and he did enjoy a little snooze in the blankets; a little straight-haired fellow, some sort of terrier . . . there's a cat here with 6 lovely tabby kittens . . . beauties, but too wild to catch . . . You will know that our work here has frightened Mr Fritz. He can't face another spring carnival . . . I wish it were all over, if not, the sooner we are there the better . . . Pay goes on for 4 months after being reported killed I think. Glad you are getting the money alright. The way things are now a chap is unlucky to get killed but they will. Had a 12 mile route march with full kit, blanket and waterproof today. It catches me on the shoulder bones. I shall always be bony. We passed a crop of broad beans. They were in flower. The breeze was blowing off them.'

The breeze blew for only a few weeks more for the sensitive bush boy. His letters are very cut about – evidently the censor was displeased with a backwoods' boy's joy in describing the villages and fields to his people. All the top of this letter had been chopped off by the censor's scissors. 'I went to church this evening. We sang a Christmas carol, "God be with you until we meet again" and "Nearer my God to thee" etc. I wondered what you have been doing today. I'm sure I don't know what to write about without offending the censor.' Then he talks of his pets at home, 'I can picture Darkey at the cream and the little thrush at the butter. It is getting dark now. Much love to you all, your loving son and brother, Higham Pepper. P.S. I often think of Bessy Creek in this place, and this evening would be good for fishing in the Ararat. Charlie Olsen is safe and well. I would be glad to hear the same about a few more I know. Yes, we all did our bit at the place you mention.'

His recently widowed mother received the visit from the clergyman as other mothers did. He had been reported *Missing* at the battle of Villers Bretonneux on 9 August 1918, the deciding battle of the whole, horrible war, and his last letter arrived after news of his death.

Three months later, when war ended, the mother sought his grave. On a slip of paper she wrote, 'Lt Crow said 97 men and officers were buried in the one grave. Tom Ellis said it was between Pozières and Harbonnières and a cemetery was there by a little wood.' The family were still searching in 1924, when his sister, Ivy, went to France.

On 21 July 1924, the Imperial War Graves Commission wrote to Ivy: '... in possession of evidence that leaves no doubt that your brother is buried in Heath Cemetery north of Harbonnières but unfortunately his actual grave cannot be located. In these circumstances the Commission have erected a special cross inscribed with your brother's name and regimental particulars and reading "Buried in this cemetery, actual grave unknown".' The family later arranged for the following words to be carved on this cross:

> Lance Corporal H. H. Pepper,
> 7th Battalion, Australian Infantry
> 9th August, 1918, aged 25.
> Glory, Honour and Peace to every man that worketh good.

After war comes the reckoning. There were the women without men, the children without fathers. Twelve months after the guns were silenced, the plight of these mainly helpless people was evident. In New South Wales alone there were 1641 boys and 1579 girls left orphaned, a total of 3220.

The *Sydney Morning Herald* of 29 November 1919, told of the 'Anzac Appeal', when the widows and children of dead soldiers and sailors were exhibited in the streets in Sydney. 'A heart rending sigh of a man in the street: "Good God! Is that what the war has left us?" The pathetic procession with its tally of orphans went by. There was no mistaking the solemnity of it all as one looked at the number of women in mourning, some moved to tears, or regarded the serious faces of the older children. District after district paraded its fleet of cars bearing the orphaned, "Father's Colors" on every hand. A little fellow waving a flag bearing the words, "welcome home". But there was no welcome home for his man.

'The appeal of these innocents made Sydney respond nobly ...

'Sir William Cullen, on the stroke of noon, declared the day open from a platform in Martin Place. "Our soldiers," he said ... "Never forget them as they were then ... in that spirit, my countrymen, I commend to you this appeal, made by the survivors of our gallant men ... for the memory of dead comrades ... all who treasure the memory ... can show their gratitude by responding to this appeal for the orphaned children of our heroes".'

The committee formed to administer the bursary fund received letters that revealed a little of the desolation in the homes of dead men. 'At a meeting of the education committee of the Anzac Memorial Fund held yesterday afternoon a case was cited which shows how vital the education of the fallen sailors' and soldiers' children is.

'Recently one of the large private schools gave a bursary to the son of a fallen soldier, and the principal of the school referred to the committee a letter just received from the mother of the lad. This soldier's widow wrote: "I find that I cannot afford to give Jack any more schooling. I have been ill again myself, and my expenses are so heavy that I will have to send my boy to work. I would really like to send him to school for a couple of years yet, but I can no longer keep him clothed and pay his expenses without assistance. If I only had the one child it would be different, but there are three others to educate yet, and Jack is just on 16, and that is the best I can do for him. I was wondering if my second boy could take Jack's place. He is only 12 years, and will thus have about three years' schooling before he need go to work. I would be very thankful if Bob could take Jack's place." '

Driving through Ballarat (Vic.), one of Australia's loveliest cities, the motorist passes beneath an arch bearing the legend: The Avenue of Honour, Ballarat 1914–1919.

> *All ye who tread this Avenue of Life,*
> *Remember those who bowed beneath the strife,*
> *Each leaf a laurel, crowned with deathless fame,*
> *And every tree reveals a hero's name*

This famous, 22 kilometre long avenue of 3700 trees was begun on 4 June 1917, and completed on 9 June 1919, by the staff of Lucas Lingerie, Ballarat.

The girls planted a tree for every man who enlisted from 'the Beautiful City of Ballarat'. At the end of their service, they published a booklet listing the number of trees, the name of each soldier and his battalion and the name of the person planting the tree. An asterisk is beside the name of those 'who paid the supreme sacrifice' – and there are many asterisks. Over the years, they planted 56 varieties of trees, from 380 elms and 150 North American maples to 16 cypresses.

*We catch but broken strokes, and try*
*To fathom all the mystery*
*Of withered hopes, of death, of life,*
*The endless war, the useless strife . . .*

CHAPTER 7

# The White Feather

*I meet the men who do not go,*
*But make no sign*
*That in my heart is quiet scorn,*
*That I thank God they are not mine,*
*Not of me born!*

During the two conscription referenda campaigns of 1916 and 1917 the country was in all truth ripped apart. The two opposing camps spilled out the hatred that only civil war can provoke in people of one race, and this was that type of war. Those for conscription wanted 'the wastrels, the loafers, the blackguards and traitors' sent to the trenches; and those against it declared this to be 'a sordid trade war', and said 'Australia has already lost more men than such a small and so young a country can afford'. Indeed she had. But both campaigns were run at the end of years of most terrible deaths among Australians.

In 1916, remnants of battalions were lined up and counted after battle and found to be only 28 per cent of the men who had gone into the fray 48 hours before. At the battle of Fromelles, 82 per cent of the Australians overrun by the Germans were casualties. In 1917, the battles of Ypres were fought, wars of attrition to see which side had men left standing. 'Wearing the enemy down' it was called. But it wore us down, too, and the terrible casualty lists rolled down column on column of the newspapers all over Australia. Women hastened to embrace one who had 'got word', with the dread of such a blow falling on themselves. 'The lives of all of us are full of grief, and none of us know that it will not be her turn tomorrow to unload a heavy heart in tears that scald.'

A woman finds much of what happened during the two referenda campaigns hard to understand and harder still to forgive, for much of the hatred was engendered by women. It has been said – and I lean to this belief – that these women, denied an active role in this war, ridded themselves of the violence war arouses in all, even those who sit and wait. Their intelligence, their pioneering background, their pride in being the youngest, newest nation on the battlefields, needed release – and erupted. They were so far from the sound of guns and smell of cordite – all the excitements and dangers of which they read – that to wait patiently in this vortex was impossible.

There are few men whose nerve-ends do not tingle at the sight of brave pennants flying and men marching to battle; few who, in the days of Empire, could resist falling in to follow a drum along the street. Women have always been considered 'different', 'delicate' and lacking in the fire that drives men to war; but that is not true. We are made as men are made, but convention has forced us to show a different face to the public.

Harder to understand is the fact that many women who had lost a son, husband, brother or friend at the war, were the worst of the pro-conscriptionists. But no situation is black and white and this was no different from any other.

The following letter to the editor appeared in a number of newspapers:

'Women in Australia are chafing to be of more use to the nation. The women of Great Britain have been truly mobilised for war – as completely and practically as if they were under conscription.

'Four thousand American medical women have been requested to register for active service in ten American women's brigades.

'British and American women are being used for war work. When will the Federal Government make full use of equally willing, and equally able, Australian women?'

Not for the whole of that war, lady, not at all for the duration. Groups and individuals were begging to offer themselves in the way men had gained immortality, but they were ignored. All that was left was for them to fight in whatever other way possible. They could not withdraw or deny the right of a country to send a man to war, because their sons and brothers and lovers were already there. To cause chaos, confusion or doubt now might well endanger their men, so they went to war in another way. One path taken was that of groups such as the Australian Women's National League.

'The Australian Women's National League has had to fight to maintain their existence as a League of women, inspired by Imperialistic Patriotism, resolved to give the best of their time – the best of their strength and mind – for the sake of God and country. They have won through, and are acknowledged as a powerful factor in Australian politics.'

Letters, said to be from 'somewhere in France', were circulated throughout the campaign: 'Don't worry about me Mum, for I'm alright. It is a bit rough to come back in the trenches while the wound is still tender, but it only aches occasionally. I can "stick it" alright until conscription goes through – as it surely will this time. I hear that all of us Anzac chaps get a rest then ...

'The French women and girls are all of them heroes – heroines we learnt at school, but I like heroes best – but I bet our Australian girls could be – and would be – just as brave if the call came; but I tell you, Australians ought to go down on their marrow bones every day of their lives and say, "Thank God our men go to the war – the war doesn't come to us". Australians don't know that they are alive (or in danger, the fools!) until they go outside our own ring-fence. A ring-fence built by the people of dear old Blighty, and which protects the – cold-footed gentry, just as much as the dear little kiddies in happy Australia.

'... Mother, I know all you League women will work hard for a "Yes" vote. I think it will go through, but don't take any risks ... And, Mother, you take it from me, that there will be many and many a coward (man and woman) will wear a "Yes" button and record a "No" vote. I'm afraid of Australia.'

Anything and everything was thrown into the battle.

> *Britain sent forth a message to her people over the sea –*
> *'Ye have done full well, my children; there is more ye can do for me.*
> *For your sons, and sweethearts, and brothers, your kindred as well as mine,*
> *The worn-out men in the trenches – the boys who are holding the line!*
>
> *'I, who have watched you, loved you, given you freedom of sea,*
> *Ask this now from my children, who have done so much for me –*
> *Respite for worn-out warriors, your kindred as well as mine;*
> *Sleep for the men in the trenches – the boys who are holding the line!'*
> – Gertrude Hart

A Mother's Answer to 'a Common Soldier':

'Sir – As a mother of an only child – a son now in training and waiting for the age limit to do his bit – may I be permitted to reply to "Common Soldier" ... Perhaps he will kindly convey to his friends in the trenches, not what the Government thinks, not what the Pacifists think, but what the mothers of the British race think ...

'To the man who pathetically calls himself a "common soldier", may I say that we women, who demand to be heard, will tolerate no such cry as "Peace! Peace!" where there is no peace ... The blood of the dead and dying, the blood of the "common soldier" from his "slight wounds" will not cry out to us in vain ... Send the Pacifists to us and we shall very soon show them, and show the world, that in our homes at least there shall be no "sitting at home warm and cosy in the winter, cool and 'comfy' in the summer". There is only one temperature for women of the British race, and that is white heat. With those who disgrace their sacred trust of motherhood we have nothing in common ... We women pass on the human ammunition of "only sons" to fill up the gaps ...

'The reinforcements of women are, therefore, behind the "common soldier". We gentle-nurtured timid sex did not want the war ... We would have much preferred to have gone on in a light-hearted way with our amusements and our hobbies. But the bugle call came, and we have hung up the tennis racquet, we've fetched our laddie from school ... We are proud of our men, and they in turn have to be proud of us. If the men fail, the women won't ... Yours, etc., A Little Mother.'

The address given at a speech night at the Presbyterian Ladies' College in East Melbourne by the Reverend J. T. Robertson, Moderator of the Presbyterian Church of Victoria, is indicative of the temper of 1917. The address, reported in the *Argus*, begins amiably enough with an almost liberated, 1980s flavour, referring to the '... commercial tendencies of women's education as being a significant recognition of the changing place of woman in the world, and the necessity for fitting her for those responsibilities which she was being increasingly called upon to bear in common with men'.

'Women have undoubtedly taken a new position in the life of the world, and have developed a new consciousness of capacity and service ... '

And then, we have the clever, machiavellian twist.

'The future of Australia lay literally in the hands of the women, upon whose votes next week the honour of our land and the vindication of women's citizenship most surely rested.'

One week before the referendum a 'great rally of Women' was held in the Auditorium, Melbourne, by the AWNL. 'A magnificent demonstration,' reported the *Woman*.

'The Auditorium was crowded in every part by 7 o'clock and the doors closed against a still greater crowd who vainly endeavoured to get within the building ... The Right Hon. the Prime Minister (who was accompanied by Mrs W. M. Hughes) received a well-deserved ovation by the vast audience ...'

After telling the women of 'the great responsibility laid upon the nation's Enfranchised Women', Mrs Hughes announced 'the grand old Hymn "Oh God, Our Help in Ages Past", which has been sung ... by our race in all great crises of national history ...

'This meeting was arranged ... to appeal to the Women of Australia to use their judgment and reason before they cast their votes either "for" or "against" on the 20th of this month.'

With a call to the women packing the hall to 'play the game tonight!', the President asked them not to create 'disturbances'. All over Australia violence had broken out at referendum rallies. Platforms were wrecked, speakers punched, kicked, tarred and feathered. The President was determined to avoid this at her meeting, and from her we learn of the strength of those other ladies, the anti-conscription women. 'So anxious was a certain section of the public to honour the meeting with its presence, that, having by some means procured one ticket as a sample, this was taken to a printer and an order given for 200 facsimiles, "never mind what they cost!"

'No doubt a few of this class of women did get in, but thanks to the action of the printer ... Miss Bridget O'Dea was interviewed by the police instead of receiving the expected bundle of tickets for the AWN League meeting.'

The speakers pointed out in their speeches that 'in our hands must lie greatly the issue of the 20th. To those of us who intend to vote "YES" I have only to say: "Well done." But to those of you [who] intend to vote "NO" I ask you, between this and the 20th, to give the matter more earnest consideration ... think of the husband, son, brother, or sweetheart, who is fighting for your honour ... would he not turn to you with reproachful looks, and his pleading voice sound in your ears: "Why desert me in my hour of trial? Send help lest I never see your face again." Women electors, think of this!

'We would like to say a word to our young sisters, many of whom have listened to the voice of the young man ... perhaps pleads with you for a hasty marriage that he may hide himself behind the curtain of a "married man". Think, if you yield to him, of the years to come – there will be no happiness in store for you, I fear. You, on your side, will have no respect for him for what he has asked you to do to save himself. He, on his side, will have no respect for you, who will have proved weak when you should have been strong in helping him in the right path, and to do his duty.'

By voting 'yes', every woman was helping to save the lives of 'our brave, war-worn men now fighting in the trenches'.

When the counting was done and it was seen that for the second time Australia had turned down conscription, the AWNL was vitriolic. In their 1 January 1918 issue of *Woman*, they castigated the NO voter.

'Australia answers – NO! By a majority of 164 794. Victoria, New South Wales, Queensland and South Australia record a "NO" vote. Tasmania, a small "YES" majority. West Australia holds the honour of the Commonwealth. W.A. records "YES" in unmistakable language. A majority of 34 314. Is the Women's Vote responsible for Australia's debacle? America's Verdict – SOCIALISM, PACIFISM, SINN FEINISM.'

(One has to wonder why Australia would be concerned with America's 'verdict', seeing that America had entered the war only a few months previously and her men – all conscripts – were yet to show their mettle. Australian troops, toughened by three hard years of war, were more likely to see it as unconscionable cheek by the as-yet-untried America.)

Handing out white feathers was yet another way women felt they were serving: with this most mundane, ludicrous symbol of cowardice, they launched forth to humiliate those they saw as being fit enough to 'join the boys at the front', the men 'shirking their duty'. Certainly, many women did not shirk what they saw to be their duty. They went forth as if they were going 'over the top', 'off for a hop-over' to defeat the enemy, and passed out white feathers to such a degree that every white chook in Australia must have trembled with the cold.

It was a terrible thing. A few women concentrated on sending the feathers through the post; others, more honest, handed them to their victims and, as many letters and reports show, often made the mistake of handing a white feather to a young, fit-looking man in the streets only to learn that he was a hero, discharged with wounds too severe for him to be used again in battle.

The feather was used in advertising; imitation feathers were made; the term 'white feather' became a part of the speech of the country in the way 'a yellow streak' had previously been.

One of the most tragic results of the handing out of white feathers – and there were plenty of cruel things – was the young Melbourne man who had twice been accosted in the street and given a white feather. On the second occasion he had been reviled in front of a crowd of people. He enlisted under a false name, because his past record would have prevented his being accepted into the forces, and was killed at Passchendaele in 1917.

His mother, Mrs E. Ritter, told me: 'He didn't want to go. He was frightened. He was sure he would be killed if he went back.' Back? Yes, back. He had been sent to hospital from the battlefields twice before being discharged and returned home unfit. 'He was frightened.' And why not? His only two brothers were already dead. But such was the disgusting power of a white feather plucked from some miserable hen, that he rushed to what his heart told him was death.

Mothers were powerless to help their sons when compulsory training was brought in. A young man might claim exemption from service if he was an only son. But to do so could mean a court appearance, as young Mr Heine found on 9 September 1916. The Sydney *Telegraph* reported his case under the heading 'Only Son Case at Exemption Court'.

'*Melbourne, Thursday.* At the Brunswick Exemption Court, Ferdinand Johann Heine . . . of German parentage, applied for exemption. His application paper stated that he was the only eligible member of his family, which consisted of three girls, and two boys, his brother being only three years old. Applicant was the only one in the family who was working. He told the Court that he did not wish to fight against his relatives in Germany . . .

'The Magistrate (sternly): You are an Australian. You're prepared to live here under the British flag, and enjoy its benefits and freedom, and yet you are not prepared to go and fight because you're of German descent.

'Applicant: I don't want to fight against my relatives.

'Magistrate: That will do. If you take my advice you will keep those sentiments to yourself. If you go away and give expression to such talk you will find yourself in serious trouble.

'The application was refused.'

Immediately after the defeat of the second conscription referendum, the following appeared in *Woman*.

'From 1st January to 31st December, 1917, the Victorian enlistments were 7062 metropolitan, and 4503 country, making a total of 11 565 for the fourth year of the Great War.

'A marked peculiarity in these enlistments is the fact that these volunteers are mostly forthcoming from districts which are already well represented at the front.

'The Grampians has the unenviable position of holding the lowest percentage in Victoria.

'Of the recruits actually obtained 75 per cent are below the age of 21, married men or returned soldiers.

'Of the 81 men per month required from the Grampians, only an average of 21 has been obtained.

'Many of the farm holdings in the Grampians are owned by Germans.'

It was a time when young women could 'go public' without risking social disapproval. In some country towns, young horsewomen and girls in white rode four abreast down the street, rallying men to enlist. 'Remember the women and infants in Belgium!' cried their banners, whilst their white frocks proclaimed them to be as yet unviolated. They carried posters of kneeling Belgian women pleading with the ape-like Hun against rape of their white-clad bodies, while 'no less' than *five* babies were skewered on the one Hun bayonet. The riders expected – and maybe got – some approval, but many people thought it was 'all for show'.

They were indefatigable in their attacks, though, and would stoop to anything, as this rather suspect 'letter' of 1917 shows. It purported to be from Private Douglas Lloyd to his mother in Myrtleford, and was headed up: A Soldier's Letter. No Class, nor Creed. 'Don't worry about us mum, we are all right. Just hold up your head, bravely and proudly, and say: "My two and only sons have been wounded in the two greatest battles the world has ever known." You and our sisters will never have the finger of scorn pointed at you like some of the Australian mothers will. Why don't the men enlist? . . . Surely to God they will never wait to be conscripted. Surely they have pluck enough when they hear of all the wounded and the killed to come forward . . . Our priests are grand men . . . The parsons are splendid men, too. No one ever asks your creed; all are treated alike.'

The final sentiment of the letter was doubtless true of the trenches, but certainly not at home. The vicious sectarianism that flared up during the 1916–17 referenda on conscription was so deep as to remain in the nation until after World War II. Archbishop Mannix, the fluent, articulate leader of the anti-conscription campaign, was the most reviled man in Australia. Catholics generally were reviled and considered to be against the war effort. Yet the figures prove nothing of the sort, and show an evenness of religious persuasion amongst the volunteers. But there must have been a strange dichotomy in Catholic mothers, such as my Grandmother Adams and Great-Aunt Byrne; both of them lost their sons, yet both were devout Catholics: both were anti-conscription.

A mother in these times was in a perilous position. Seeing other mothers' sons setting off to be killed, she trembled for her own.

> When I lie quiet in my bed
> And think of you dear lads out there;
> The thoughts that crowd my heart and head
> Are almost more than heart can bear.

In Melbourne, the Australian Women's National League took in 'all classes of women, rich and poor'. 'It does not matter what their employment or what their denomination is, if they love Australia, and want to work for her prosperity and for freedom of thought and action, the League will welcome them as members. The platform is a broad one and the work disinterested.

'The members of the League do not seek place or power; they do not wish to send women into Parliament. They wish to educate themselves and others to use consciously and intelligently the vote the country has given them, and they wish to keep their homes pure and united, their faith in God undisturbed and unshaken, and to see their country free and prosperous.'

That introduction, from their own magazine, *Woman*, would alert today's woman to their true aim, which would repel or attract her, according to the way she voted. But it would be silly to dismiss them as having been merely a strident political party. Like many other such organisations that flower in war-time, what appears to be their almost trance-like, enthusiastic jingoism hides many another fear and passion.

### HER CHRISTMAS

> No, Do not pity me nor call me sad.
> Indeed you are in error – I am glad!
> Glad that I bore and glad as well I gave;
> Glad that my blood may help to free, to save.
> 'Somewhere in France?' – E'en that I do not know;
> He heard a call; my lips close whispered: 'Go!'
> And now 'tis Christmas Day – and he is there –
> And earth's most precious hour I've learned to share.
>
> No, do not sympathise – your eyes are wet!
> Indeed, you do not understand – or you forget.

> *I gave him freely – as my cheerful gift –*
> *And now no doleful song my voice shall lift.*
> *No! Help me to be brave, deny my tears;*
> *Think of the glory and allay my fears;*
> *For this is Christmas Day in every land,*
> *And over seas of space I touch his hand.*
> – Roscoe Gilmore Stott

By 1917 'the total amount collected for war purposes by the League exceeded £14 000'. As well, the AWNL War Work Party met every Friday to make shirts, socks and other clothing not provided in sufficient quantity by the army. 'Newspapers for the troops were wrapped and addressed by a voluntary worker at the rate of 1300 a quarter.'

In common with other groups of women working all over Australia, the League collected funds for groups ranging from French Red Cross, Prisoners of War, French babies, Belgian babies, Navy League, Polish Relief, Wounded Soldiers, Italian Red Cross, Motor Ambulances, 38 spinal beds. A travelling kitchen was donated by the Koroit branch. On Australia Day 1917, they collected seven tons of goods and over 2000 articles for the British Red Cross. Earlier, they had collected Christmas gifts for soldiers, nurses and all the men on HMAS *Melbourne*, a whole host of things: '14 420 2lb Tins of Fruit, 500 lbs Canterbury Cake, 23 cases Tomato Soup from Malvern Branch (to soldiers at front), plus 1 gross Atkinson's Eau de Cologne, 15 doz. tins Cadbury's Chocolate (to Nurses abroad, Xmas, 1915).'

Some country branches took on responsibility for specific work, such as Toolamba, who cared for the Toolamba Cot at Caulfield Military Hospital. The little town of Romsey, up country, collected £344 7s 6d and spread it all round – to the October 1914 Belgian Relief Fund, the Milk Fund for troops in the trenches, and on walking sticks.

The Deniliquin branches, as well as the usual comforts, raised funds for 'the fighting men, the wounded men and the nurses. For God and country'.

|  | £ | s | d |
|---|---|---|---|
| Four Motor Ambulances sent to the Front | 2138 | 0 | 0 |
| Three Y.M.C.A Huts from Deniliquin Branches (known as the Kitchener Huts in France, Moascar and Salisbury) | 1050 | 0 | 0 |

| | | | |
|---|---|---|---|
| Milk Fund for Men in the Trenches – to date | 5755 | 0 | 0 |
| A.W.N. League Ward in Caulfield Military Hospital | 900 | 0 | 0 |
| Sun room at Caulfield Military Hospital | 350 | 0 | 0 |
| Furnishings in Caulfield Hospital – about | 200 | 0 | 0 |

'It is almost impossible to enumerate all that the League has done. Everywhere – whether it be in town or country – the women of the AWNL are the backbone of the Red Cross Society, and, indeed, there is scarcely any branch of patriotic work or endeavour where League members are not to be found ... up and doing for her country and Empire in this, the greatest war in history.'

The last phrase gives us a clue to another, equally urgent reason for their being. It *was* the greatest, or largest, war fought. Australia had the highest casualty rate of men in the field on the allies' side in World War I. Sixty-eight and a half per cent of her men were casualties. Naturally, this affected the women who had been left widows, childless. To have damned the war would have seemed to them like admitting that their men had died in vain. And no bereaved woman could easily live with that. 'As the war rages the more fiercely on, so must the League's efforts be the greater; so must the women uphold their soldier sons and say in very truth –

> *Women's souls shall march beside you; women's love shall hold you fast;*
> *While you fight the fight of honour, till your triumph come at last.*

Their patriotism spilled over. From our viewpoint we look back and see a side of these hard-working women that we wish was not there. But hard, inhuman, hysterical times are mirrored in the people swept along in the wake of the storm.

> *Then when in loneliness I sit,*
> *With grief-worn eyes,*
> *But strong in pride of mine, these lines*
> *By one who knew man's heart so well,*
> *In my mind rise –*
> *'Cowards die many times before their deaths,*
> *But valiant never taste of death but once.'*
> — Janet Spark, *Maffra*

# CHAPTER 8

# *The Bride Ships*

With the Australian soldiers away from their own country for five years of their young lives there were romances, marriages and children with both English and French women. When the war ended, these families had to be got to Australia and so the 'bride ships' were requisitioned. Among the hundreds of young women who braved the voyage to the other side of the world was Lily Crighton, a Scots girl who had served in the English Queen Mary's Auxiliary Corps. This corps of women had staffed such places as the British Officers' Rest Houses, replacing men who could then work close to 'the front'. Lily and 16 other girls were at such a rest house when she met and fell in love with Lou Bayer of the 5th Battalion.

'I knew a lot about Australia, because my brother Alex had been to Australia and enlisted there and fought at Gallipoli with the Aussies. He used to write to me. He told his Aussie friends in hospital to visit the Crighton family in Glasgow if they got leave, and four great big sergeants turned up at our house one day, and mother told them to come and see me when they returned to France. So they did. Lou Bayer was with them.

' "Your brother Alex told me to look you up," he said. I fell for him. But Lou and the other diggers went to the firing line and my corps went to the forest of Crecy.'

We know what happened here, for a report was sent back to England of the girls' courage. 'The Tommy WAACs have thoroughly justified their existence. They have been through raid after raid at Boulogne, Abbeville and Etaples. Abbeville, their camp was totally demolished before their eyes, big bombs, while they took shelter in trenches. Another time their hostel and all their possessions were destroyed while they encamped in the neighbouring woods.

'They were moved to another camp that was also wrecked in front of them and, 20 minutes later, while they were congratulating themselves, a small bomb fell in their midst killing eight. The others immediately went back to work. After that, each night at 11 p.m. after work, the girls were taken by lorry to sleep in tents in the forest 15 miles away and brought back next morning to begin work at 5.30 a.m.'

Lily remembers, 'There would be six to seven hundred men lying wounded on the steps waiting for us to give them their breakfast. Then, one morning, we were handing food out and a big London bus rolled up and took us away and we learnt the Big Push was on and General Monash was about to push the German Army back. When we got back ... the next day it was all gone, Abbeville had been bombed out and our clothes with it. There were only a few of us there, us girls and grave-diggers. They dug open trenches for us to shelter in. There was only part of one wall of our dining-room left, another aerial torpedo hit. We slept on the floor with our greatcoats over us. One night bombs scattered our things everywhere and I found my corsets in a field. They had about 70 holes in them. They were no good after that.

'We always knew when someone was killed because we were lined up for roll call on those occasions. We had to move. We began to walk. At a ruined village a poor old chap looking after a canteen gave us a cup of café au lait and we lay down on the floor and waited till we got some clothes again. I'd had one girlfriend killed. Now another said to me, "I wasn't very good to my mother but once I get home I am going to be really so much better". And then she was killed.

'Oh, you saw a lot. One day the Australian general, Sir Carl Jess, came and asked, "Who is the Scots girl here?" and I said, "Me, sir". He had come to thank me. "My boys tell me how you looked after them and made them laugh."'

War ended on 11 November 1918 and Lily and Lou found themselves in London three days later. 'He said we'd get married, but I said we were supposed to be four weeks in a parish to get married. "And would anyone be enquiring whether we had been or not?" this Aussie says to me, and off we went and got married. Louey Conyers of the Australian Nursing Service was my bridesmaid. We knew one another in France.'

Lou Bayer was sent home three weeks later and Lily followed on the *Osterley*, a bride ship. Her cabin mate, another bride, was pregnant and sick. 'But we at least were in second class. This girl's husband was third class and the food was terrible. So I went off to the Officer-in-Charge and said, "Mrs Brown is bad. Her husband must be brought to her", and he came at mealtimes and ate the food she couldn't get down.'

The ship arrived in Australia on 23 February 1919. 'Lou was on the wharf. I was home.'

With so many casualties among the Australian troops, the girls at home resented 'war brides' who, they believed, had robbed them of prospective husbands. An Australian soldier, Oliver Coleman, wrote to his family about his 'coming alliance with an English girl': 'I believe that many of the Australian girls feel they are not getting a fair deal. I suppose the girls under the same conditions would please themselves. They had a fair run with me anyhow...

'I wish you well, father, and keeping the old home squared for my Dolly who is going to be a worthy successor of my dear mother and I'm sure you will like her. I expect someone will know my business better than my own and feel it's their place to say I should not marry an English girl. As it happens, young folk generally please themselves in that manner and I am no exception, and can face all hostile criticism.

'You know we all want to have a few little soldiers & nurses to fight Fritz next time because he will surely come again, if in 50 years time.'

CHAPTER 9

# People in the Storm

*'Even in a quiet little country town a young girl could be aware of the tumult in the lives of others in Europe, people in the cold eye of the storm.'*

'My dear Australian friend', wrote Edith, the Viennese pen-friend to 13-year-old Jean Doig of Colac (Vic.). It was June 1935, and spring was warm in Vienna. 'I have never written to any Australian girl yet and as I learn English only two years, I beg you to excuse all the mistakes I make.' In September it is too cold to swim, 'so I play inside with my little brother who is very sweet and amusing'. 'Vienna is a very pretty town. I am sure you would like it. I hope you will come to Austria. That would be fine! Tell me what Colac is like.'

And in this way, two girls wrote as pen-friends until 1 June 1938. 'Things have changed for us here lately, not for the better you will know from the papers. Daddy will have to leave the country and begin life elsewhere. We cannot take any money with us, every penny must remain here.' Her father, Jacob Roll, was a Doctor of Medicine, as was Jean Doig's father in Colac, and Edith asks for information about opportunities to come to Australia, what positions are available, 'for any salary be it ever so small! Please don't be angry with me for asking so many questions dear Jean but this is a matter of life and death for us.'

Dr and Mrs Doig wrote to Dr Jacob Roll, and the girl wrote to Jean. 'Oh Jean, you cannot imagine how difficult it is to leave the country one loves so much, but we are not allowed to let sentiments overwhelm us. I have already said goodbye to school and am trying to learn manual work. Many of our friends have left Austria already, so I am lonely now.'

Dr Doig wrote to the Commonwealth immigration authorities, the Pharmacy Board of Victoria, the Department of the Interior, the Victorian Refugee Immigrations Appeals Committee, everyone who could possibly help rescue the family.

In January 1939, Edith wrote, 'I am very sad that I have no possibility ever to get to Australia. I should have been ever so happy to make your acquaintance Jean.' The family are going to try to cross into Slovakia. Mrs Roll writes to Colac saying that if the Doigs could help get her husband out she would be willing to stay in Slovakia with the little son and try to get Edith to England to one of Dr Roll's ex-patients.

The Doigs wrote many careful, courteous letters appealing to the authorities, eventually offering to stand guarantee for the family or for any member of the family – not a small undertaking, since such a nominator would be bound by law to support totally any persons they had guaranteed if the persons could not support themselves, and Dr Doig had four children to educate on the income of a small town practice.

At the Malvern branch of the Australian Women's National League on 9 May 1939, the President of the Legislative Council, Sir Frank Clarke, stated, 'the eastern European Jew is deficient in some of the qualities that made citizens of the British empire.' The Leader of the State Parliamentary Opposition, Sir Stanley Argyle, agreed with his political opponent.

Another letter arrived from Vienna. The Roll family had not been successful in crossing to Slovakia. 'Can you kindly induce a quick decision from Canberra,' they plead. Dr Roll enclosed references and degrees from universities and major hospitals in Vienna. Mrs Doig is informed from Canberra that such refugees would be required to bring 'a very substantial amount of capital – say 1000 Pounds.'

'We are in highest despair,' writes the pen-friend. 'Do help to a desperate man,' Dr Roll writes, 'You are saving four lives. I beg you, forgive my boldness, please take the terrible situation we are in as an excuse. I apologise for causing so many inconveniences.'

Letter after letter arrives from authorities in reply to requests by Mrs Doig. She is tireless in her efforts. But, 'There is a Jewish sub-quota in the total of 5000 refugees annually, but more than twenty times that number of applications are received.'

Jean Doig kept the letters; she has them still. 'We heard no more,' she says. 'We wrote to many addresses but – nothing.' The final letter in the brief file on Edith Roll, pen-friend from Vienna, is from the Secretary, Department of the Interior, Canberra. It is 15 September 1939 and war has been declared. 'In view of the existing international situation, consideration of the application for Dr Jacob Roll, a German national, has been deferred indefinitely.'

'And ... we heard no more. I was young, sometimes I forgot Edith for months at a time but then I'd wonder ... I still wonder. I still think of her. I still keep the correspondence.'

# CHAPTER 10

# *Après la Guerre est Finie*

The soldiers had sung it during the four worst years armies had known – 'After the war is over'.

The day dawned that the women who waited at home had feared would never come. It was peace. They spelt it 'Peace' in the newspapers. Armistice Day, when the guns stopped on the eleventh hour of the eleventh day of the eleventh month, 1918. In those days before radio the first the waiting women knew of it was the sound of bells.

My mother, Bridget Smith remembers: 'I was working, living in Warragul with Mr and Mrs Gay's family. I ran out on the verandah and stared down at the town. Mrs Gay ran out. "What is it? What are the bells ringing for, Mrs Gay?" I asked. "It's the Peace, Birdie. The boys will be able to come home." But my brothers would not come home ever again, those noisy, naughty, laughing boys, and I went inside and knelt by my bed and put my head down and cried and cried as I prayed. Then I felt movement beside me. It was Mrs Gay. She was Church of England. I was Catholic. She fell on her knees beside me and put her head beside mine and we knelt there praying till her children came and found us.'

The war was over – or so the leaders said. 'That war never ended,' say the wives of men who came home from it. 'No man returned from that war unmarked.'

Australia, with a population of under five million people when World War I began, had been the only country to send into battle an army completely made up of volunteers. In round figures, over 400 000 volunteered; 340 000 saw battle. Of these, our casualties were the highest on the allied side. We sustained 68.5 per cent casualties, a stupendous calamity for so young and small a nation. 'Those not marked in body, or put away in lunatic asylums,' the elderly ladies say, 'were marked in other ways. All were marked.'

When I published *The Anzacs*, three, separate, elderly women telephoned me, each with the same story: 'You forgot the women who had to live with these men'; 'The most loving and the most awful men were marked'; 'No man came home unmarked.' We can only imagine what kind of country, what type of nation we would have had, had these men been able to build it for us. 'They walked like princes, they looked like kings,' wrote poet laureate John Masefield in 1915. But that was before Ypres, before Villers Bretonneux ...

Those still alive returned to the 'Land Fit for Heroes' (as the recruiting posters had called it) and tried to earn a living. Young, they married, had children – and walked straight into the worst Depression Australia has known, the world-wide slump that began with the collapse in 1929 of Wall Street in New York and remained until World War II broke out in 1939. 'Just long enough for our babies to grow to men and be sent to fight.'

Men took to the roads as they had in depressions of the 1890s, 'humping the bluey', the blue blanket rolled as a swag that they carried. Like a leaderless army they wandered across the land. By 1930, unemployment was running at 19 per cent; by the following year it had jumped to 28 per cent.

Mrs Jean Hayes told me: 'My husband was awarded a Military Medal for bravery. I often wondered what our two boys thought of that when they saw him sitting with his head in his hands, too scared to go out again to try for yet another job when he'd been knocked back for years of trying. Humiliated, ashamed in front of his own sons.

'For the first few months he used to be just angry, then he was violent, but after that time he just got ... he cried sometimes. If he cried in front of the boys he took it out on all of us, me and the kids. He was ashamed of not being a proper man with a job. That's the way he saw it. He was so angry with the world he had to take it out on someone, and we were nearest him, so we copped it. I understood and I think the boys did too, although they left home young and went to the country and enlisted from there in 1939.'

Women were left at home alone to bring up families much as the early pioneer women had done; but, in many ways, they were worse off than those much-admired founding mothers had been. Bridget, my mother, says: 'There was a stigma about accepting the dole and these women felt it keenly. There was a stigma about being "on the wallaby", whereas in the early days we could boast about our father and grandfather and great grandfather "going on the tramp". It had been a way of assessing country according to the earlier men – although my Mamma always declared it was just their excuse for leaving the cares and toils of home life back in the 1890s. But in the Depression the thing was to keep up appearances and that was hard for these women to do with no man, no money and no work for women.'

Dad was never out of work and calls for help came to those families who had a salary. Mum had never forgotten one incident.

'I remember this poor man, a returned man. He had been at the Landing and right through the war until 1918. He came to the railway siding at Nowingi where I was station caretaker. He wanted me to give him a ticket to Melbourne, 400 kilometres away. "A ticket for me, the missus, and we'll nurse the kids and you can have everything in our hut and the tent."

'His home was miles away towards the salt lakes. I'd been there when his first baby was dying. Furniture made from White Rose kerosene cases and a tea chest for a table. But it was home to that poor family.'

She of course could not give away railway tickets.

'What I did was to phone the SM [station master] at Ouyen and ask which guard was on the train next day to Melbourne. It was Jim Casey. I knew him. He was all right. The train came in and the railway gang were working in the yard, and they helped secrete the little family under a tarpaulin in an empty truck. I'd made pasties and ginger beer enough to keep them going until they could hop out close to Melbourne – they would walk the final miles. They left with a bedding roll, a big basket with a strap around it and the woman had a bottle of powdered milk in her hand for the baby.'

Mum never said it, but she must often have thought that had her brothers not been killed in that war, it might have been one of them under the tarpaulin. 'You did all you could. You never knew but what you would be in their shoes tomorrow.'

In this area, where we lived then, soldier settler blocks had been offered to the returning heroes. The land, on the edge of the desert west of the Mallee, had been denuded of its sparse vegetation by great steam rollers, and now it stretched as far as the eye could see to the horizon – a dust bowl.

'One poor fellow, Mr — , used to go quite mad. He had been badly shell-shocked. He ripped the pickets off the railway fence one night and took a swing at your father.' But dad had been in the navy for seven years and could look after himself. 'Your father held him on the ground until he calmed down, then let him up and rolled him a smoke and they went off talking race horses.

'He was a good man, and handsome, but the war had unseated some part of his brain and we would hear him coming the miles across the dusty desert, roaring. He would disappear for days, weeks. When Mrs — was having their second baby he cleared out. We heard him sobbing as he went by on the rail line one night, sobbing and roaring and swearing. I went to her and she had the baby in the tent and Bobby, the two-year-old, kept trying to sit on my knee while I attended to her. When I left the tent to walk the four miles back to Nowingi to attend to the daily train, she asked me to phone her father. He was a Methodist minister in Melbourne. I couldn't use the phone for personal messages, so I told the guard and he phoned when he reached Melbourne, and next week her father came and took the whole family away.'

Mrs C. R. Saxton went east of this area to the Murray River with her husband in 1922. 'Few of the men had done farming, but all of them felt the country air must help them. All were unwell. The men who were suffering the after-effects of gas did no better there than in the factory-polluted air of the city.

'At first we lived in tents. In those days no dwelling or the likes was in the Land Settlement deal. Later the men worked with one another and built log cabins. They cut down Murray pine for this. It was good for that area. But the problem was, we were there ten years and only got one good year in those ten and the government took our subsidy back because of this.

'My sons were born there. Before Dick was born I set off for Red Cliffs. My father had brought an old car up for us for this very purpose. We had to carry water and spares. Anyway, we bumped away throughout the night on the dirt roads. I had a clean bath towel and I had it like a great diaper between my legs in case the baby came. When we got to the bush nursing hospital eventually, the boy was about to be born but I wanted to go to the toilet. The midwife was snappy. "Why didn't you go before this?" she said. I was a bit snappy myself by this time. "If I'd got out of the car for this purpose," I snapped, "more would have come away than ever I intended."

'We all left. No one could stay. No one has attempted to work that land since the day we all straggled off. It has gone back, now, to desert and salt lake. It remains only in the minds of we women who saw our soldier husbands struggle and fail – and, for some wives and widows, that meant forever. I was lucky. My man survived. But the statistics were not good, the men were too exhausted, too . . . oh, they saw too much, heard too much, left their strength and youth along the Somme and on Flanders Field.'

There were the women without men. Every war leaves these women behind, the Miss Havershams of battle. For some years they were singled out by comments such as 'her fiancé didn't come home', or 'She expected to marry'. At first, they were expected to mourn, but when they recovered the chance never came again.

In some ways men – fit men – saw the Depression years out differently from women. A sort of 'manliness', as it was called in those days (macho today), was exhibited. Not only in the 'Returned Men', as they were called, but in all fit men there was an air of what Anzac, Gallipoli and the Somme had proved Australian manhood to be: something to be lived up to. As well, the shrunken job market, and the absurd social disapproval of working women, kept women in the singular position of being entirely dependent on men on whom was thus bestowed either real or imagined power.

Elderly women (including some of my aunts) have told me of their feeling that not enough 'strong' men (their word) had come home from the war. One woman told me, 'We took what was left'. That is all she would say. Another, younger than the first, said: 'That is why she was so bossy. It's why I am so bossy. All the strong men, emotionally as much any other thing, went to that war. We married others. Someone had to run things and we became bossy.' Today, we would not consider these women as being 'bossy', but strong, brave and stalwart.

One of my father's sisters told me long ago that she believed 'nature planned wars to balance the population'. She thought more male children than females were born after regular wars. She also believed that war 'was for fools', even though five of her own brothers went and her son as well, and from those six only five lived through it, and one of them, Uncle Dick, died when I was a small child, 'coughing his lungs up' as he had done since he was gassed on the Somme.

In an attempt to meet with men of like minds and thus ease the loneliness of not speaking of a large and dramatic part of their lives, the men formed what is now the Returned Servicemen's League (RSL). They pressed for preference in employment for returned men, but when jobs were scarce, that did little to help the true battlers. I have told elsewhere of my father's struggles. Sent home before the end of the war on a hospital ship, discharged as medically unfit and put on a pension, he married my mother, promptly told a doctor he was fit, refused the pension, and took the only job then offering – shovelling coal into railway engines from the coal stage at Warragul.

The hours were long, he was weak, and then one night he didn't come home at 2 a.m. as expected. Before daylight the young bride went to the town, climbed up on the high coal stage and, finding him collapsed, got him down into a wheelbarrow and pushed him two miles home. He could not work for some time after, but the pension was not renewed. After his death, my mother asked for a war widow's pension. I asked, why? Why not when he was alive? 'It would have embarrassed, humiliated him to beg,' she said. And there was the crux of it as far as many were concerned.

Popular literature has given us to believe that 'the poor' struggle and strive to educate their children so they will ascend to somewhere else in the world that the parents were not able to go. I have seen no sign of this in my working class life. Certainly not in the Depression. Any working-class man with a job would be proud to have his son as well off as him. The little boys swaggering round with dad's crib tin, his old Gladstone bag with tools, his cloth cap, even falling over in his Blücher boots, were evidence of that. 'A fair day's work for a fair day's pay,' was said in many homes.

Some children got to high school, a few to university.

For the bulk of the population it was a relief when each child turned fourteen, the age when they need no longer attend school. Then they could go to work for the few shillings offered such young workers. Unions were unable to help. They knew that in such times, every man must help himself and not count the moral or social cost.

As for girls, they were still seen as being the future mothers and wives, so there was little pressure put on them to add to the families' difficulties by asking for further education.

In depressed areas of the country, things were bad. In those parts of the cities that many avoid, it was tragic. Families, often mothers and children with the father 'away looking for work', were evicted for failing to pay rent. They squatted in empty houses, tenements. They were thrown out again, any stick of furniture of value sold. Abortions were the only means of preventing the arrival of another mouth to feed, another head to house.

Several women who served in World War II in the armed services have told me of this. A Sydney woman remembered: 'I saw my mother with her foot up on the bath. I was about twelve. I knew it was something terrible but I didn't know what. Mum saw me at the door. She slammed it. It hit me. She screamed to get out. I hated her for it. I ran away. When I got back the next day, she was in bed. There were towels and sheets and things soaking in the bath. She had put old newspapers on top of the water to hide it but the blood was seeping up.

'I had two brothers and two sisters younger than me. Dad was away half a year or more that time, being moved on from town to town to get the dole. He sent some of it home to us.'

There were signs on the locked gates in these industrial areas: '*No Labour Wanted. No Men Needed*'. The level of unemployment was disastrously high in suburbs dependent for generations on industrial work. It would have been remarkable if such families could have gathered the energy, will power and faith, or simply have found the desire to sit to think about education or even the well-being of their children.

'Wherever you trade buy Australian made!' shouted the posters. But with what? asked those smitten by depression. The German Ruhr was silent; a postage stamp on a letter from Germany to Scotland cost some million marks; Liverpool in England had one million unemployed for the whole of the Depression until the next war began.

The movies tell us of the roaring twenties, cigarettes, booze, Clara Bow lipstick, the Charleston, fast, shiny cars and money to burn. True, some did have these things; but the majority did not. For the latter, it was the slough of despair; a courageous ignoring of calamity by day and hunger by night.

For most of us whose parents had a job, it was just as courageous in a different way. For us, it was a striving to survive on the reduced wages, a determination to prevail, never to show patches, mended shoes, onion sandwiches or slates, when you were aged 11 and, unable to afford an exercise book for school, must use the wet thumb to rub the slate pencil from the slate so it could be used again. It was a time when someone like me, whose mother was scrimping to get the two shillings and sixpence a week to have me taught to play piano and violin, was extravagantly in demand. Everyone wanted to dance, to sing, to move, to try to forget so very much.

It was 3 September 1939. On the Sunday night there was to be a dance in the Catholic school, in Penshurst where my family lived. I hoped to go but I was too young to do anything but wait for my parents to say they would take me. My father had hovered round the wireless set all day. Prime Minister Menzies was to make an announcement. We sat waiting, Mum, Dad, my sister aged 19 and her husband aged 22 and their baby John, and Grandmother, whose sons had been lost at Lone Pine, Gallipoli, 8 August

1915. 'Missing', the army notification had said. Now, through the static, we heard that Britain had sent an ultimatum to Germany to withdraw her troops from Poland by this date or . . . 'We are now at war with Germany.'

They played 'God Save the King'; my mother said 'God save us all', and Grandmother said, 'Wouldn't it be funny if they found the boys wandering round over there and they got their memory back?' In all these years, the mother's heart had never accepted the loss, without evidence, of her noisy, naughty sons.

It has been said that war is about mothers searching the battlefields for their sons and, suddenly, I knew it.

Dad wouldn't go to the dance, he said. Mum reminded him he was doorkeeper. My brother-in-law suggested we all go. But my sister, with her first baby on her knee, was staring, unseeing, at him. He had said when the news was announced, 'Well, it will be a job anyway.' She sat and stared.

> *Last night as I lay on my pillow,*
> *Last night as I lay on my bed*
> *Last night as I lay on my pillow*
> *I dreamt that my bonny was dead.*

We had sung it round the piano often enough. The young men Dad had helped during the bad days came. 'Did you hear the news?' they yelled, their eyes as bright as those of the boy married to my sister. They were off to the dance. 'Come on! You never know what we'll be dancing over there!'

We danced to the big bands in the city and whatever made a noise in the bush. The shimmy, Charleston, black bottom and such-like that Hollywood movies of the between-the-wars period have made much of, were rarely seen in public dance halls, but were more the province of those whom the Depression scarcely troubled. Sets – four couples in what later would be called square dancing – were what we danced, and half a dozen more, some graceful, some wild. We waltzed, did the barn dance, Pride of Erin, Highland schottische, polka, mazurka and, as well, the modern dances of the day which of course included the foxtrot and modern waltz. But as 1938 and 1939 had rumbled towards war, silly, fun dances had begun. Under the Spreading Chestnut Tree, a thing using one's hands and body as in a child's game. 'Not proper dancing at all,' our parents sniffed. The Lambeth Walk took on. 'If you go down Lambeth Way, Any evening any day, You'll find us all, doing the Lambeth walk, Oi!', we swaggered along the polished boards roaring out at the top of our voices. 'Everything's free and easy, Do as you darned well pleasee!' and our parents clucked again.

But, in retrospect, there was not much chance of doing as 'you darned well pleasee'. Any girl who 'left the hall', as it was put, was damned by the community in those pre-pill days when sex was equated with pregnancy and pregnancy outside marriage with social suicide. Even more immediate retribution befell a girl who left the hall. Few boys, if any, would dance with her on her return – or, indeed, at future events because, if they did, the 'good' girls would not then dance with them. We young had to expend our energies in dancing vigorously, as amorously, closely pressed, body to body, as the gimlet eyes of our watching mothers permitted.

Astoundingly, a tramp of feet came down Penshurst's main street. And trucks were rumbling by in this sleepy backwater. It was the Light Horse off to bivouac in Hamilton and now 'because of the news!' they would stay for the dance. Their plumed, cocky hats were romantic. No one thought of the anachronism of horses in this age of the aeroplane. We loved it. A Light Horseman gave me a flower as the band played the last tune, 'Goodnight Sweetheart Goodnight'. And then the lights went out.

When the fit, wild, lively boys and young men left for the war, a dreary change drifted over our lives.

# CHAPTER 11

# *Would My Heart Tell Me?*

*(If You Come to Die)*

The first Division of this war, the 6th Division, was formed and sailed for the Middle East on 11 January 1940, although as far as we were concerned they had left us by mid-December 1939, when their final leave to their home state ended. In the country we saw them 'jumping the rattler' (stealing a ride on a goods train), and in the city they left the dole queue and volunteered to die.

The 7th and 9th Divisions sailed to the Middle East, the 7th to fight in Syria, the 9th to go with Montgomery across North Africa and gain fame as the Rats of Tobruk, while the 6th Division was sent to Greece and Crete. The 8th, the other of the four divisions formed at the beginning of the war, went to Malaya, to islands to the north of Australia and to the south-west Pacific areas.

Suddenly the dance halls felt deserted; all the lively, noisy, flirtatious boys had gone, or so it seemed to us young girls just embarking on this side of life. There were farewells in the Mechanics' Institutes in the bush and the town halls in the cities. 'Our gallant boys' were spoken of in speeches as 'fighting the foe'. 'We will pray' and 'make ourselves worthy of their sacrifice by working to make Australia an even better country on their return'.

They were heady days and stirring nights, but when the boys went it always seemed they had been spirited away, they were lost to us, then weeks later someone would say, 'Bob Whitehead must have gone. He hasn't been back' or 'Mrs MacGregor hasn't heard from Jack, reckon he must be on the water'.

The bush towns and the city suburbs missed their noise, motor bikes, push bikes and rattle-trap cars; their hanging around shop verandah posts and light poles; we missed their singing, for we were still singers in the 1930s. 'She was sweet sixteen little Angeline,/Always dancing on the village green./When the boys passed by,/You could hear them cry:/Poor little Angeline' – although often in the dance hall you would hear a pack of them alter that final line to, 'Whacko! There's young Angeline!'

It was loving time, and the songs reflected it: "Twas on the Isle of Capri that I met her,/Neath the shade of an old walnut tree'; 'South of the border,/Down Mexico way', and now we heard Gracie Fields singing on the wireless. We could scarcely sing the song ourselves for the tears that suddenly, surprisingly, choked us:

> *Wish me luck as you wave me goodbye*
> *Cheerio! Here I go on my way*
> *Give me a smile I can keep all the while*
> *In my heart while I'm away.*
> *'Til we meet once again you and I*
> *Wish me luck as you wave me goodbye.*

In some ways, events moved swiftly. From the great distance from which we saw the war in Europe it appeared electric. Germany had invaded Poland on 1 September; on 3 September Britain, France, Australia and New Zealand declared war on Germany – and on that day the British liner *Athenia* was torpedoed, with a loss of 112 lives.

By 17 September Russian troops had marched into Eastern Poland and two days later Germany and Russia partitioned that country between them. (They were allies at that time.) By the end of 1939 our first men were preparing to leave for 'overseas' and Australian troops landed in the Middle East on 12 February 1940. Within the next three months Denmark, Norway, Holland, Belgium and Luxembourg were over-run by Germany, and by 22 June France had capitulated. The Empire was now alone. General de Gaulle had broadcast from London. Dunkirk had been evacuated by the British between 30 May and 4 June, becoming a legend to rival Gallipoli, Mons, Thermopylae. We were Empire to the core, and the drama of that embattled army on a narrow beach thrilled our loyal nerve ends. Our thoughts were with England, no matter what our country of origin. With her back to the wall, she awaited invasion. She alone among the 'free' nations now stood against the victorious German army, who had swept across Europe in these few months, seemingly invincible.

Some of our AIF were already in Britain, but none of our men were yet in action until 19 July – and then, what headlines! HMAS *Sydney* sinks *Bartolomeo Colleoni*. Like her namesake of World War I who sank the German raider *Emden*, the *Sydney* had sunk the Italian ship in true, traditional, navy style. We were ecstatic. She would sail back to Sydney

Harbour in 1941 for a tumultuous welcome. In the meantime we were still far from any scene of battle, any loss of loved ones, any adulation of heroes or consolation of the vanquished.

On 8 August 1940, the Battle of Britain began. Churchill was later to write of that handful of men who took to the air: 'Never in the field of human conflict was so much owed by so many to so few.' For 20 weeks those few airmen, including Australian pilots, went up night after night, day after day, until they died.

On 24 August London was bombed, and on 7 September the night raids began. On 16 December the AIF went into action at Sollum and Fort Capuzzo, but the fire blitz now burning London was of greater moment. It may have been what Churchill called 'our finest hour', but it was equally our darkest.

King George VI, who had unexpectedly come to the throne in 1936 when his brother Edward VIII abdicated for love of Wallis Warfield Simpson, now broadcast to the Empire – and we in Australia were part of that Empire. As that year without hope, 1940, died, his voice came over our static-charged wireless sets:

> *'I said to the man who stood at the gate of the year*
> *Give me a light that I may tread safely into the unknown.*
> *And he replied –*
> *Go ye out into the darkness and put your hand in the hand of God*
> *That shall be to you better than light and safer than a known way.'*

By the end of the year that we were now about to begin we would remember his words; they were copied into the scrap books many of us kept and, by December 1941, there was, in truth, no light for us to follow.

But all that was still 12 months away and the martial music, street marches, flags, trumpets, banners and drums accompanied our reading of the headlines of the valour of our Australian friends and brothers now in action, triumphant.

On 6 January 1941 they captured Bardia. Our new fashion colours became Bardia Brown and Derna Red, and our hats were Desert Gold. Before that month ended they had captured Tobruk and taken 25 000 prisoners. Lord Haw-Haw broadcast from Berlin to what he called the Rats of Tobruk, 'living like rats in holes in the desert'. When they were first besieged we were afraid for them. As the months went by and they could not be budged, we grew proud of the Rats.

Then, on 6 February, Benghazi was captured. We pored over maps of the arid lands of northern Africa. On 18 February troops of the 8th Division with their oval colour patches landed in a lush, tropical land closer to home – Singapore. 'Impregnable Singapore', we called it. A true bastion of Empire, its great guns bristling out, facing the sea, a warning to all who meddled with Empire. All this seemed a little more like war to patriotic Australians, isolated with New Zealand in the southern hemisphere far from the scene of battle and sacrifice.

When HMAS *Sydney* came home, steaming through the Heads on Tuesday 11 February, our pride tumbled out in a tumultuous welcome. Two hundred thousand lined the streets as the sailors marched from Circular Quay to Sydney Town Hall for lunch. We shouted, waved, threw kisses, girls, women and kids, and the lesser number of men in the crowds, as Captain Collins swung into view leading his 'Jolly Jack Tars in a Victory March'. Dressed in summer whites they were young, beautiful, proud – and winked at us. No girl aged 15 watching them swing past would believe, had she been told, that every one of them would be dead in nine months time. Yet, surely, some mother's heart stopped for a second as she watched her son's face go by, some sweetheart gasped with foreboding?

'Would my heart tell me if you came to die,/And should I see your spirit winging by/A swift white bird against grey sea and sky?' Helen Power wrote.

> *Ah! love, be sure my inmost soul would guess,*
> *Warned by the stirring of a strange distress,*
> *The meaning of its sudden loneliness.*

For indeed, they were all dead men. But in the meantime, there was plenty for them to do in Sydney and Melbourne.

It was 12 February 1941 and the lights were still on in Sydney. Bette Davis and Charles Boyer were starring in *All This and Heaven Too*, James Stewart and Rosalind Russell in *No Time for Comedy*, Gary Cooper and Madeleine Carroll with Paulette Goddard in Cecil B. De Mille's *North-West Mounted Police*. In Melbourne there was a Gaiety Dance at the Brunswick Town Hall, 'where dancers meet with joy complete', and at the Palais Pictures Myrna Loy and William Powell appeared in *I Love You Again*.

March and April were not so good. The enemy re-occupied Benghazi in April, as well as Bardia, and attacked Yugoslavia and Greece. By 11 April,

Australians were fighting in Greece; but by the 27th of that month, the Germans had entered Athens and, within three days, all British and Australian troops had been withdrawn to the island of Crete. One must remember we were not yet the great travellers that the wealth and comfort and convenience of the 1960s later made us. We had scarcely found Crete on our maps when, on 20 May, the German paratroopers began their attack on the island and overwhelmed its defenders. Brave boats, ships and submarines loitered in dark of night, attempting to rescue our beleaguered battalions, but by the final day of that month, which heralded the coming of winter to Australia, we knew the casualty lists would begin to appear. Added to the names of the wounded and dead were those of the 'missing, believed POW'.

On 2 June 1941, we were told that the position on Crete was 'desperate'. Crete! The headlines didn't tell us the tragedy it was for us. 'Half Crete army saved!'

'But on which half is my Raymond?' my Aunt Maggie cried.

'Crete evacuation an epic!' the papers heralded. 'The entire evacuation was an almost incredible epic that gave the world a new record of courage and daring.' HMAS *Perth* had taken 1300 men from Crete. 'They did not see a single British plane for days.' But they had seen 600 German planes as well as transports landing paratroopers and foot soldiers. 'After she left Crete with the men she rescued, she was bombed solidly for seven hours one day and 13 the next.'

The difficult thing for the women waiting at home was that the news releases were so shamefully gung-ho, and so wickedly censored, that the reader could neither believe nor sift the truth from the propaganda. But they did know one thing: it was bad, and the Australians had been hit hard, and that indeed it would be true that the gallant HMAS *Perth* had been plastered for as long as the news item said it had.

'No official estimate of killed or wounded, or of those taken prisoner has been issued.'

Long, long after, the truth came out: 3102 Australians had been taken prisoner by the Germans and there had been 781 casualties. In April 1984, I spoke again to Aunt Maggie, now 91 years of age, about Crete. 'They must have thought we were all stupid,' the bright old lady snapped. 'We knew the 6th Division was there – our boys had written to us from Greece, "Saw the Acropolis today". The papers were careful not to say *all* the troops had been rescued. Well, we thought, how many have been taken off? And how many left behind? The papers said, "18 000 Germans dead".

Well then, if that were so, how many of ours were dead, taken prisoner, or lying wounded in the valleys and on the scrubby hills? That's what made the war bad for us, waiting at home here, you know. We were so far from everything.'

Aunt Maggie was one of the lucky ones. 'Two months later I received a letter from Raymond. He was in hospital in Egypt. I'd prayed night and day for him. Now I prayed for his friends in the POW camps in Germany, and for their mothers.'

Prisoner of war! It sounded a vague thing, a no man's land our minds could not yet encompass. But not too many of them were prisoners, and the Germans had been fair to the Australian POWs of World War I, so the three-letter abbreviation was not yet the chilling hand clutching the heart that it would become before another year was done.

In June, on the twentieth, Germany attacked Russia. Hurrah! We read between the lines of the report. Now we had an ally. We became total admirers of the gallant Russians and sang: 'Curl a mo Uncle Joe! Curl a mo!' in reference to Josef Stalin's famous moustache. His portrait appeared on our hoardings; we stood for the Russian national anthem.

We took little heed of Japan landing in Indo-China on 27 July. We said we didn't trust that country, Japan. We knew of their brilliant defeat of the Russian navy at Port Arthur in 1904, the first time a 'yellow' race had defeated a 'white' race. And we knew of their cruel rampage through China but . . . no, it did not thread fear through our veins at all. Japanese cameras were still music hall jokes, as were their 'bandy' legs, bloodthirsty manner of ritual suicide, short-sightedness and 'inability to walk because their legs are not strong, owing to babies being carried too long on their mothers' backs'.

However, we did send troops to Burma, dressed, as were the Australians in tropical Singapore, in good Australian woollen khaki. Throughout September and October the valiant Russians held our attention. Leningrad was under siege and there was no doubt even then that these people would stand fast to the end. We now stood with genuine pride at being allied to this nation as their national anthem was played. As the newsreel screens flashed scenes of their most terrible suffering in the midst of their brave stand, we wept.

But our own time was now nearing and, as if to prepare us, in November the great HMS *Ark Royal* was torpedoed and sunk. Five days later, on 19 November, HMAS *Sydney* was sunk 'with total loss of personnel'.

Dear God, we prayed, not those boys we had cheered as they marched through Sydney so few months ago? Not *all* those lovely boys? Not our cousin Bertie, not those golden boys who winked at us girls as they marched up the steps of Sydney Town Hall? Not that boy Nugent we went to school with at Warragul? But yes, they were gone; the sea had devoured their ship and we saw them no more.

We had three weeks left to mourn. Then, it seemed to us, 'out of the blue', as people were saying, Japan attacked the American fleet at Hawaii and declared war on Britain and the USA.

CHAPTER 12

# No Foe Shall Gather our Harvest

Now it all moved too fast for us to follow without fear. It moved too inevitably, too disastrously. Day followed day, bringing only bad news. Islands were over-run and our men who defended them disappeared. The day after Australia entered the war against Japan, Nauru and Ocean Island were attacked, as were Singapore and the Gilbert Islands, and Japan had begun its offensive in Northern Malaya. The following day, 10 December 1941, HMS *Prince of Wales* and HMS *Repulse* were sunk off the coast of Malaya. Guam, the Philippines, Hong Kong, North Borneo, Sarawak, Papua, New Guinea, Penang, Rangoon, Wake Island – all were under attack and, of these, most were administered by Britain or Australia. That Christmas Day, the Japanese took Hong Kong. By New Year they were advancing steadily down the Malayan Peninsula and, on 2 February, the AIF were in action in Malaya.

The first bombs to fall on Australian (mandated) territory fell on Rabaul, where our young, 2/22nd Battalion was awaiting attack. The Americans were pushed from Manila to the island of Corregidor; Kuala Lumpur, Dutch Borneo and the Celebes had fallen; 100 aircraft had carried out the second raid on Rabaul and it was still only 20 January. The next day Lae, Salamaua, Bulolo, and Madang were bombed, as were Manus Island and New Ireland.

We made no new ground; we just kept losing it. Then, on 22 January, a Japanese invasion fleet was seen approaching Rabaul and the civilians were evacuated into the jungle, as the young men of the 2/22nd Battalion manned their machine gun posts on the beach under Mt Vulcan.

We heard no more of that battalion for some time; they managed to hold out for 24 hours, we later learned, and then the remnants took to the jungle and waited their chance to escape from the island. On 23 January the Japanese occupied Rabaul and, by the last day of that month, the British and Australian forces had been pushed off the Malayan peninsula to Singapore Island. And the enemy had seized Amboina. Here, on this small island north of Darwin, the 2/21st Battalion had met the invasion fleet and now they, like the 2/22nd, were lost to us. We heard no more of their fate for three and a half years.

And so it continued. Singapore fell on 15 February and Darwin was bombed on the 19th. Darwin shocked us, but Singapore had shaken us to the core. Impregnable Singapore! With 17 000 Australian men and nurses prisoner, a devastating number, given our small population of seven million people. Those of us who were here at that time experienced a surge of rage that only Mary Gilmore, that great patriot–poet, could articulate for us:

> *We swear by our dead, and captive sons –*
> *Revenge for Singapore!*

She spoke for us all in 'Nationality':

> *I have grown past hate and bitterness,*
> *I see the world as one;*
> *Yet, though I can no longer hate,*
> *My son is still my son.*
>
> *All men at God's round table sit*
> *And all men must be fed;*
> *But this loaf in my hand,*
> *This loaf is my son's bread.*

And, in the dramatic 'No Foe Shall Gather our Harvest', she expressed our fierce pride of being one with our country:

> *Our women shall walk in honor,*
> *Our children shall know no chain,*
> *This land that is ours forever*
> *The invader shall strike at in vain.*
> *Anzac! . . . Bapaume! . . . and the Marne!*
> *Could ever the old blood fail?*
> *No foe shall gather our harvest,*
> *Or sit on our stockyard rail.*
>
> *We are the sons of Australia,*
> *Of the men who fashioned the land,*

> *We are the sons of the women*
> *Who walked with them, hand in hand;*
> *And we swear by the dead who bore us,*
> *By the heroes who blazed the trail,*
> *No foe shall gather our harvest,*
> *Or sit on our stockyard rail.**

We did not know until war's end of the great loss of life in the raids upon Darwin, and of course we didn't know the truth of Singapore or Amboina, but those two islands had held the darling boys of many an Australian home, as had Rabaul and other islands where the 8th Division had been scattered. There was no respite, scarcely time to register one shock, before another struck. On 14 March, John Curtin, Prime Minister, announced: 'Information has been received from the Naval Board that HMAS *Perth* and HMAS *Yarra* are overdue on their return to Australia from waters around Java. In view of the circumstances surrounding operations in that area it is with deep regret that I announce that these two ships must be presumed lost. An enemy claim to this effect was made some days ago. There has been no news of survivors.' Brave, brave *Perth* that had survived 21 bombing attacks in her bid to rescue the living from Crete. Brave, drowned boys. Again, Mary Gilmore spoke for us:

> *We are the women who mourn our dead.*
> *Yea. Let us weep for them.*

Eight hundred and thirty-three men had disappeared with the two ships.

It was the season for tears. Each day brought its dark, drear news. General MacArthur had left his men on Bataan and Corregidor and reached Australia by boat and Flying Fortress. He was now in Melbourne. His melodramatic 'I shall return' utterance became an American legend – and an Australian catch-phrase. Indeed, Ellis Finney (who was an army physiotherapist in World War II) overheard the following in a Melbourne restaurant:

DINER: Can you serve us now?

---

*\*Author's note in the original edition*  In the early days of Australia, in the good old cattle days, the stranger was entertained in the parlour (no one knew who he might be), and the friend down at the stockyard. No *gentleman* ever saw hide, hoof, or brand he should not see.' – Mary Gilmore

WAITRESS: I shall return.
DINER: Thank you, Mrs MacArthur.

At the same time, the Japanese were making their second raid in two days on Port Moresby, a short hop from the top of Australia. On 22 March Japanese planes attacked Katherine, 210 kilometres south of Darwin.

The press repeated MacArthur's every word with reverence, even to the effect that he was 'surprised and disappointed' to find no army in Australia. Hell, we said, doesn't he know that although America has only been in the war for three months, we have been fighting for two years six months, and our fighting men have been the other side of the world for most of that time? Our Prime Minister would now order them home – to the unforgiving anger of Winston Churchill: but the enemy was now at *our* gate and this time it was *our* survival that was at stake.

> *When our last ship's been torpedoed,*
> *And our last plane drops in flames,*
> *When our one last friend has ditched us*
> *And we're lonely in our shame –*
> *When deserted, bankrupt, weakened,*
> *We're exhausted, tired and blue,*
> *Then we'll have to take the white flag out*
> *And tell the world we're through.*
>
> *When bereft of our resources,*
> *We are robbed of all our strength,*
> *When we pray for one last fighting chance*
> *Before we sink at length,*
> *And it's denied us when we're ready*
> *To hoist the white flag high –*
> *Hold on! there's still one better thing,*
> *And we'll do it first – we'll die!*
>
> — When, *by Phillip Lyons*

## CHAPTER 13

# *Australia is Fighting Mad*

*For the South must look to herself for strength in the storm that is yet to break . . .*
*And is it our fate to wake too late to the truth that we have been blind,*
*With a foreign foe at our harbour-gate and a blazing drought behind?*

– Henry Lawson

In the early days of the war in Europe they called it 'the Cold War' because of a lack of obvious activity. In Australia, women had been waging their own cold war from some years.

Since the first rumour of war in 1938, groups of women had trained with considerable difficulty and expense in order to be ready at a time of national crisis. Signallers, nursing aides, motor-drivers and mechanics were being trained to a high standard of efficiency.

On 27 February 1938, the Minister for Defence, the Hon. G. A. Street, had the following placed on Cabinet Agenda: 'It is considered that the general manpower available for the Armed Forces is sufficient to obviate any great demand for the utilisation of women's services in the way of substitution for men in the early stages of war.

'Women's services, it is thought, would be restricted in the first place to relief and mercy work; canteen work; transport work for these services; and various auxiliary non-Government activities.

'Registration of women, therefore, not being a matter of urgent national necessity, should be maintained on a voluntary footing, guided by the Government . . . without stultifying the efforts of the several women's organisations desirous of taking part in the work. All women desiring to register would be asked to associate themselves with one or other of these organisations.'

In 1939, the Federal Government, in response to pressure by women's groups, set up a Women's Voluntary National Register as co-ordinating machinery. Because of this, women believed Government recognised the ultimate need of using women's services.

But war came in September that year and the women still waited.

In 1940 there was such demand to assist that the Women's Australian National Services was established in New South Wales, under the leadership of Lady Wakehurst, 'to bring the various independent training groups into closer co-operation and to extend general and specialised training over a large area so as to ensure a maximum amount of efficient service'. By co-operating closely with the Women's Voluntary National Register, the WANS received the approval of Federal Government and a small yearly subsidy from the New South Wales Government. Within this comprehensive organisation, some thousands of young women were prepared for just such a national crisis as was now approaching Australia. They were disciplined and efficient; 90 per cent were wage earners, who willingly gave up their Saturday afternoons and up to four nights a week to training. Similar organisations co-ordinating training were set up in other states and affiliated with New South Wales.

The Women's Australian Auxiliary Air Force began enlisting between March and May 1941 – a few only, and those because male recruiting could not provide men to fill certain musterings. By October 1941, recruiting was stopped. The Women's Voluntary National Register wrote on 28 October to the Hon. F. M. Forde, Minister for the Army: 'The proposal of the Federal War Cabinet to stop enlistment of women in Service Auxiliaries will bring dismay and keen disappointment to hundreds of women, who at great sacrifice have been trained for such work.

'The Prime Minister, on behalf of the Government and with full approval of the Commonwealth, has emphatically pledged the total effort of this Country to the winning of the War. This would seem to imply the employment of *all* trained personnel, both men and women, in such a way that the necessary Services, the Army, Navy and Air Force, as well as industrial undertakings, might be given the greatest support.

'Great effort is being spent on recruiting campaigns to bring men to the Services. The establishment of Women's Auxiliaries will release all the young and fit men now in routine jobs for the work that they alone can do.'

This letter was received six weeks before the bombing of Pearl Harbor, four months before Australia itself was bombed.

When the Japanese came into the war with their surprise bombing attacks, women were suddenly in demand, this time urgently and in great numbers. At the outbreak of the war with Japan there were 2 755 000 working women over the age of 14 in Australia. Of these 3600 women were in the Defence Services, 71 200 were in government, semi-government, munitions, shipbuilding, aircraft works and defence work in factories.

As well, approximately 128 000 worked in factories not involved with war, but this number was already 21 000 less than when the European war broke out in 1939 and, within the next two years, it would drop dramatically as the country was geared into almost total war effort.

Enlistment records showed that women who were not normally employed now joined the services or war production. The manpower problem was suddenly so acute that it was not a matter of skilled workers being needed but *any* and *all* labour. 'One clear possible source was a more effective use of women . . .' wrote S. J. Butlin.

The coming of war to our shores and the need to harness all possible labour did not automatically bring about a change of attitude to women in the workforce. There was the fear that competent and versatile women would be more acceptable to employers if their labour was cheaper than men's. There were still doubts as to whether women were as 'strong and reliable' as men and deep doubts about the dangers of paying women a man's – that is, an equal – wage. There was a cry for 'equal pay for equal work', but an equal cry for the banning of women from certain work or at least for provisions to be made so that women would leave this work immediately the war ended.

It was a dilemma which caused the Labor Party, in power for only one month before the Japanese attacked, to writhe. On 15 December 1941, one week after Pearl Harbor, Cabinet decided to approve 'as a war measure' the principle of the 'extensive employment of women in industries when men are not available . . . to attain the scale of production approved as a war objective'. Prime Minister Curtin gave a public undertaking in the name of his Government that 'all women employed under the approved conditions shall be employed only for the duration of the war, and shall be replaced by men as become available'. He promised that a sub-committee would deal with the matter 'with full regard to prevention of an invasion of men's work by cheap female labour'.

On 24 September 1942, John Curtin announced in Parliament that in order to release more men for the fighting services, his Government expected to bring at least 64 000 more women into factory employment during the next six months. 'We have to ensure,' he said, 'that men who are displaced do not have their economic standards eaten into by the incursion of women as a permanent economic feature. But,' he added, 'we must also keep faith with the women of this country and ensure that, if they are capable of doing as much work as men, they should be paid as if they were men.'

The Women's Employment Board, hedged in with political fighting (the Opposition regarded the Board as a political body), nevertheless assisted the smoother employment of women in war industries, interesting itself in the new problem of the transfer of thousands of women to jobs and industries in which they had not previously been admitted.

All the while, the Curtin Government was forced to reiterate that they would 'prevent an invasion of men's work by cheap female labour'.

By June 1943 there were 190 000 women in direct war work and, altogether, 840 000 women occupied. A further 127 000 women, who had not been working when Japan attacked, now were either in the services or involved in war work. Forty-four thousand seven hundred were in the defence forces and 39 400 in munitions, ship and aeroplane building.

By June 1943, enlistment in the women's services had grown to 16 243 WAAAF, 18 210 AWAS, 1408 WRANS and 8846 nursing services. As well, by September of that year, the Women's Land Army had 2205 women in the field. Almost the whole of the fabric of the nation had been blasted into wartime endeavour within two years.

Paul Hasluck wrote of this period, 'Only very small numbers of persons "not gainfully occupied" remained to be drawn into useful work (at least if it were assumed that married women could not be called up for national service).'

A resolution carried by the ACTU Conference in 1941 had stated that 'The federal Labor Women's Conference required for any section of work in the Army, Navy or Air Force units, that the equivalent male rates shall automatically apply, together with all the privileges and status of the men enlisted for service in the same group, and that no sex differential of any kind be permitted to be introduced into the pay, conditions and privileges of defence force ranks.'

Such brave endeavours remained on paper (although each of the women's services appears at some time to have brought the matter up). At war's end, women were getting up to two-thirds of male rates of pay. As for privileges and status, few women then or now could complain: it was all so much more than we had got in the Depression years, that it seemed the golden age had arrived overnight.

Before the war, except in some large factories, very few girls were paid the stipulated wage. And in the country, where there were virtually no factories, a girl was lucky to get a job 'for keep', which was supposed to include 'spending money'. My sister Kathleen 'worked' in the country; there was never a need to say 'housework'; just 'work' was enough, when everyone knew that was the only paid toil open to girls in the bush. In 1937, aged 18 years, her 'spends' went up from 7s 6d a week to 10s 0d with 'live-in'; the last supposedly made the wage up to an acceptable figure.

'For that I worked in the cow shed in the morning from 6 a.m., then indoors washing children, scrubbing (on my knees with a bucket, a scrubbing brush and floor cloth), polishing, washing up, washing clothes and ironing until the tea dishes were put away about 6.30 p.m. One day a week – after milking my share of the cows – I was permitted to walk home two miles to spend the rest of the day with my family. Mum supplied my clothes and shoes. Whatever the girls got in the army and factories during the war had to be a damned sight better than we got pre-war, so they would be fools to complain, wouldn't they?'

At the turn of the century, almost 50 per cent of the female working population was engaged in domestic service of some kind. (In the country, the proportion was much higher, perhaps 90 per cent.) Between 1933 and 1947 the number of women employed in private domestic service fell from 170 000 to 42 000 and much of that was service in regulated areas, such as hospitals, restaurants, guest houses and hotels. The drudge of the private home had gone forever.

Earning a living, 'work', became respectable for all unmarried women, widows or the few divorcees. They could claim patriotism as their motive. During the early part of the war, married women were excused from this womanly lapse of decorum but from the day Prime Minister Curtin broadcast the truth of the nation's peril, 'It is war to the death ... the honeymoon is over', even married women were permitted by society and anxiously welcomed to help in 'turning the foe from the door':

'No foe shall gather our harvest or sit on our stockyard rail!'

The day had arrived, when girls could leave home, and hundreds of thousands did just that.

Much had changed in the attitude regarding the enlisting of women. On 22 February 1942 the *Sunday Mail* reported: 'Army Staff Purge Canberra: All physically fit men under 45 at Army Headquarters Melbourne and at the headquarters of all States' military commands are to be removed from their present positions and appointed to positions in the field. Their places on staff are to be filled by others not physically fit for active service, by older men and by women.'

Army Minister Forde had issued this instruction 'in view of the serious shortage of manpower. Women appointed to the jobs will be members of the AWAS.'

Officers in each state were working around the clock. With instructions to speed up enlistments they moved from town to town interviewing girls. Dorothea Skov and Hazel Moloney, both captains in the AWAS in early 1942, made what newspapers called 'whirlwind tours', as they travelled the vast state of Queensland: Caboolture, Maryborough, Mackay, Bundaberg, Somerville, Rockhampton, Gladstone, Cairns, Southport. In one week, these two officers visited sixteen centres. Their immediate quota was 666.

Among the 26 applicants for enrolment in the AWAS being interviewed at the YWCA rooms in Brisbane on 3 March were Beverley Bassingthwaighte from a country property, Diamondy, Jandowae. 'She has been driving for a number of years and is able to carry out running repairs which are part of everyday life in the country, and is a good horsewoman.' Other women in this batch of volunteers had already served in such organisations as Women's Auxiliary for the Fighting Services and most had brothers serving overseas in one or other of the services. The fathers of some were serving.

The first batch of 'women motor drivers' was already on the road. Aged from 18 to 45 they had been given 'an intensive course in engine maintenance, map reading, driving and army discipline'.

Many were experienced drivers before enlisting. 'Two earned their living by driving and one had driven across Australia a number of times [no mean feat, considering that the first motor road had been graded across the Nullarbor only a few years previously].

'One girl has driven heavily loaded wool trucks for months at a time. Others have a detailed and practical knowledge of farm machinery. Each girl must maintain her vehicle on the road and do minor repairs. Night driving is one of their duties. Every girl will release a soldier for combatant duty.'

But already complaints were being made of discrimination against women. 25 February, 1942, *Courier-Mail*: 'Eighteen months ago my daughter volunteered to drive motor vehicles if her services were required. Her husband is with the AIF in Malaya, and her only son has just joined up, having reached the minimum age.' The woman had gone to Victoria Barracks, Brisbane, and had been told that married women would not be accepted until all single applicants had been enrolled.

Another wrote: 'My daughter, who is Australia's first aviatress and cross-country flyer, aged 40, has an experience of motors from her cradle. She can drive any motor vehicle, car or truck, diagnose any irregularities of engine and make the necessary adjustments. But experience evidently does not count.'

Within a week, the Queensland WATS, Women's Auxiliary Transport Services (a volunteer group, part of the Women's National Emergency Legion) were rejected when they applied to train as tram conductresses and drivers. 'We could relieve a larger number of men. Even if we are not needed now, our members should be given a month's training so that we can take over in an emergency. It would not be necessary to spend money on uniforms. We have them,' the State Commandant, Mrs R. C. Philp said. They were rebuffed. However, machinists for tent and tarpaulin making and those having knowledge of factory power machines, were being called for.

The YWCA was beginning to establish hostels for servicewomen. 'Rates of pay for members of the AWAS and WAAAF begin at 3s 6d a day for minors, and 4s 0d a day for others. If the girls are not rationed and quartered they are allowed an extra 2s 5d a day and if away from their home town maintenance is increased to 3s 6d a day. Girls must balance their budget on £2 9s 0d a week, a convincing argument for the establishment of hostels at reasonable costs. The welfare of the women behind the men in the fighting services is the concern of the YWCA throughout the English speaking nations.'

They would, for the duration of the war, offer bed and breakfast, meals, use of a sewing machine, iron, hot bath, writing tables, home newspapers, cups of tea, radios, lounges, club rooms, games' rooms. Girls would be able to bring their men friends in to the club for refreshment and talk. At weekends there was hospitality and entertainment; again, women could bring their men friends in. These YWCA clubs were staffed by voluntary workers.

On 7 April, the Prime Minister 'told the world "Australia is fighting mad".' Newspapers reported the following day, 'That applies to Australian women. For the first time in the history of the Commonwealth women are on the march. They are making history.'

'Thousands are in uniform,' said the press. They were aged between 18 and 45 and now could be married women if they had no children under the age of 16. Darwin had been bombed, so had Broome. Army Minister Forde issued a proclamation (15 April) stating that women in the army were now subject to active service discipline wherever they were stationed. 'All members of the Australian Army are now on active service.' The whole of Australia and its territories were proclaimed a theatre of war. 'All the legal consequences of soldiers being on active service now apply.'

Certainly, attitudes had changed. 'You are part of the army itself,' General Sir Thomas Blamey told the women the first time he inspected them on parade in May 1942. 'Every member of the Army is happy to have you coming in to help. You have earned the right to serve, and the greatest thing any person can do is to serve his country ... There will be many more activities for the women's Army.'

On 31 August 1942, War Cabinet decided that Women's Auxiliaries were to be established as part of the Forces enlisted under the Defence Act. Earlier that month it had been agreed to prefix the letter F to the army numbers of servicewomen. 'The moral fibre of society' and woman's 'natural function' (of being a wife and mother) was to be put in mothballs for the duration of the war while the ultimate survival of society – indeed, of mankind – was in peril.

According to *Truth* (12 April 1943), 'war must be classed as the vilest of evils, but this particular ill wind has blown much that is good in the way of women in Australia'.

Henry Lawson had died in 1922, but prophetically he had written the following lines in 'The Storm that is Yet to Come'.

> *By our place in the midst of the farthest seas*
> *we are fated to stand alone –*
> *When the nations fly at each other's throats*
> *let Australia look to her own.*

CHAPTER 14

# From Tobruk to Tokyo

The Australian Army Nursing Service was naturally the first of the three army women's services in the field, and its members served in every battle area where the Australian army fought – in the sands of the Western Desert, in Greece, in the mud of New Guinea, and in the jungle of Malaya. They served in hospital ships, troop transports, in general, base and camp hospitals in Australia, and they, like the men, spent three and a half years in prison camps in Malaya and Japan.

The service was mobilised on 4 September 1939, and the first contingent of nurses embarked for overseas in January 1940. In 1939 the uniform of the service was modernised from the ankle-length, high-necked and high-hatted style of the 1914–18 war to the short-skirted, shirt-necked style and low-crowned hat of 1939.

The first overseas contingent sailed with the 2/1 AGH (Australian General Hospital) which accompanied the 6th Division to Palestine. The hospital was established on Gaza Ridge, a spot full of memories of World War I for the AANS.

The next overseas contingent also went to Gaza Ridge, where the sisters were detached to British hospitals, until 2/2 AGH was moved to El Kantara to establish the hospital in the desert on the edge of the Suez Canal. This hospital received the wounded from the first Libyan campaign, the famous 'Bardia Boys'.

Members of the next draft of sisters to sail are still known as the 'Battle for Britain Girls', they having arrived in England in time to serve during the 1940 blitz. Later, these and another batch of sisters who went to England served in the Middle East.

By the end of 1940, members of the AANS attached to six AGHS and three casualty clearing stations (CCS) were serving in the Middle East. In 1941, AANS units were working in England, Australia, Palestine, Libya, Egypt, Greece, Eritrea, Syria, Malaya and Ceylon under many and varied conditions, and in all kinds of hospitals, tents, underground dugouts, huts, evacuated civil hospitals, and even palaces, such as the Kaiserine on the Mount of Olives.

That year, the sisters were evacuated from two hospitals, 2/AGH and 1/CCS, in Greece, and an AGH and a CCS in Tobruk. During both of these arduous operations the sisters 'gave magnificent service and were, with difficulty, made to evacuate'. For her leadership during the evacuation from Greece, Matron Kathleen Best received the Royal Red Cross, the first to be awarded to an Australian in this war.

All through their service in the Middle East the sisters worked at high pressure, often during air raids, caring for the acutely sick and seriously wounded from Libya, Greece, Crete and Syria. During the Syrian campaign, they had their first experience of nursing malarial patients in large numbers, and during this campaign, too, they were attached in teams to field ambulances in Syria, when these units were being used as small hospitals holding their own sick and wounded.

One unit of nurses attached to a CCS actually moved up with medical units in the wake of General (later Field Marshal) Montgomery's forces after the victory over Rommel at El Alamein.

During their service in the Middle East, five Royal Red Crosses were awarded to members of the AANS, as well as one Associate Royal Red Cross.

The collapse of Singapore in 1942 brought the greatest blow the AANS had suffered. Sixty-five sisters were posted as missing after the fall, 32 of whom were officially listed as prisoners of war held by the Japanese in Sumatra, while 33 were posted missing, believed killed.

For their magnificent courage during their escape from Singapore, when the ship they were on, the *Empire Star*, was dive-bombed and they went on deck to attend to the wounded men, under fire, two members of the AANS were decorated, Sister M. Anderson receiving the George Medal and Sister V. A. Torney the MBE.

During 1942, the majority of the AANS from the Middle East returned to Australia, in many cases to conditions more primitive and difficult than they had experienced abroad. One hospital in northern Australia was blown to pieces by a cyclone, the wreckage then being saturated by torrential rains.

Central Australia and the Northern Territory had become operational areas, and the sisters serving in them, from Alice Springs to Darwin, had to undertake the care of the civilian and native population as well as of military personnel, even to the extent of providing an obstetrical service, maternity centres and infant welfare centres. These services were also supplied by members of the AANS in north-west Australia and in the Torres Strait area.

At the end of 1942, the first draft of sisters arrived in New Guinea where conditions were 'grim', and 75 sisters were soon coping with over 2000 patients. They were hampered by mud, malaria and insufficient and inadequate equipment. Six members of the AANS who were stationed in Rabaul were taken prisoner by the Japanese during their drive southward in 1942.

By early 1943, sisters were working in hospitals in Port Moresby, and over the range at Buna, Lae and Finschhafen. Working dress became a problem in areas infested with malaria and scrub typhus, so the uniform that had been modernised in 1939 was adapted further in 1943 to meet the needs of tropical service; the nurse's tropical suit was devised, consisting of safari jacket, slacks, boots, gaiters and broad-brimmed hat.

The service of members of the AANS in hospital ships also brought losses to their numbers. In the sinking of the hospital ship *Centaur* in 1943, 11 sisters, including the matron of the ship, were lost, and in the bombing of Darwin Harbour in 1942, one sister was killed and another seriously wounded in a hospital ship.

Members of the AANS served in various other campaigns. Six sisters were on the staff of the No. 2 AAMC training battalion, where they assisted in the training of male nursing orderlies and stretcher bearers, and AANS tutor sisters formed the entire instructional staff of the AAMWS Nursing Orderlies Training School. When this service was formed from the enlisted VAD in August 1944, six sisters were trained in all aspects of nutrition at the LHQ catering school and worked as mobile teams with the assistance of an AAMWS W/O caterer, visiting hospitals in all areas to check on the nutritional aspect of the hospital's work.

In January 1943, Colonel A. M. Sage, RRC, was posted matron-in-chief, AMF. Since May 1941 she had been matron-in-chief, AIF, succeeding Miss Grace Wilson, CBE, RRC, and Florence Nightingale Medal, in this post. Miss Grace Wilson was a World War I veteran who had been matron-in-chief, AANS, for several years before the present war; she went overseas in that capacity early in 1940, but ill health had forced her retirement.

In each line of communication area, in Western Command, and with Northern Territory Force and in New Guinea, there was a principal matron with the rank of lieutenant-colonel, while a principal matron was appointed to any expeditionary force sent out of Australia. Until 1943, members of the AANS did not hold commissioned rank, although they had always received all courtesies extended to officers. But from March that year, all members of the AANS were commissioned and automatically became lieutenants on appointment. None used their military rank as a form of address. Those with the rank of colonel, lieutenant-colonel or major were addressed as matron, and those below the rank of major as sister. Members of the AANS were subject to military law and to the provisions (other than those applying in terms to males only) of the Defence Act, the Army Act and the Rules of Procedure, as are all other enlisted women.

On 7 May 1942, Australian military regulations were amended to increase the age on entry of nurses to the army. Until that date, age limits were 40, with 45 as the retiring age. Now nurses could enter the service up to 50 years of age and retire at 55.

While most people see those enlisted in the AANS as healers of the sick and wounded, few know of the many members of the service who have been in the vanguard of advancements in the civilian nursing profession. In World War I, most of the original Reserve women were prominent in reforming hospital procedure and there was a similarly high percentage from World War II.

Sister Victoria Hobbs of Perth (WA), was one of these women when she wrote her treatise on *Rat-caused Diseases through the Ages*. Her book, *Look You Westward*, is a fine survey of nurses and nursing in her home state. In September 1940, Vicki left in a convoy of Dutch ships and arrived in Palestine, from where she went to Tobruk to the 2/4 AGH.

'On 10 April 1941, the hospital was strafed by the Germans. Two doctors were killed that day. On 6 April, the commander of the force in Tobruk was advised that on the following day, the siege was to be declared. All nurses must leave. We refused, but were ordered out. Twenty-four hours later the great siege commenced. We were still in the harbour.' Because of this, these sisters do not qualify as 'Rats of Tobruk', the sobriquet given during the siege by Lord Haw-Haw to those 'living like rats in the ground'.

As with male enlistments, some nurses joined up with other members of their family, although there could not have been many families with three sisters in the army. The small town of Angledool (NSW) saw the three Hatfield sisters join up. Joyce and Nancy joined the AIF and their sister Ruth, who was in England when the war broke out, joined the Queen Alexandra Imperial Military Nursing Service.

Ruth, the eldest, served in France, Egypt and on the East African coast; Nancy, the youngest, was in Greece and Palestine; and Joyce was at Concord, nursing returned men.

Nancy Hatfield experienced both the evacuation of Greece and of

Crete. 'We went from one Greek port to another trying to find a ship to take us off. We ate nothing but bully beef and army biscuits for days.' Finally an Australian destroyer picked them up and took them to Crete where the wounded were pouring in. Nancy's tent alone had 200 men to be nursed. In 24 hours, the nurses were evacuated again – back to Alexandria and the usual nursing round, while at the side of their mind all day and night was the memory of the patients they had been forced to leave behind.

Among those women serving in military hospitals, the work of the masseuses was little known outside the wards. These qualified women were in many hospitals performing tasks under medical supervision that they would have done in ordinary civilian public hospitals back home. They accompanied hospitals to all parts of Australia and overseas and were at the evacuation of Greece.

Leah Knowles was a senior masseuse with the AIF in Greece in May 1941 when the Luftwaffe began bombing and strafing the towns and areas near the hospitals. Only a few weeks before, she had sailed from Egypt, through 'Bomb Alley', the route from Alexandria through the Mediterranean. At first, in Greece, the women were billeted in a small hotel, the operating theatre being in another hotel.

'Machine gunning woke us regularly every morning and dive bombing sang to us at night. Curfew was 8 p.m. For four weeks this went on. We couldn't leave the hospital area. Wounded men came in too tired for anything but food and sleep.'

She had scarcely arrived in Greece when the successful German push began. She slept four days and nights in her uniform ' . . . with my tin hat on my head. I suppose I shall wear said tin hat to the races when I get home, it's become such a part of me.

'We were always packed and ready to go in a hurry, slept in our clothes. Suddenly we were told to go. Quick. Couldn't take our kitbags and cases. We all volunteered to stay. I longed to stay behind even though I am so fond of my family. Many cried. Thirty of us were packed like sardines into military trucks, only room to stand.'

Like others who escaped from Greece and Crete (before the Germans marched in and took those who stayed prisoner), Leah Knowles was forced back to Alexandria, 'only four and a half weeks after we left there!'

Among the first women physiotherapists to enlist in 1939 was Captain Alison McArthur Campbell. She was called up in 1940 and left Australia with the 2/4 AGH for the Middle East, where she stayed in Egypt, Libya,

Tobruk and Palestine. By 1944, Captain Campbell became the first appointee to the position of chief physiotherapist on the staff of the Director-General of Medical Services, and she acted as liaison officer between the DGMS and all physiotherapists working in Australian general hospitals and convalescent depots.

Her jobs also included inspecting the work of the physiotherapists employed in medical units, and keeping a check on the adequacy and suitability of the wide range of equipment used in army physiotherapy departments. This appointment was the result of the growth in the use of physiotherapy among sick and wounded soldiers in this war. Women had made physiotherapy so largely their field, their numbers growing from four to 150 in the army in just over four years, and it was just recognition of their important contribution that a woman should be appointed to this post.

These women were enlisted through the Australian Physiotherapists' Association. The DDMS, General Rupert Downes, was the first president, which made their passage into the army much simpler than was the case for most of the women's services. 'Our *raison d'être* was simple,' Alison McArthur Campbell says. 'We were to work to restore as quickly as possible the muscle power and joint mobility of wounded and sick men.' The women were attached to the AAMC. They served in hospitals in Australia, in the Middle East and in New Guinea.

Jocelyn Growse and Ellis Finney went over in a convoy that left Sydney on 4 February 1941. 'One day en route we saw a destroyer on the horizon and, at the same time, the great *Queen Mary* gave three loud blasts of her siren, and next we knew this fast ship had pulled out of line of the convoy and was off to deliver her passengers, the 8th Division, to Malaya – Singapore. Of course, Japan wasn't in the war yet, so those boys felt they were being left out of all the fun, as we were off to the land of the pharoahs.

'The *Queen Mary* did a lovely thing before she left us. With all our soldiers and nurses and us crowded on the decks of our ships and the 8th Divvy lining her deck, the Queen circled swiftly round each of the ships in the convoy, her speed delighting us. And then she was gone and, in a moment, it seemed we couldn't see those boys any more. They went so fast over the curve of the horizon. I often thought of that during the three and a half years those boys disappeared from our sight, lost in the prisoner of war camps.'

Ellis was senior physiotherapist. 'We all did much the same thing in the

Middle East: helped make plaster casts, exercised limbs and muscles, went sight-seeing as often as we could get away. But the work was long, sometimes twelve hours at a stretch. It was all exciting for me. I hadn't been anywhere but Adelaide until then!'

They set off for Greece, but on the way both Greece and Crete fell. 'Sisters and Masseuses to be fed and returned,' was the message on the notice board.

Back in the desert in Egypt Jocelyn found so many men complaining about their feet that she set up a flat-feet-class to meet every morning. This soon became so popular that the CO asked her to discontinue the exercises, as it was a great scheme for the men to escape being allotted tasks for the day.

'One of the terrible things about being away from home in time of war is to learn in the worst way that your homeland is under immediate threat. We read it in the Egyptian newspapers. It was not exaggerated. It was cabled from Berlin. They listed the string of islands the Japanese had overrun and their determination to take the south-west and south Pacific. As soon as the 9th Division could be pulled out, we all set off for home.'

Jocelyn sailed on the *Aquitania*. 'A Dutch luxury liner: the Dutch called her "the fur coat".' On returning to Australia, the girls were sent to New Guinea and other islands where the AIF were fighting. 'We worked fearsome hours. We had boys coming down from the Kokoda Trail, wounded, weary, covered with mud. Of course the hours were long. The sisters worked long hours standing on their feet most of the time.'

When Ellis marched in the Anzac march in April 1984, wearing her wartime uniform of navy blue with the smart crimson cockade on the hat and rows of ribbons on her chest people asked: 'But what service were you with?' An old digger of World War II called out, 'They're the girls who were hard on us in the Middle East. But you'd softened up by the time you helped us in New Guinea!'

CHAPTER 15

# The Ultimate Crime

On Wednesday, 19 May 1943, news was released of the deaths of all but one of the nurses aboard the hospital ship *Centaur*, off the Australian coast. The newspapers mirrored the cry of the people: 'The Ultimate Crime', they called it. 'Torpedoing of Hospital Ship' ran the headlines, reporting the sinking five days previously of what had, until that Friday, been known as 'the Luck' ship. One of the last ships to leave Singapore before it fell to the Japanese, she had escaped all air attacks without damage. The *Centaur* had been anchored in Darwin harbour when the Japanese made their first devastating attack in 1942.

During the ship's war career she had survived more than 70 near misses from enemy bombs. Throughout these adventures the 3286 tonne vessel had been a freighter, but in early February 1943 it was converted to a hospital ship with accommodation for 250 patients, as well as medical and nursing staff and 70 crew. Among the latest fittings were modern ventilation and refrigeration, X-ray apparatus, 'ultra-modern' surgical and medical equipment, rows of double-tiered cots and electric lifts.

Three months later, she was gone, and had taken 299 Australians with her. Australia was outraged. The sinking of a hospital ship was considered the ultimate crime among civilised nations. The barbarity of this deliberate attack (and what other ship at sea would have all lights blazing? they asked) etched even more firmly in Australian minds the conviction that their Japanese foes were savages. By flouting this most sacred convention, the Japanese had set themselves outside the ranks of civilised nations who went to war according to the rules. 'This act gained for the perpetrators a deeper stain of the infamy their nation had already earned,' read the leader of the Melbourne *Argus*, 'a fiendish act'.

John Curtin said, reporting the loss of the ship and all on board her: 'Notice of intention to use the *Centaur* as a hospital ship with particulars of her dimensions, markings and appearance, had been communicated by the Commonwealth to Axis Powers early this year – in Japan's case on February 5. In addition, full publicity, including photographs of the ship, was given in the Press and particulars were broadcast in news from Australian stations.

'There was therefore no reason to suppose that the Japanese Government and naval authorities were not fully acquainted with the existence and purposes of the ship.'

In a statement on the circumstances of the sinking, Mr Curtin said: 'The *Centaur* was at 4 a.m. on Friday, May 14, a short distance off the Queensland coast. Weather was fine and clear and visibility good. The ship was brightly illuminated, in accordance with the Geneva Convention. Illuminations, in addition to usual navigation lights, consisted of red crosses on each side of the hull, red crosses on the poop, and rows of brilliant lights along the side of the hull to illuminate the characteristic green painted band – in this case 5 feet wide – which encircles hospital ships.

'On board the *Centaur* were 363 persons, consisting solely of ship's crew and medical personnel, including 12 nurses. There were no wounded on board. In all there were only 64 survivors, including one nurse. The remaining 299 persons, including members of the ship's crew, nurses, and other medical personnel, lost their lives.'

International law, which owes its authority to general acceptance by the nations of the world, is explicit on the inviolability not only of hospital ships but also of hospital personnel, such as comprised the sole complement of the ill-fated *Centaur*, apart from its crew. This principle was adopted at a Hague Conference of 1899, when it was sought to apply to naval warfare the principles already applying to land warfare by the Geneva Convention of 1864.

Briefly, it is laid down that hospital ships may be neither attacked nor seized. They must be used solely for the succour of wounded, sick and shipwrecked, and they must, if necessary, afford relief and assistance to the wounded of either belligerent. At a further Hague Conference a few years later, at which Japan was represented, a code of rules was adopted, one of these specifying that a hospital ship must be painted white outside, with a horizontal green band about five feet in width all round, and must hoist, together with its own national flag, the white flag with a red cross provided for by the Geneva Convention. It is the practice, too, to give the opposing belligerent particulars of hospital ships.

All these rules had been scrupulously obeyed by the Australian authorities. There could be no doubt, therefore, that the sinking of the hospital ship was, to quote the Prime Minister, 'an entirely inexcusable act, undertaken in violation of the convention to which Japan is a party and of all the principles of common humanity'.

There were no patients on the vessel, which was bound unescorted for New Guinea. Survivors included one medical officer, one nurse, 32 other medical personnel, and 30 members of the crew. Eighteen doctors, 11 nurses and 193 other medical personnel were killed. Excepting members of the crew on duty, everyone was in bed when the torpedo struck. Survivors estimate that about 150 people succeeded in getting into the water. More than 200 were trapped below decks by water and flames, and many others were sucked down with the ship as it plunged to its doom.

Anger and grief were experienced by the families of those who were lost. Mrs A. E. Johnson of North Fitzroy (Vic.) recalled that both her husband and her brother, Warrant Officer Williams, were never recovered from the sea.

A number were killed by the explosion and by falling debris, many were terribly burned and collapsed in the water; several were taken by shoals of sharks. Survivors said that before they got away they heard 'agonising cries of nurses' caught by flames billowing up to the promenade deck and of men trapped below. There was no chance to send out a wireless SOS or to get any lifeboats free. Some, on deck, in the few minutes it took the ship to sink, saw the outline of the submarine at close range. Apart from those burned while escaping, many suffered severely from hot oil scalding their eyes in the water. Some spent the whole time on planks, but the majority were able to form into two parties on rafts and wreckage which they fastened together. Several rafts and the top of the wheelhouse were lashed together by another party numbering about 30 and including the only nurse who survived.

Ronald Moate, chief pantryman, of Williamstown, said he was on the boat deck, where Captain G. A. Murray, Jack Stutter and Charlie Carey were trying to launch a lifeboat. 'Fire belched up and covered the bridge,' he said, 'and the ship started to slide down. I saw a mast break away, and then we were sucked down. Only Stutter and I came up. I caught hold of a hatch cover, but it was torn out of my grasp. I then got a rubber raft, and Stutter and a badly burned fellow joined me. About three hours later we were joined by another raft, on which were Stan Morgan, donkeyman, of Melbourne, and another badly burned man. This man died at sea, and we buried him at dawn on Saturday. We were joined by two other rafts on Friday afternoon. Sister Savage was on one of them. She was so magnificent that we did not even know she had fractured ribs. There were finally over 30 in our party. We had 2000 milk tablets, 2 lbs of chocolates, a tin of prunes, a tin of raisins, some meat extract, and 2 gallons of water.'

The fortitude and courageous conduct of Sister Eleanor Savage was one of the dramatic features of the stories told by survivors. With grim detail they described their terrifying ordeal as they jumped or were swept from the sinking vessel into shark-infested waters. Sister Savage, of Sydney, only survivor of the 12 nurses aboard, suffered fractured ribs and lacerations to the face, apart from suffering severely from exposure, exhaustion and shock. She had been an AIF nurse for two years, having previously served on the hospital ship *Oranje*, then operating for the Commonwealth to the Middle East.

Sister Savage and her cabin mate rushed to a window when the explosion awakened them. They saw the ship was on fire, so they seized their lifejackets and made for the deck. Sister Savage also snatched up her rosary beads. 'My best friend, Sister King, was in the next cabin,' she said. 'We had often talked over what we would do if we were ever torpedoed. Sister King could not swim, and it had been agreed that I should crocodile her – that is, take her across my shoulders – if we ever finished in the water. So after meeting on deck we jumped into the water together.

'Sister King was apparently killed by some debris, for I never saw her again. It was then that I apparently injured my side, but I never realised it at the time. I am a strong swimmer, and immediately struck away from the ship when I realised Sister King had disappeared. I climbed on to a section of the deck house with Robert Westwood, 15-year-old cabin boy, who had burns. We worked our way to two rafts, on which nearly 20 men were huddling.

'I had only torn pyjamas on, but one man gave me his khaki trousers, and another a greatcoat. I gave Westwood what attention I could, and sheltered him against me with the greatcoat. The greatcoat undoubtedly saved my life, for I could never have survived the cold otherwise. I had always wondered what I would do in such circumstances. My reaction was quite different from what I thought it would be. I had no thought of panic, but took immediate comfort in prayer. My first thought was to say a prayer that we might be saved, and that my friends might be saved too. Later I led the prayers as we recited the Rosary, even those who were not Catholics joining in. It did much to brace our morale.'

Alex Cockrane of Subiaco (WA) was saved by an oil drum. He said all joined Sister Savage in reciting the Rosary. 'They were for many of us the most fervent prayers we have said in all our lives.'

Dr Leslie Outridge, medical officer, and other men rescued with Sister Savage, highly praised her courage, describing it as an inspiration. They said she took charge of the rationing of what food and water they had, working on the assumption that they would not be picked up for four days. 'She must have been in great pain all the time but never said a word about it, and her leadership was a great factor in the morale of her party.'

Jim Waterson, storeman, of Bassendean (WA) said he was trying to get to the boats when the stern reared up about 20 metres and the ship plunged down. He was swept off the deck and grabbed a raft on which there was another chap. He could hear screams of some of the nurses on the burning promenade deck and of men trapped below. During the morning he saw Sister Savage on the hatch cover about 50 metres away and swam over with a rope, and the others dragged them back to the main raft.

Two planes passed over shortly after 9 a.m. on Friday. Flares and smoke candles were lit, but visibility had declined and the survivors were not seen. Later they saw two more planes and two ships, which were too far away to see distress signals. Before dawn on Saturday an engine was heard. At first it was thought to be an aeroplane, so lights were shown and flares lit. Then noise of a submarine coming to the surface was heard. Some survivors saw the silhouette of the submarine, realised it was an enemy craft, and all lights were doused, as it was feared the enemy would open fire with machineguns. After a short while the submarine disappeared.

There was almost continuous rain on Friday night and all suffered severely from cold. Although there was not very much sun on either day, all suffered from sunburn, against which few had any protection, as most had lost their pyjamas in the water. They had food enough in the form of milk tablets, chocolate, meat extract, prunes and raisins, but fresh water was the main worry. All had only enough to wet their lips on Friday evening and a mouthful just after dawn on Saturday.

A fifth plane was sighted on Saturday morning and another ship. Then at 1.45 p.m. they were sighted by a plane, which guided an allied vessel to the rescue. The first survivor was picked up about 2.15 and the last shortly after 4 p.m.

'Those Yanks from the small allied rescue vessel were marvellous,' Trevor Hoggins said. 'Ignoring the sharks, they came overboard into the water to help those who were injured, burned, or otherwise too weak to climb aboard. They gave us clothes, food, and all the medical attention possible, and even their beds. They could not have done more.'

Many of the nurses had been on the hospital ship *Oranje* for up to two years before transferring to the *Centaur*. Among the 11 nurses who went down with the ship was Matron S. A. Jewell, who had served in the Middle East and with Sea Transport, going backwards and forwards to Australia on troop transports. The sad irony of her death was that while on the transports she had no protection, such ships being fair game to an enemy. Yet her life was taken while on a ship guaranteed safe passage by all nations, including those whose submarine crew sent the torpedo into the unarmed vessel.

Captain Hajime Nakagawa of the Japanese Imperial Navy submarine 1-177, which torpedoed and sank the *Centaur*, has consistently refused to speak of the event. A journalist from the Melbourne *Herald* asked Nakagawa's daughter in Japan in 1981 for help in speaking with her father, but the request was refused. The daughter, according to Ken Merrigah, the reporter, said that there was no point in resurrecting the matter. 'The winners of the war can talk about anything they wish . . . I think a winner is a winner and a loser is a loser.'

Mr Nakagawa was arrested after the war and tried as a war criminal. He spent four years in Sugamo prison for his part in activities in the Indian Ocean when he (and other Japanese captains) fired on survivors of torpedoed ships.

## CHAPTER 16

# *RAAFNS*

*You can say what you like, but it does a man a world of good just to be able to look at a woman.*
— *An airman, when the* RAAF *Nursing Service arrived in New Guinea*

For the first few months of the war, RAAF sick and wounded were treated at army hospitals. Then, in the winter of 1940, an outbreak of influenza and bad throats in the southern states forced the creation of the Royal Australian Air Force Nursing Service, RAAFNS, a few weeks after the appointment of the Director-General Medical Services, Air Vice-Marshal Hurley.

On 29 July 1940, Miss Lang was appointed Matron-in-Chief to form the RAAFNS. She was a Salonika veteran of World War I, who had been in charge of the Victoria Police Hospital for several years. For this new service she chose her own nurses, travelling from state to state selecting from the hundreds who wanted to join. During the first year, the RAAFNS took on 120 nurses. By 1945, there were 616 members.

The uniform was founded on that of Princess Mary's RAFNS, which was formed in 1918 and established permanently in 1921, but greatly modified. The ranks run from four rings for matron-in-chief, three rings for principal matron, two and a half rings for matron, two rings for senior sister, one ring for sister, all ranking as officers.

By the end of 1940, RAAF nurses were overseas. Fifty-two members of the service set off with the Empire Air Training Scheme escort parties to Canada and the United States.

In the following year, October 1941, four nurses were sent to Darwin, then regarded because of the posting's monotony as being almost equivalent to Siberia. But within eight weeks of their arrival, the Japanese had entered the war and Darwin was in the firing line.

Perhaps the posting that pleased these women most was New Guinea, humid, hard and isolated though it was. It was exclusively male when they arrived, but the men were so glad to see them that they had prepared for their personal comfort 'quite touchingly'. Their quarters were tents high on the hillside overlooking a kunai grass-covered valley, with the tented camps of combat squadrons and the sound of roaring aircraft engines in the distance.

It was a strange chance that brought them their first patient for a major operation in the little theatre that had been set up on the station. He was a Papuan with 15 centimetres of spear buried in his back – the result of a domestic quarrel, not of war. Unable to pronounce his name, the theatre sisters called him Laurabada, the Papuan name for the south-east traders which blow for half of the New Guinea year and which break the stillness of the equatorial day.

*Wings*, the RAAF journal, wrote that 'The hospital has been changed since we have had women on the station . . . the nursing staff had the feminine trick of making the best of any situation. They would soon have the men digging small garden beds around the theatre, around their own tents. In a very short time there would be flowers and vegetables growing where only kunai grass had waved before.

'There, women had brought an enduring quality to a temporary scene. Many men will remember so long as they live; the debt they owe these women comrades in war.'

In Darwin the nurses were ordered to do practice evacuation of their hospital each day and to keep respirators and tin hats handy, along with emergency clothing, beside their beds. The moment came at 9.45 a.m. on 19 February 1942. The air siren screamed and, within ten minutes, the staff evacuated their patients from the hospital. A description of the Japanese attack on the RAAF station was given by Senior Sister I. M. Smith.

'As we were going to our trenches we could see high up, nine clusters each of nine planes. We were in the trenches for about half an hour when a formation flew over. They came down very low and stayed for 40 minutes, which seemed like two hours. The relief was wonderful when we heard the all clear. We all went to our posts and attended to quite a few minor casualties and evacuated the patients safely to the 119th AGH. After a short interval, we were back to our trenches to undergo a most awful experience.

'The planes came over in perfect formation, and let us have it. The noise was terrific. A bomb exploded ten yards from our trench, and believe me, we thought our end had arrived. Although our trench was of rock formation, the vibration caused it to tremble, and the dirt and rubble fell on our backs and tin hats.

'When the all clear sounded, our SMO, Squadron Leader Howle, called for Senior Sister, and was surprised when we all hopped out of our trench in good condition. Apparently, he thought we had been buried when the bomb exploded so close to our trench. We shall never forget the sight which then met our gaze. The huge hangars were burning, also the equipment store, post office and the administrative block of the hospital, dental section, X-ray and dispensary. We went back to the hospital and rescued equipment which we had packed and stored in trenches.

'Later we went to our quarters to prepare a meal for the staff and medical officer and found the water and light were cut off. Our home had been strafed and there were bullet holes in our uniforms which were hanging in our rooms. Just as we were going to have a snack the alarm sounded again and the sisters were ordered on to a truck and were taken out to the bush. Fortunately we had been packed for several weeks previously. We stayed in the bush for two hours waiting to know our fate.'

After this, they worked at the 119 AGH which was overflowing with civilian, army, navy and air force patients. The RAAF nurses helped out at the army hospital until it was decided to transfer the air force station back to Daly Waters, south of Darwin.

'We went back to the RAAF Station for the first time since the raids', wrote Senior Sister Smith, 'and boarded a Hudson and left for Daly Waters. It was the first time for many a year that they had had no rain. It was very hot and dusty. We walked about one mile from the aerodrome to the little hotel which was the station sick-quarters, officers' and sisters' living quarters.

'There were several patients with dysentery, dengue and malaria and an American airman very ill with blackwater fever. We firstly attended to the patients and secondly to the washing as there was not an atom of soap to be had anywhere. When we first arrived we had an out-patients of 100, but they gradually decreased as conditions improved.

'Flies were there in millions. The keeping of food was a problem as there was only one refrigerator for hospital patients and staff, but after the first week the Americans delivered ice daily, their camp being 20 miles away. Things were very quiet for the patients as there was nothing there for their welfare until the Red Cross representative arrived from Alice Springs.

'The sisters adapted themselves fairly quickly to tropical conditions but, for the first few weeks, sandfly bites and minor skin conditions were troublesome.'

Eventually, a hospital was set up at Coomalie Creek, 96 kilometres south of Darwin, and here were brought the men involved in accidents, some of the airmen suffering from severe burns. This nursing was heavy and the patients required special attention. Conditions, as always in the 'wet' in the Northern Territory, were trying. There were only primus stoves on which to cook special meals for the very sick, or to boil water for sterilising. On occasions, the women had to do the hospital laundry when the mobile laundry broke down.

As did the nurses in hot, humid climates in World War I, they found their veils going limp in the moist heat – 'it was hard to appear neat'. Sleeping in the daytime was difficult, so night duty was limited to only one week on, if at all possible.

Up to this time, the RAAFNS wore white uniforms, but it was then realised that this made too clear a target for enemy pilots and the nurses were ordered to dye them khaki – with strong tea.

By November 1942, the RAAFNS were in the semi-arid June Valley, Papua New Guinea. Wards at No. 3 MRS (Medical Receiving Station) at Ward's airfield were tents and the night after the arrival of the nurses there was an air raid, the first of many. Sleep was disturbed and work was heavy. Mosquitoes were so bad that the women were issued with long-sleeved shirts, slacks, gaiters, boots and fur felt hats for wearing between sunset and sunrise in this malaria-prone area.

At the beginning of 1943, the sisters took over the training of male nursing orderlies as well as training WAAAF as sick quarters' attendants and nursing orderlies.

In February 1944, a medical air evacuation transport was inaugurated and in the following month, No. 1 MAETU came into existence. Nurses were included, and applicants for air evacuation duties were called for from nurses within the service. When applications closed, 100 sisters had volunteered, and the first 15 were selected and posted to the Medical Training Unit for two weeks' special training. Senior Sister N. I. Kendrick, an original member of the RAAF Nursing Service, was appointed Sister-in-Charge.

Later, a second medical air evacuation unit, No. 2, was formed and nurses were included in this also.

Even when hostilities ended there was still the need – and danger – for nursing sisters. RAAF Nursing Sister Marie Eileen Craig, aged 33, was killed in 1946 when the Dakota on which she was flying with patients from Biak to Australia crashed in West Irian. All 27 Australian servicemen, 9 RAAF crew and Marie Craig were killed, but their remains were not recovered until 1971, when Jerry Reeder, an American missionary pilot, found the hitherto undiscovered wrecked plane in inaccessible mountains. Later, two RAAF helicopter crews established a landing pad some 3000 metres up the mountain so that the wreck could be reached and the bodies retrieved. The body of Marie Craig from Drummoyne (NSW) was given a military funeral.

# CHAPTER 17

# RANNS

*I*n the main, it was the demands by nursing organisations and relatives of sailors for the recruitment of female nurses that brought about the formation of the women's Royal Australian Naval Nursing Service in October 1942. Earlier it had seemed inadvisable, even undesirable. It was impracticable to have female nurses in sea-going ships or remote shore establishments and a male sick-berth branch was necessary. Its competence depended not only on training but also on opportunities for practice. 'If all specialised work was done by female nurses', the Naval Board believed, 'the sick-berth staff would be found wanting in experience.' When World War II broke out, there were 59 sick-berth ratings in the RAN. When the sudden call for the navy to expand tenfold came, Miss A. I. Laidlaw, who had been an army nurse in World War I, was appointed the first matron, and nurses were chosen initially from Sydney and Melbourne only.

Regulations were modelled on those of the army and air force. The matron was given rank equivalent to that of a lieutenant-commander; nurses on entry had the equivalent rank of a sub-lieutenant, and on promotion that of lieutenant. Saluting, however, was obligatory, the RANNS being the only one of the three Australian nursing services in which this was so at the time.

The first RAN nurses were not unnaturally a little timid as they entered the depots, for they were invading what had hitherto been an all-male service, and most of them spent their first week studying the 'Bible', a mighty tome of naval rules and regulations. However, they quickly adjusted and were soon talking unaffectedly in the naval vernacular. The rooms in the hospital became 'cabins', the floors 'decks', the windows 'scuttles', and they did not leave the hospital, they 'went ashore'.

At Melbourne, 12 nurses under Matron Laidlaw took up their duties at Flinders Naval Depot, living in two cottages there. In their first weeks at Flinders the nurses found that they were really needed. Many of the recruits travelling from other states in the winter without adequate clothing caught chills, and infectious diseases among them spread rapidly. At one time the nurses were in charge of five wards with approximately

150 patients. When the WRANS entered the depot, a ward was made available for them, which added still further to the nurses' duties.

At Sydney, where Miss M. L. Rae had been appointed the superintending sister, there were some initial difficulties. At first the navy had no hospital of its own, and the nurses worked in two – and, for a time, three – wards of the Prince of Wales Hospital, Randwick, accommodation being provided for them in the quarters of the Repatriation Department sisters. Later, when the navy took over 'Canonbury' as a hospital, Sister Rae, after much difficulty, succeeded in finding a cottage at Darling Point to serve as living quarters. At first the nurses received a victualling allowance and were responsible for their own cooking and housework. This was a most inconvenient arrangement, for often a nurse who was needed at the hospital had to be sent home to prepare meals.

After they had been at Darling Point for about six months the Director of Naval Medical Services came to inspect the nurses quarters. He was horrified to see fruit cases round the table instead of chairs, and almost immediately afterwards the navy took over the cottage; it was furnished properly, and a cook and WRANS stewardesses were provided. The RAN nurses in Sydney looked after not only Australian but Royal Navy, Free French and American patients (although the last only came under their care until the US Navy set up its own hospitals).

The service benefited greatly in 1943 when a limited number of physiotherapists and one biologist were admitted to work in Sydney and Melbourne.

The nurses took a prominent part in the training of sick-berth attendants. At Flinders, Sister B. V. L. Swallow took over the theatre, where she supervised the training of SBAs.

Only one of the nurses, Sister J. E. W. Tame, was appointed to a ship; she made a voyage to India in the hospital ship *Manunda*. Numbers of them, however, served overseas. In April 1944, when the military position at Milne Bay had become stable, six nurses under Sister V. E. Kelly were posted there to take over a 40-bed ward at the RAAF hospital. Later, the navy took over the hospital completely. The establishment then had to be refitted, a task for which naval organisation was not well adapted, but after unavoidable delay and difficulty, a satisfactory hospital unit was formed, capable of taking between one and two hundred patients in palm-thatched wards. The nurses, with sick-berth staff and other ratings, continued to work there under the direction of two medical officers for more than nine months. Other nurses were posted to 110 AGH, Perth, the naval sick-quarters in Brisbane, Townsville, Cairns, Canberra and Fremantle, and to Darwin.

The sick-quarters at Brisbane, Townsville, Cairns and Canberra accommodated up to 25 male and 12 female patients, and also treated outpatients. Usually two sisters were stationed at each, and, as the more serious medical and surgical conditions were not treated there, all needs could usually be met. The navy took over Kahlin Hospital, the one-time civilian hospital at Darwin, in 1945, and naval nursing sisters served there until the end of the war.

The author of the official history of the Medical Services of the RAN, writing only 23 years later in 1961, gave no indication that female nurses would ever find a place on board a ship at sea. 'The influx of highly trained nursing sisters into the navy presented problems to the officers administering hospitals and sick-quarters. Goodwill played a large part in avoiding friction, but more than that was required. It was always necessary to be on guard against relying on skilled female nurses and relegating the male staff to subordinate positions, which would obviously militate against efficiency at sea. It was found advantageous to place some wards in charge of petty officers, and to see that the operating theatre was not entirely the responsibility of a theatre sister, no matter how skilled she might be.'

Although the number in the service never exceeded 60, there was no question that the naval nursing service was successful, and that its members added to the general comfort and well-being of the sick and wounded in naval hospitals.

# CHAPTER 18

# *The VAs Who Became AAMWS*

Most bush families were closely knit before World War II and many sent their sons and daughters to war when the call came. Of my own family, none lived in the city; all of us were living in isolated areas of the bush and, as each reached the age of 18, we 'joined up', boy and girl cousins alike.

Some of us 'jumped the gun' and did not wait for our eighteenth birthdays. Instead, we coaxed our mothers to sign the enlistment form and filled in the details ourselves – in private. We four girls were very dear friends, more like sisters than cousins. Margaret and Victoria Buick went into the WAAAF, Sheila Adams enlisted as a driver in the AWAS, and I enlisted at the close of 1941 as a VAD (later to become AAMWS). We corresponded with one another throughout the war, scattered though we were from one end of the continent to the other. There were many families enlisted like my family.

The World War II service whose names are most confusing to almost everyone who did not serve in it – and just as confusing to those who were later enlistments in it – is the VAD/AAMWS. To those of us who were VADs we remained, in our estimation, VADs until war's end, even though by then we were officially AAMWS. Such is the camaraderie of men and women at war that, even though they continue to unselfishly work in a cause, they have a fierce loyalty to their original unit. Nothing, not even time, lessens this commitment.

This service, formed by Red Cross to work in army hospitals and convalescent homes in World War I, had a long and honourable history before the outbreak of World War II. Girls were enlisted to work rather as orderlies or aides to the trained sisters of the Australian Army Nursing Service, as limitations in army hospitals made it impossible to enlist and train nurses as in a civilian hospital. In Britain, Voluntary Aid Detachments (VADs) were formed in the early part of this century. When World War I broke out, the women, already trained in first aid and home nursing, manned hospitals at home and crossed the channel to serve in Flanders and France, often within five kilometres of the firing line. Several Australian volunteers were with the VAD at that war, but the best known VAD of all time is the Englishwoman, Vera Brittain. She is the author of *Testament of Youth*, a book loved by those of us young enough to serve in World War II and by another generation in the 1980s.

The Order of St John of Jerusalem (of the famous St John Ambulance Association) collaborated with Red Cross in instruction classses and examinations in first aid and home nursing. Certificates in both, as well as a period of part-time work in civilian hospitals, qualified a girl to enrol as a VAD if she had her Commandant's blessing.

Voluntary Aid Detachments were recognised by the Australian Government in 1916 as auxiliaries to the Medical Service and, from that time, a considerable amount of voluntary work was done by members of detachments in military hospitals. After the war, the work of Voluntary Aids continued as a peace-time activity in hospitals throughout Australia.

When war was declared in 1939, Voluntary Aids soon began to take an active part. The Director-General of Medical Services first sought approval for the employment of female Voluntary Aids in camp hospitals in Australia, and then for their inclusion in military hospitals for service overseas.

VADs did not have to furnish references of good character on enlisting. Their character was already vouched for by their community. Each town and suburb had its Voluntary Aid Detachment in peace-time. They had enrolled under the very simple but time-honoured practice of being invited, either by the Commandant of the district or by a friend who was already a serving member. Clergyman, employer, teacher and parents – all would be known to the Detachment or the Commandant.

Approval for overseas service was obtained on 27 June 1941, the number of personnel authorised being 800. It was arranged that the women should proceed in drafts of approximately 200 each, and the first draft sailed for the Middle East in October 1941. Later, a detachment was sent to one hospital in Colombo and a number were to serve on hospital ships.

On Japan's entry into the war in 1941, the services of many more women were required in medical units. Approval was therefore obtained for more extensive employment of Voluntary Aids in hospitals, and a system of army control was developed.

A VAD officer (Commandant) was appointed to the staff of the

Deputy-Director of Medical Services in each state to carry out the duties of selection, enrolment and allotment to units. A Commandant was also appointed to the staff of the Director-General of Medical Services at LHQ to co-ordinate the administration of Voluntary Aids on full-time duty.

There was a strong, but by today's reckoning, outmoded sense of service about the VAs. Their motto was:

> *Not of men sought we Glory*
> *For Ye are our Glory and Joy.*

While everyone who trained wanted to carry a lamp, training early taught these girls that it was tea-trays, scrubbing brushes, pans, bottles and soiled linen that would be carried until war's end released them.

Wearing the Cross of St John of Jerusalem on their hats and a Geneva Red Cross on their arm in honour of the two services who bound them, their workaday dress was the traditional garb of those who fetched and carried for the sick and injured: the veil of the nun, the apron of the maid-servant, and the cape of the gentlewoman.

But Voluntary Aids in no way formed an exclusive group, a society who could *afford* to be seen doing the most menial work as a sort of ultimate offering of themselves for their country. On the contrary. When the best known of the yellow press of the day hinted at such, there was no need for a rejoinder. For those 'who never previously soiled their hands' could point to girls such as myself, the daughter of a railway navvy. It was different. It was the tail end of the *old* tradition of service for one's country and mankind – or, with hindsight, perhaps it could be said to be the connecting link between the old and the new woman's version of service.

There was a special quality about the relationship between the VAs and their Commandant. None who trained with (Mrs) Major Appleford could forget her. Some of us who 'got our time in' in Gippsland (Vic.) knew her well, as she and Dr Appleford lived at Lang Lang and had ministered to many of us in childhood illness and accident. Others knew she was the rare woman: she had a Military Medal. This medal was awarded to men only, but Alys Ross King (as she was when in the AANS in World War I) had been considered brave beyond any decoration awarded then to women.

She was twice mentioned in despatches, received the Royal Red Cross, and after her work with the VAD in World War II the FNM (Florence Nightingale Medal). She had left Australia in 1914 on the first convoy and nursed Gallipoli men in Egypt. In France at No. 3 Casualty Clearing Station behind the lines she remained with the surgical cases who were too dangerously ill to be moved back to base hospitals, even though the CCS was being bombed and the enemy was advancing.

On her return to Australia in 1919 she married Dr Appleford and assisted him to set up a first aid military unit and, in the 1930s, she became involved with the Voluntary Aid Detachments. I was a little girl when my family lived in her district, but without precise words she left the impression on me that, if war came, my country-girl's energy and strength would be needed.

Another famous World War I nurse who became a well-known Commandant of a VA Detachment was Effie Garden, who first enlisted in 1914 and nursed in Egypt, France and Belgium. During the Second Battle of Ypres in 1917, she nursed in a casualty surgical team at 'the front' and was from there mentioned in despatches and awarded the ARRC. In World War II she became a VA Commandant and, as well as lecturing in home nursing, she set out the Medical Nursing Examinations for enlisted women. She too, was awarded a FNM.

Every town of any reputable size in Australia had its VAD with a notable local woman as its Commandant, and when war came, many of them enlisted, along with their girls, in the army.

In 1941, as the shortage of manpower became more apparent, and in order to release as many men as possible for duty in forward areas, it was decided that women should be employed in hospitals to the fullest extent. So in addition to working as nursing orderlies and operating theatre assistants, Voluntary Aids were now posted for duty as cooks, clerks, messwomen, telephonists, seamstresses and tailoresses, laboratory assistants, dispensers, radiographers, storekeepers, dental clerks, dental orderlies, orderlies, laundry workers and as administrative and general duties' personnel.

It was then decided that, in order to facilitate administration and to distinguish between Voluntary Aids employed on full-time duty in the army and those still engaged on unenlisted part-time duty, a change of designation for those in the army was desirable. In December 1942, the Adjutant-General approved of the establishment of the Australian Army Medical Women's Service (AAMWS).

From that date, the Service's officers and soldiers were subject to military law and to the provisions of the Defence Act, the Army Act and the Rules of Procedure. (Although this approval was given in December 1942 it was late 1943 before it became effective.) 'The majority of the original recruits for the AAMWS were drawn from the ranks of Voluntary Aid Detachments, and the experience they had already had was of great benefit in their work in military hospitals, both home and overseas.'

It was all very well for the official unit history to gloss over the transfer, but the feelings among the rank and file were bitter. It is not easy to relinquish one's place in a time-honoured Service, indeed, to be in at its death. We were to change from our navy uniform and greatcoat and hat with the badge of St John of Jerusalem to khaki (although we were permitted to retain the Geneva Red Cross on our sleeve). There was little understanding or sympathy for the sense of loss felt by these women – many of us young girls, and all of us proud, perhaps too proud, for it could only have been pride in this honourable service that made us perform the menial, often unpleasant, almost always heavy work, often for such long hours that the weekly *Truth* wrote of us in 1942. 'Slaves. Young girls work 17 hour day.' (Our only comment had been, 'And what's it got to do with them!')

We, who had never drilled or saluted, were sent to a training camp, and there the efficient and well-trained AWAS NCO taught us – now privates – how to belong to the army. We were a recalcitrant bunch. VADs who had seen service in the Middle East and nursed the 9th Division after Alamein and Bardia were now told, 'Smarten yourself up, soldier,' while crossing the parade ground. When the time came for us to escape there was to be a passing-out parade and – oh joy! a camp concert! The Middle East girls were all saying they were 'browned off', a saying they had brought back with them from overseas.

I, and my companions from No. 1 Australian Orthopaedic Unit were spared it all, for we were suddenly commanded on parade, told we were to have final leave and, after three days, to head 'North' with our hospital. So we missed the item some of the returned girls had prepared to the tune, 'Bless 'em all'

> *So we're saying goodbye to you all*
> *The long and the short and the tall*
> *You got your promotion this side of the ocean*
> *So cheer up you——Bless 'em all!*

From this distance in time one can appreciate the commonsense of the change, the economy, the uniformity – but many a girl wore her blue ward uniform till it was worn thin rather than don khaki. Again, in retrospect, khaki was preferable to both our navy outdoor garb, or pale blue, indoor, button-through uniforms.

We did some fearsome rail journeys, cramped eight to a carriage day and night, side by side except for those who slept on the floor, out in the corridor, or up in the luggage rack. Meal stops were often as not pandemonium, and in the heat of Queensland one could be shunted into a siding and left there for hours on end while trains carrying the fighting men forward were clear-lined north on the single-track rail system. The solitary hand-basin at the end of each carriage was always without water within an hour or two of our setting out; there was nowhere to wash so much as a pair of army knickers, let alone a shirt. The white shirts worn with our navy uniforms had stiff starched collars – so those of us who travelled a lot were rather quicker to change to khaki than our pride would admit.

As the demand increased, the AAMWS rapidly expanded and its field of service extended. As these girls had no prior training, an intensive course of preliminary nursing training was given at Darley (Vic.). VAD/AAMWS were posted to medical units all over the Commonwealth. Early in 1943 it was decided to send them to various units in the Northern Territory, and they served continuously there from that date and, from July 1943, in hospitals in New Guinea. More than 400 members served in those areas.

For a time, specialists such as physiotherapists, occupational therapists, dietitians and biochemists were members of the AAMWS, but in September 1944 they reverted to the AAMC. Many of them, like the original VAs who formed the nucleus of the AAMWS, had overseas service in the Middle East, Ceylon, Malaya and New Guinea, and in hospital ships.

First Controller, AAMWS, was Lt-Colonel K. A. L. Best, who originally transferred from the AANS to become Controller VAD before the AAMWS was formed. Previously she had been Matron of No. 5 AGH overseas and received the RRC for devotion to duty during the excavation of Greece and Crete. She directed the administration of the VAD and the AAMWS from June 1942 until February 1943. This period saw the rapid expansion of the Service, including the change of VAD to AAMWS, and the return of members from the Middle East, a vast and unenviable task for any woman.

Lt-Colonel May S. Douglas was appointed Controller of AAMWS in July 1943. In the early days of the war, Colonel Douglas served as a VA, and was subsequently one of the first group of officers selected for the AWAS in which she served as Assistant Controller, SA and Queensland Line of Communications Areas before her appointment as Controller.

In November 1943, AAMWS in New Guinea flew across the Owen

Stanleys to Buna, where they played a large part in establishing the hospital, receiving and treating patients and carrying out all the hospital work until the arrival of the sisters eight days later. As the hospitals moved forward in the wake of the Australian forces, the AAMWS accompanied them from Moresby to Dobodura, Lae and Finschhafen. In the concluding stages of the war, members of the Service were sent to New Britain, Bougainville, Hollandia, Morotai, Borneo and finally Japan.

The first members of the women's services to come to Port Moresby, the AANS, often spent their nights in slit trenches, tin hats on their heads. By the time the AAMWS arrived, there was not much bombing, but over the range, at Buna, they were often subjected to air attack. They also suffered the usual hazards. In 1945, 16 of them, members of the 2/9th AGH at Morotai, had a narrow escape from death. The aircraft in which they and nurses from the hospital were returning to Australia on leave burst into flames soon after leaving Darwin. The pilot managed to land and the crew smashed the Perspex machine-gun turrets at the sides and rear, allowing the girls to jump clear seconds before the plane blew up.

From July 1942 onwards, AAMWS were posted to medical units in the Northern Territory – at Alice Springs, Katherine, Adelaide River, Tennant Creek, Larrimah, and Mataranka. The climate during the wet season was very trying, but most of them stood up to it very well, even when on duty in kitchens and laundries. Because of the severity of conditions, service in the Northern Territory, except at Alice Springs, was limited to 12 months.

A few of the AAMWS were also posted to a camp hospital at Mount Isa and others to a mission hospital at Halls Creek in the far north of Western Australia, possibly the most isolated place in which the AAMWS served.

When off duty in the tropical islands, the AAMWS naturally were popular with the troops. A special club was built at Port Moresby; there, and elsewhere, they could go swimming, picnicking and dancing. Their tropical uniform – a khaki overall, white veil, and ankle socks instead of regulation stockings if they so wished – had to be changed after 6 p.m. for the anti-malarial rig of safari jacket, trousers, woollen socks and boots. In this attire they would set forth in the evenings, with no make-up but lipstick (which had to be applied frequently as it melted so quickly). They were not allowed to go out except in parties of six, and male escorts had to be armed. This posed quite a problem for would-be swains among artillerymen and naval gunners who had access to 25-pounder field pieces and 6-inch naval guns but not to small arms! This rule was later altered to parties of not less than 6 AAMWS and male escorts, with a senior NCO (male) in charge and armed with a revolver.

Many AAMWS married whilst still in the islands and other areas. With the help of fellow AAMWS and army personnel, most of them had a traditional wedding. Dental units would often produce the wedding ring made from gold used for dental fillings. Formal dresses and veils were conjured up in the most unlikely places and some couples even had honeymoons on plantations.

Apart from those VADs enlisted in the army, there were thousands of civilian members of detachments and these women worked for the duration of the war in a voluntary capacity manning hospitals, hostels and buffets. Detachment 610 Devonport (Tas.) met every ship docking with troops on board and served tea, coffee and biscuits to the men before they were taken off by ambulance or boarded the train for home leave.

In each state, these women worked in any field connected with hospitals or the welfare of soldiers, including the collection of funds to finance their labours. And when the enlisted girls left for the war or came home after it, the warmth of the comradeship was shown in their greeting.

While some talents certainly withered and died with neglect, in those days there were other women whose total talents were not only recognised, but used unsparingly. Joan Richardson of Perth (WA) was one of these women. Joan, a ballerina, joined the Red Cross in 1937. 'We all felt that war was coming, that we should be *doing* something. I did the course in first aid and home nursing. It just seemed natural to think we would be needed.' When war broke out she worked with the concert parties and entertainments for the servicemen, and then, in 1941, she enlisted as a nursing VAD in the army and served in Egypt, Syria, Rehoveth and Gaza with the 9th Division, and later in New Guinea. In 1945, Joan transferred to serve on the aircraft carrier HMS *Formidable*. She was, at the time of writing, an executive member of the Western Australian Branch of the RSL, the third woman to be elected to the executive.

She held both the Distinguished Service award and the Long Service medal of the Red Cross, and the MBE. The *West Australian* reported her departure on her first trip away as a VAD, describing her as 'a well-known member of Perth's younger set'. Another paper commented that 'Many who do not know Miss Richardson personally will remember her graceful dancing'.

In 1983 Joan recalled, 'After four years at the war there was none of "the younger set" left in me nor were there many dancing years left'. Yet

When Gallipoli was evacuated in December 1915, Australian nurses who had cared for the wounded on nearby Lemnos Island were taken off by barge.

These South Australian ladies may look prim, but the Misses E. and V. Williams daily cooked food and drove it in their wagon to the 7th AGH Keswick, to succour the returned wounded, 1916.

Major Jean Wood and Lieutenant Colonel Sybil Irving, AWAS (centre), interviewing Joan Braithwaite, whose husband was serving in Malaya.

Sheila McClemans, Director, WRANS.

Clare Stevenson, Director, WAAAF.

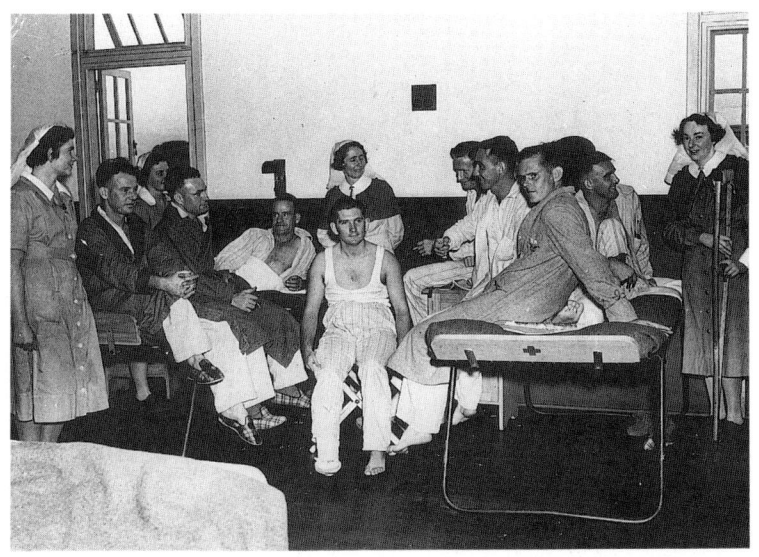

Nursing sisters, with the help of nursing Aids (Australian Army Medical Women's Service), saw service in many areas.

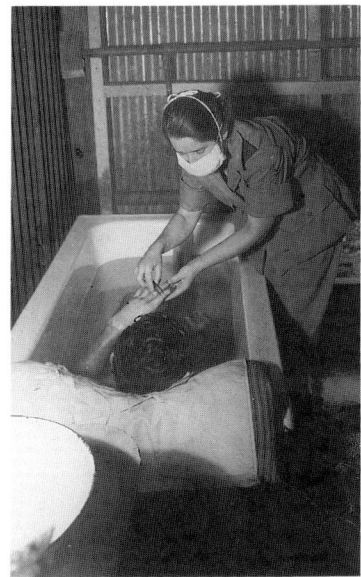

Sister Everett attending to a burns patient.

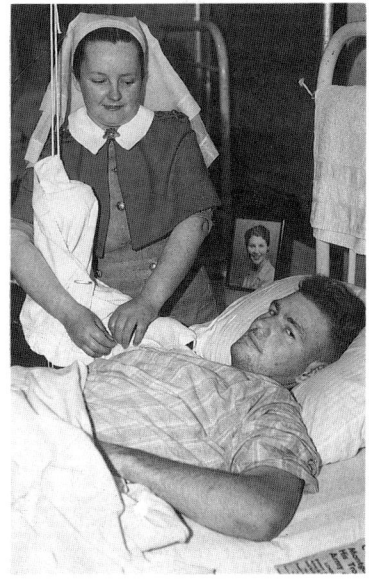

Sister Una McDonnell, a typical nurse, skilled and caring.

'The Invisible Crew'. The young girls building the Beaufort Bombers were told: 'Their lives are in your hands.' Jean Page is second from the left.

Renee Barlow and Marie Purvis oxy-welding belly tanks, thereby giving planes a wider range.

Refuelling wagons at RAAF stations were run by WAAAFs.

AWAS height-finder crew with their anti-aircraft battery. At one time 3577 members of the AWAS helped man anti-aircraft and searchlight defences throughout Australia and in some instances completely manned entire stations.

AAMWS reinforcements en route for the island of Bougainville.

Women from the Royal Australian Navy warming up before going on parade.

Medical ward, New Guinea.

Casualties from the Pacific were nursed on their journey home by the RAAF Nursing Service (Medical Air Evacuation Unit).

Matron A. M. Sage (left) searched for her imprisoned nurses in Singapore and Sumatra.

on the way 'overseas' and 'over there', as the newspapers called it, she had put on a concert on board ship and danced the Sailors' Hornpipe and arranged ballets to the songs, 'Wings over the Navy' and 'There's Something About a Soldier' and 'Nursey':

> Nursey! Come over here and hold my hand.
> I feel oh so blue
> Nursey when I look at you
> My heart goes ooh ooh ooh
> Nursey! Nursey! I'm getting worsey
> What am I going to do?

When the girls reached the 2/7th AGH in the Middle East there was little time for dancing. Wood-fired coppers had to be stoked for boiling up anything from bandages and tea towels to veils, uniforms and bed linen. While she was in Egypt, her beloved brother Frank, a RAAF pilot, was able to get a day's leave to Cairo, and there they met for the last time. He was killed in Burma shortly afterwards.

Joan did dance at least once in the Middle East, as we learn from a letter from Mrs Mary Dodge of the American University of Beirut, Lebanon, to Joan's mother: 'It was a pleasure to meet your charming daughter with the artistic members of the 7th AGH. They entertained troops in our garden. Joan's costume and dance were lovely in the moonlight. She was so sweet about repeating the dance. We were so grateful to the group for coming to us on the actual eve of their transfer to [cut out by censor] and my heart went out to them all and Joan in particular, and I said I would write you a note. I hope before too long you will have your dear girl back.'

The VADs arrived back in Australia with the 9th Division in 1942 and became pioneers once again when they went to New Guinea to the 2/5th AGH, the first contingent of VAD/AAMWS to be sent to Port Moresby. Here, they tackled any job. 'First task of the day was to clean the kitchen, then tidy the wards, sponge the patients, take temperatures, prepare special foods and sometimes go on mess duty in the sisters' quarters.'

Like all the others who enlisted as VAD, Joan found the life to be little different from the way Vera Brittain had described it in World War I.

When she transferred and became Assistant Superintendent Red Cross Field Force in March 1945, she set off on the first of several voyages on the 23 460 tonne aircraft carrier HMS *Formidable* – straight into a typhoon.

'It wasn't anything. The big ship rode it out, standing out to sea from Manila.'

The Japanese were being pushed back from the islands and the vessel was able to bring back 1300 Australians and a large contingent of English and New Zealand ex-prisoners of war. As well as her other work, Joan again organised shows and concerts. 'There were 200 cot cases aboard and that took up some time.'

On the outward journey the ship had transported Indian prisoners of war from Rabaul to India and picked up the Australians on the homeward run. 'These Australians had been stranded at Manila for three weeks and more and that of course seemed a life-time to men who had already had three and a half years in prison camps.

'The two English and we two Australian Red Cross officers were stationed on the flight deck near the reception desk as the Indians came on board, and we distributed cigarettes, matches and chocolate to each as well as a note of welcome. When they were all on board we then went to the hospital and gave each man there the same, plus barley sugar for the Sikhs, who do not smoke.

'From then onwards the routine was for us to open the Red Cross cabin from 8.30 a.m. daily. We'd set up our gear on tables in the aircraft lift-well each day and get them to the flight deck by lift, where the Indians queued up for toilet gear, peanuts, handkerchiefs, dilly bags, washers, boot brushes, pen, paper and envelopes. All the simple, everyday things they had not had for so long. The rest of the day we spent in the hospital wards helping with handicrafts.

'When we got to Bombay the Indian Red Cross were on the wharf to help them to the hospital train drawn up waiting for them.'

The British OC troops, thanking Joan Richardson for her work, said the men were sorry they could not show their appreciation in some way. 'In the Indian Army it is an order that when a man receives anything he stands to attention and says nothing.'

'Well,' says Joan now, 'that certainly explained to us the unusual experience of a daily distribution to 1100 men, with no verbal acknowledgement at all!'

Then it was off to Batavia. 'On the way there we helped with the ship's mending. It was all part of the job. Then, when we picked up the 1300 long service veterans from the islands, we helped the doctors and nurses and kept the library open for the troops.' And naturally Joan organised a concert.

When her service ended, she went back to Bombay to marry John Dowson, an army engineer. 'We honeymooned in Poona.'

> *If you can make the orange drinks and egg flips,*
> *About the diets knowing all there is to tell,*
> *And get the* MO*'s morning tea and heat a poultice,*
> *And maybe sponge a man or two as well.*
>
> *If you can take a 'ticking off' from Matron,*
> *And realise she doesn't mean it – much,*
> *If you can bear to see your rec. leave vanish,*
> *When you thought you had it safely in your clutch,*
> *If you can take the trials and tribulations,*
> *The good times and the bad all in your stride,*
> *If you can do all this and keep good tempered,*
> *Then you're not a* VAD*, but a saint who hasn't died!*
>
> – *The* VAD*'s "If"*

## CHAPTER 19

# *Calls for Blood and Serum*

Jean Kahan, who served from 1940 to 1946, came into the army in a different manner to most. A member of a well-known Western Australian family, her uncle, Harry Kahan, was an original Anzac before he returned to his occupation as a headmaster; her aunt, Douska Kahan, was visiting America when World War I began and went to France as a Red Cross nurse for two years before coming back to Australia. When World War II began, Jean had graduated in science with a major in zoology and was teaching. She was asked to work in the mustard gas section of munitions at Maribyrnong (Vic.) 'Stringent blood tests were necessary before acceptance for this work, as mustard gas can affect the blood of those working with it.' Her tests were done in Perth by Dr C. Fortune of the AAMC, who was interested in blood serum and transfusions. 'He performed the tests but talked all the time, trying to persuade me not to go. "Stay here. We must get our own serum laboratory here. Stay here and work on it!" '

In those days, all serum came only from the Commonwealth Serum Laboratories in Melbourne and, with the transport of the day, this seemed almost as great a distance as was London from Perth. But, because Jean had promised her services, she believed she must go. She began work – not enlisted, of course, but as a scientist – and later that year Dr Fortune wrote to her saying that it was now possible to set up a laboratory in Perth, and she was to gain experience in the work in Melbourne – buy equipment, 'all sorts of equipment, anything you can get' – and then come back to Perth, where he had a handful of VAD working with him.

Jean went first to the 'Walter and Eliza [Hall] Institute, where they were awfully kind to me', and studied the then-new techniques. 'The first blood transfusion I saw, I was told to hold the bottle while they drained the blood from a man. I sat holding the bottle in my hands and the warm fluid coming from a body – I felt things going black and I said to myself that I wouldn't be much help in a war if I fainted at the first trial, so I got firm and pulled myself up. It was just the warmth; it was strange to me.'

When Jean finished at the Walter and Eliza she went to the

Commonwealth Serum Laboratories. 'They were good to me too.' Jean was now instructed to contact Dr Julian Smith, who would discuss the process with her. 'I wanted to meet Dr Julian Smith. He was as well known for his photography as for his work in the medical field. He made a direct blood transfusion set; until then, we used to get blood from a donor and bring it to the waiting patient. Dr Smith made one set for each blood and serum unit for direct donor to patient transfusion.

'He also made a mechanical needle sharpener. Until then we sharpened needles by hand with oil stone and varying degrees of sandpaper after each use – some could sharpen and some could not! The doctor demonstrated various parts of the process to me.'

Remembering Dr Fortune's injunction, Jean took back to Perth, by train from Melbourne, a complete blood transfusion set. She had bought any and all equipment she could get her hands on, and she had a great amount of luggage. A friend helped her to Spencer Street Station.

'Take great care of that,' said Jean, indicating the transfusion set. 'It is a treasure to be taken to Western Australia.' When she was finally seated, she looked up to see a notice scrawled on the huge ungainly bundle. 'Eggs, Handle with Care!'

And so the valuable cargo came west. She had also bought yards of stainless steel piping, glass tubes and any other equipment available on the rapidly shrinking market. 'Other army travellers kept asking "Who owns all that junk up there that is taking all the space?" I pretended to sleep. In civilian clothes I was suspect. There was no space for anyone else's luggage at all. I'd taken the lot.

'On arrival in Perth, all of it worked in well. The serum was separated from the blood in the ordinary domestic cream separator – one of us turning the handle like farmers' wives have always done. Then it was filtered, stored for a period to be sure antibodies were absent. Washing the blood from the separator – none of us cared for this job.'

She was still virtually a civilian; she belonged to no part of the services, although the army paid her. Eventually, Dr Fortune threw his car keys over to her and said, 'Go down and get yourself enlisted'. Jean joined the AAMC, which already had several women part-time with the corps.

'Get yourself a tailor and get something made,' she was told, so Jean went to Mr Mendelsohn, a Perth tailor. 'He was diligent. Kept saying, "For the army it must be so!" He sewed the buttons on the wrong side. "You're in the army, you've got to wear it that way," he insisted.

'Donors were coming in – Red Cross got them for us. It was all new.

A mobile unit got the donors from factories. We stored the transfusion serum when ready for use in refrigerators in a number of hospitals, so that supplies were dispersed for safety. I was phoned one night for permission to use the first batch manufactured in Western Australia, as some patients had come in with burns. And I still remember the anguish I felt after giving permission, wondering if the product was all right.'

Blood and serum preparation units had been established in each capital city by early 1942. These were army units working in conjunction with Red Cross. Campaign conditions in New Guinea called for special conditions for the supply of stored blood.

Jean was transferred to Sydney. 'There were calls for blood and serum from all directions. Sydney General Hospital, hospital ships coming in, matrons and sisters coming in from transports to learn the technique. There was plenty of action. Blood was being sent to Port Moresby in ice boxes. It had been collected into the standard "soluvac" flask using saline citrate anti-coagulant. It was all innovative for the time.' The bottles were filled to capacity to allow no space for shaking and so save the corpuscles from damage, and sealed with cellophane and wax.

As the battles moved further north in 1943 so, too, did the blood-collecting centre – and Jean. 'In Brisbane, messages were coming in [requesting] serum or whole blood by plane, flying boats or ships for New Guinea. Again the glass flasks went off in lead-lined wooden boxes packed with ice. The main function of the unit in Brisbane was to supply New Guinea and Queensland.' On top of all this exacting work, Jean had her staff to consider. 'One of my girls, a VA had seen her husband for two weeks between his returning from the Middle East and his departure for New Guinea. A few weeks later I had the job of telling her he was dead. It was an officer's job. It had to be done. There was no easy way to do a thing like that.

'The train trips from Perth to Brisbane were a thing to remember. Ten days – not counting the days in Melbourne to clean up and do some washing. We were fed on the Nullarbor, slept sitting up.' By the time Jean was to return to Perth to serve there, she had got to know some of the pilots who carried blood to the islands, and they helped her home. 'Standing in the bomb bay, then sitting on the cold metal floor of the plane the whole trip. These bombers were, of course, not heated. We had to go in stages – no real long hops in those days. We went from Melbourne, Adelaide, Ceduna, without food. There were no ladies' toilets of course. Overnighted at Kalgoorlie, then home on the third day.'

By now the American navy had a submarine base in Western Australia and submarines were coming regularly to Fremantle. Most of these men had not been blood-grouped and the unit at Perth arranged to blood-group each man and supply the vessels with serum. (Serum is given for shock and burns, blood to replace blood lost from a body.) Eventually, two American naval technicians were assigned to the unit to help with preparations and this enabled the unit to supply any ships that came to the port. 'When the subs came in *everyone* wanted to go down to Fremantle.' But it was Jean who must go. 'I didn't know how to salute. Hank said, "You must salute the fore-deck." "Where's the fore-deck on a submarine?" I wanted to know.'

Jean enjoyed working with the Americans. 'The technicians were superbly trained. Sergeant Cooper would have a flask of coffee percolating on lab equipment all day! I lived with my Aunt Douska, and Cooper would sometimes come for an evening meal, and Aunt Douska and I loved that, because he brought all sorts of American things, some things that we hadn't seen in Australia since war broke out, some we had never seen.'

Jean had to make much of the equipment. 'You couldn't buy it.' She worked long hours. 'Cooper didn't have to work such long hours, none of the US technicians did, but they'd stay to help – and make coffee. We had only Sunday off and that was spent washing, going to church and then picnicking.'

Major Fortune, the doctor with whom Jean was associated, was by now in New Guinea, where he set up a special blood centre for men with serious wounds from the Owen Stanley-Buna battlefields.

A. S. Walker, writing in *Clinical Problems of War*, tells of the value of the work of the blood units. 'It was particularly necessary for naval ships, as many casualties were due to suicide Japanese bombers. Following a Kamikaze attack on HMAS *Australia* in December 1944, in which 96 casualties occurred, causing 30 deaths, fluid replacement was administered by mouth, and sometimes per rectum, in addition to plasma given intravenously. The medical officers worked continuously for 15 hours. When the Royal Navy arrived in the Pacific, the ships and shore establishments were also supplied.

'Transport of blood by air was necessary in the islands on account of the distance and the difficulties of terrain. Even after blood had been landed at airfields in good condition, its distribution was often troublesome, involving journeys over rough jungle roads only fit for jeeps. High priority of air transport was arranged and blood collected at Sydney in the evening of Day 1 reached Port Moresby on the afternoon of Day 2, and often was actually being used at main dressing stations on Day 3. It was found that blood would last up to a week if ideal conditions of transport and refrigeration could be maintained. Ideal conditions were, however, almost impossible to obtain.

'And so life of the stored blood was limited.

'The improvement in many patients was dramatic and many lives were thus saved.'

# CHAPTER 20

# *Persons and Practitioners*

Although the authority for the appointment of medical officers in the AAMC referred to 'persons legally qualified to practise medicine', the word 'persons' was not interpreted as including women practitioners until 1940.

By a special army order of 17 October 1939, the British War Office authorised the commissioning of women practitioners in the RAMC and set out the method of such commissioning in the British army. Using this order as a guide, Australian authorities introduced the commissioning of women graduates in medicine in the AAMC on 10 July 1940.

The first woman to be commissioned in the AAMC, AIF was Lady W. I. E. MacKenzie MB, BS, who was appointed 25 September 1940. Before being commissioned, Lady MacKenzie had undertaken administrative duties in the Medical Directorate LHQ for some six months in a voluntary capacity. Her appointment, therefore, was an administrative one, as Deputy Assistant Director-General of Medical Services.

There were 18 medical women officers on the Active List on full-time duty in the AAMC, some with the rank of captain and some as majors, mostly specialists in general hospitals, but some were engaged in general duties and administration. Assistant pathologists, pharmacists, physiotherapists, dietitians and occupational therapists became members of the AAMC on 1 September 1944. Prior to this date they were members of the AAMWS.

Thirteen women biochemists and all science graduates, whose duties were to assist the pathologist medical officer in a general hospital, were grouped under the heading of assistant pathologists. There were three women pharmacists in the AAMC and 150 women physiotherapists, 77 of whom served with units overseas. The first four left Australia in January 1940 as members of the staff of the 2/1 AGH. Twelve women dietitians were on full-time duty in the AAMC, as were 16 occupational therapists.

# CHAPTER 21

# *Gallant Sailor-girls*

The WRANS had to learn naval tradition and terms that this oldest of the services had built up since the time of Henry VIII. They 'come aboard' or 'go ashore' when entering or leaving the establishments where they served – yet WRANS never went to sea. If they told a story they were 'spinning a dit'; they didn't grumble but 'nattered'; food was 'scran'; the kitchen the 'galley'; laundry 'dhobying'; regulation was 'pusser'; and non-regulation 'tiddly'.

When the first girls joined the Women's Royal Australian Navy in 1941, they heard the words that scores of generations of men had listened to in the preamble to the Articles of War of the Naval Discipline Act: 'For it is the Navy whereon, under the good Providence of God, the wealth, safety, and strength of the nation chiefly depend.'

The nucleus of the service was enlisted for the wireless telegraphy branch and this was due to the work and tenacity of one woman, Mrs Vi McKenzie. As remarkable a woman as any developed in Australia, Mrs Mac had a hard opponent in the Naval Board. 'They battled against accepting women in the navy for a long time. We had difficulty getting going.'

Yet Mrs Mac had girls serving in HMAS *Harman* by 28 April 1941. She was a person who, sensing that World War II was inevitable, began anticipating, planning. She was already a qualified electrical engineer when she founded the Women's Emergency Signalling Corps.

On 27 December 1940, Mrs Mac wrote to the Minister for the Navy, the Hon. W. M. Hughes, suggesting the girls trained by the WESC be permitted to join the RAN as telegraphists. 'So I went to Melbourne to see the Naval Board. The person in charge said "Girls in the Navy? What could they do?" I told him to send an examiner to Sydney and we would show him. Commander J. B. Newman came to Sydney in January 1941 and was "astounded". Three months later, the 12 girls – and two attendants – were admitted to the Navy under the proviso that there be no publicity about this break in tradition.'

She was eventually responsible for the training in communications of more than 12 000 servicemen – Australian, American, Dutch, Greek,

Indian, Norwegian, Filipino, Chinese, plus the hundreds of girls who joined the women's services in the communication branch. The whole of this work, which they did as a voluntary contribution to the war effort, was funded by Mrs Mac and her husband.

*Smith's Weekly* wrote of her in 1943: 'Florence Violet McKenzie, with her managerial, administrative and technical ability, has done this work for the forces, for the nation. She remains kindly, genial, human, radiating an atmosphere of friendliness which must remain in the memory of the thousands of students who have become indebted to her.'

She waved no banner, but decided what she wanted to do and found the means to do it. She graduated as an electrical engineer in 1923. As there was no actual course in electrical engineering, she studied science for two years at Sydney University. When funds ran low, she enrolled at Sydney Technical College.

The course demanded that an electrical trainee student be employed by an electrical firm. No firm would risk employing a woman apprentice, so she started her own electrical supply business in the Royal Arcade and in this way was able to qualify.

After her marriage, she continued to run her own radio and electrical business. She was the first Australian woman to be granted an amateur radio operator's licence (Station VK 2FV); she formed the Electrical Association for Women; and then formed the Women's Emergency Signalling Corps because she foresaw the day when Australia would need trained signallers for the services. The work began pre-war and continued long after, always unpaid. The RAAF gave her honorary rank in the WAAAF as Flight Officer and provided her with a uniform so she might legitimately instruct air force personnel, but they did not put her on the payroll.

Her greatest triumph was getting her 'girls' accepted into the navy. Over 1000 WESC girls entered the women's services as trained telegraphists and signallers, and others remained with Mrs Mac as instructors to the 12 000 men of many nationalities and services, including the merchant navy, all of whom received free training.

The first 14 WESC were accepted by the navy and sworn in on Anzac Day, 1941. On 28 April, Mrs Mac accompanied them to HMAS *Harman* W/T station to assure herself of their proper living quarters and treatment. Mrs Mac later took eight girls to Navy Office, Melbourne, and found the accommodation arranged was too expensive so, on a 'cold, bleak, rainy day, trudged all over that city'. Finally the Traveller's Aid Society came to her assistance.

Many people, well-known in later years, passed through Mrs Mac's hands, including Captain P. G. (Bill) Taylor and C. A. Butler; Mr Howard Beale (Minister of Supply, 1950); Mr Merv Wood, former Commissioner for Police, NSW; Captain E. Gold, Professor of Maritime Law, Dalhousie University, Halifax, Nova Scotia, Canada; Captain W. A. Pearson, Principal, Navigation School, Melbourne Technical College; Captain W. D. Heighway, Principal, Navigation School, Sydney Technical College; Captain J. F. Dodwell, Commissioner, Maritime Services Board of NSW; Captain J. J. Wilson, Harbour Master, Weipa; Captain M. La Delle, Senior Check Captain Boeing 747; Captain Keith McKnight, Senior Qantas Pilot; and Captain Derek Simon, Torres Strait Pilot.

But to Mrs McKenzie, the great achievement was having made it possible for young women to train as wireless telegraphists. She pleaded their cause and, when they were accepted as part of the service, remained their friend. When Japan entered the war, Mrs Mac's girls were already working as the nucleus of a service which, at the time of its greatest expansion, amounted to approximately ten per cent of the Royal Australian Navy.

When she lay dying in 1982, aged 90, she said to visiting ex-WRANS, 'I have a Pilot Flag flying and will reach safe anchorage'. Two hundred men signed a scroll to present to her. 'In recognition of a wonderful lady from Pilots and Mariners of Australia who she has helped so much in their careers.'

The day before she died, she said: 'It is finished, and I have proved to them all that women can be as good or better than men.'

Sheila McClemans BA, LLB, the Director of the Women's Royal Australian Navy, had been admitted to the Bar when war broke out. 'Men were going to the war, and I was getting more opportunities at the Bar than perhaps I would have done otherwise.' She was the first woman to appear as counsel in the Supreme Court in Western Australia.

'But it was no use. I, too, wanted to go to war, or at least to serve. In 1942, I saw an advertisement in the morning paper for women to train as officers – if suitable – in the WRANS. I thought they were looking for someone here in Perth for HMAS *Leeuwin*. When I arrived for interview I found they were looking for a Director for the whole service! There were three terrifying naval officers doing the interviewing. They gave no indication either that I was of any value or that they could tolerate any woman at all getting into their Service.

'A week or so later I was on my way to the Police Court when I was called to the phone: it was the Recruiting Officer telling me to come for my medical. So I borrowed a dressing gown from a friend and reported. Then it was off east to officers' training school, three of us, unescorted, second class rail tickets, in civvies. There were 16 from all states being commissioned as officers. All very impressive.

'At Flinders Naval Depot a CPO had to drill us. I was enlisted as Writer McClemans, graduated from the course as 3rd Officer (Sub-Lieutenant).' She was appointed Director in May 1943. 'I "worked my way up" to Chief Officer (with three gold stripes) and the title of "Madam".

'I spent most of my war at Navy Office, Melbourne, and in the Barracks, St Kilda Road. We didn't have enough quarters and it was difficult to absorb the Service if one was living out. You learn a lot from living in with a group of girls; we were all much enriched by the experience. Better people for it. You were not just yourself, you behaved, became part of something much bigger than yourself. Girls were loving to one another. One WRAN at HMAS *Lonsdale* received a telegram reporting her husband missing, believed killed. She wouldn't believe. She just said, "No, I know he isn't dead." Blow me down, but he turned up. The WRANS at *Lonsdale* pooled their clothing coupons and stayed in the depot on leave days and made her a trousseau.

'This feeling went right through the services. Certainly the senior women of the three services had no jealousy between them, nothing but warm co-operation, never any diffidence or jealousy. We were each serving for the same reason.'

Discipline was no great problem. 'I only once had what could be termed real trouble. The Officer of the Day paraded the girls in front of me. I knew what I must do. We eventually fell them in, all the girls, and read the Naval Riot Act – it's a sort of "everything punishable by death or as hereinafter mentioned" kind of document. There was no repetition of the trouble. The whole thing about discipline was that we *wanted* to do what we were told to do. Discipline was bucking in to do what was necessary to win the war. It was the day of "My Country, Right or Wrong". We question this today, but then life was simpler for us and we did not question such precepts. We really did feel we were working for the country, for the war effort.'

There were five girls in Sheila's family. 'I was used to getting on with girls and particularly in the navy, because we were sincerely wanting to help with the war.'

The WRANS never exceeded 3000 women enlisted at one time. 'The navy is different from other services. The men cannot stay at sea forever, so there must be duties left for them ashore. Therefore, the two figures, male and female enlistments, must balance all the time. We were a service that could not expand merely for the sake of expansion. We could supply cooks, stewardesses, transport drivers, signallers, coders, writers [clerks], cinematographer operators, visual signallers, and girls working in highly classified "hush-hush" sections.

'At all times it was made clear we would never be permitted to go overseas. Mr Makin, Minister for the Navy, thought we would be raped if we were to do so. So, we were banned.' [When Sheila learned in recent years that the navy were considering permitting enlistment for overseas service for the WRANS, she laughed. 'Marvellous! It's only taken them forty years!']

In naval parlance, Sheila McClemans returned 'to the beach' in 1947 and resumed her profession. Her first duty was to arrest a ship in the time-honoured manner of fixing a summons to the mast. She practised Family Law 'until the day I broke my back in June 1980'. She now lives in 'retirement', which includes being a member of the Parole Board, Chairman of the Canteen Trust Board (WA), and Chairman (WA) of the Commonwealth Council on Discrimination in Employment and Occupation.

Margaret Curtis-Otter, one of the first 16 officers, became adviser to the Naval Board after the war, as well as Acting Director WRANS, while Sheila McClemans attended the Victory Parade in London in 1946. 'Those old grey-beards of the Naval Board were so afraid of us when we came up for interview. The girls who came into the service in March 1941 had been 18 months without officers.

Margaret had already married, 'My husband was on his ship on the East China Station. I had joined him in Hong Kong and realised for the first time what marvellous lives men lived.' In July 1940 his ship left Hong Kong, Margaret rejoined him at Portsmouth Naval Base, then returned to Australia in 1942 via the Panama Canal. 'There was nothing for it but I should join the navy. I went in in 1943 and had an awfully interesting war.'

When she was interviewed for an officers' course she was asked, 'Do you think having women mixing with men will make for trouble?' and she replied, 'Of course! You can't put fit young women with fit young men without what you call "trouble". It happens every day.' She was impatient with these outdated excuses for banning women. 'Why not ban the men? Really, it was all ridiculous.'

Margaret went into Naval Control where she assisted with the assembling of convoys and arranging for the departure of merchant ships. She then went to the Naval Office as one of the founders of the Naval Information Service. (The RAN had no public relations department until 1944.) 'They got it started in time for D Day!' The branch consisted of seven men and Margaret Curtis-Otter. 'An interesting job, interesting men, such as Asher Joel, in it.'

As an officer she, like Sheila McClemans, had to have her suit tailored. 'The tailor asked me had I worn a double-breasted suit before. "Of course not," I said, and he hissed to his off-sider, "She'll look like hell, won't she!" But I thought I didn't look too bad.'

This silent branch of the Silent Service must have smiled after Japan entered the war when they saw the advertisements suddenly appearing in newspapers: 'WRANS urgently required'. Pearl Harbor may have been a wartime catastrophe, but it opened out the services for women in Australia. Margaret Curtis-Otter, 2/IC WRANS, says, 'Until this time we had to put up with those female pillars of conservatism who spat out "all those hussies want is to get into trousers!" Now we were the gallant sailor-girls helping to win the war. The Service was thrown open to motor transport drivers, clerical assistants, storekeepers and office orderlies, still "essentially womanly" occupations, but a list of things to come when "gunnery girls" in overalls would discuss the range-finding equipment with WRANS assessing the magnetic attraction of vessels, as they crossed the degaussing* range.

'Even so, on 24 July 1942, at a conference at Navy Office, Melbourne, right in the middle of the acute man-power shortage and the fear of invasion after so many of our men had been taken prisoners from the islands off the coast – even then, the bastions of male naval tradition decided that no more than 600 WRANS could be absorbed into the Service – and of these, 280 must be telegraphists. In August, the Naval OIC, Fremantle, wrote the Naval Board requesting a complement of 100 WRANS and that three or four hundred could usefully be absorbed into that depot.'

Not until this time was the entry of officers into the WRANS seriously considered. Up till now the Service was administered by the Director of Naval Reserves and Mobilisation.

Hundreds of women from all over Australia applied and 16, including

---

*Degaussing: attending to the correction of magnetic instruments. Such as compasssses.

Margaret Curtis-Otter, began a course on 18 January 1943. 'Nine of us already in the Service, including Petty Officer Frances Provan and Leading Telegraphist Joan Furley who had the WRANS enlistment numbers 1 and 2.' The other seven were 'from the beach'.

Thereafter, the selection was made from the ranks and, in all, 124 officers were appointed. Apart from those executive officers dealing with the discipline and welfare of the WRANS, the other officers were stationed in the various War Ports around Australia in ciphers, confidential and secretarial work.

In Brisbane, Second Officer Dorothy Hill was assistant to the Staff Officer of HMAS *Moreton*; Second Officer Josephine Cox corrected and issued charts at Townsville and Cairns, and her efficiency brought tributes from the master mariners who depended on her accuracy for the safety of their ships.

In Sydney, Second Officer Muriel Cheney handled all Safe Hand Mail for this busy port; Second Officer Margaret Vaille was the RAN Press Relations Officer for three years; and Third Officer Sue Beattie, Sea Transport Officer, many times completed her work in merchant ships as they sailed, being taken off at the Heads by the pilot boat and brought ashore. In Fremantle, Leading Writer Julia Lawler boarded every ship – merchant or naval ('grey funnel' to the WRANS) – which entered that port.

Margaret Curtis-Otter knew that 'many of the WRANS held in their keeping such secret information as the movement of ships, composition of convoys, the facilities of various ports and information on merchant shipping which the enemy doubtless would have liked to know. Their work brought them into close association with master mariners of all the allied nations and, apart from the security angle, an appreciation of the vast problems of logistics in wartime. The girls on the degaussing range had an intimate contact with the sea and worked with merchant as well as naval vessels.

'On the lighter side, there was often back-chat per aldis lamp with vessels. Pertinent queries to a ship such as asking her name and details were apt to be answered by "What is your telephone number?" and on one occasion, in Sydney, an outward bound ship answered the query "Are you calibrating here?" with "No, but we have had a wonderful time – so long, honey".* One signaller at the Sydney range was flashed a signal from an

---

*To calibrate was to adjust to scale or standard of any graduated instrument; correcting or adjusting the range of guns for instance.

outgoing vessel asking if she would take a personal message for delivery. She replied "yes", and received the name and address of a girl with the message: "Consider yourself engaged to me. I love you very much. I shall see you in three months time. Bob".'

Many WRANS were engaged on technical duties of a secret nature, working long hours under exacting conditions, and this meant keeping absolute silence about their work, even after their demobilisation. To others, the post-war closing of their particular department released them from the secrecy which was imperative during hostilities. The winding-up of Allied Intelligence Bureau and the Coastwatching Service, for instance, made it possible for the first time for Petty Officer E. Ekert, Writer M. Carswell and Writer J. Hazell to explain the nature of the work that had taken them to the office seven days a week for two and a half years. To these three Brisbane girls were entrusted the Top Secret details of allied work behind the Japanese lines; not only did they type out the operational orders issued to each party before its departure from Brisbane, and the reports brought back or signalled by the parties, but they also assisted in the making up of codes and in the preparation of reports, for General MacArthur's headquarters, of the whereabouts of every man in the Allied Intelligence Bureau.

The responsibility devolving upon these WRANS was great, for even the slightest indiscretion on their part would have jeopardised the lives of gallant men, with proportionate damage to the allied cause; General MacArthur's headquarters recognised the value of their sustained effort by the award of a commendation to Petty Officer Eva Ekert, the only award to be made to any member of the Service. (Olive Boye was awarded the British Empire Medal, Civil Division, for her courageous work as a coastwatcher, but at the time of her recommendation she was working as a civilian).

The scouts of the forces in the South-west Pacific were the coastwatchers and, of these people doing most highly classified work, one was an Honorary WRAN, Sub-lieutenant Mrs Olive Ruby Boye. After the war, when their story could be told, Lieutenant Ronald Sawyer of the United States Navy wrote in the *Christian Science Monitor*: 'When intelligence officers were briefing air crews before a mission they would remind pilots, "If you are forced down, get to the nearest island and find the coastwatcher. He'll do the rest".'

Little was known of the coastwatchers on the islands of the South Seas – the Solomons, New Guinea, the Santa Cruz and New Hebrides groups, and later the Netherlands East Indies and Philippines. For the success of their work and their own safety, their very existence had to be a secret. They were equipped with short-wave radios through which they maintained contact with headquarters, sometimes 500 miles distant across the Coral Sea. They reported all enemy movements, either troop or ship, depending upon the location and size of their particular island. They organised Melanesian tribes into espionage systems that brought by word of mouth and by native canoe from island to island military information which they passed on to headquarters. Through the natives, some missionaries, and a few planters, they arranged for the rescue of hundreds of airmen. They sent daily reports on the weather. 'Japanese intelligence knew there were coastwatchers among the islanders; they had a few themselves, either Japanese soldiers or Melanesians who had been persuaded to support them.'

The constant threat of capture by the Japanese lay over Mrs Boye's life. Tokyo Radio broadcast a warning that her days were numbered. She calmly prepared to retreat to the jungle if the enemy landed. Lieutenant Sawyer wrote: 'One of the Australians whose identity was guarded during the war was a woman, Mrs Olive Ruby Boye. She was stationed on Vanikoro, an island in the Santa Cruz group about 500 miles east of Guadalcanal.

'From the earliest days of the war, she sent valuable information to South-west Pacific headquarters. At first she served Australian forces and subsequently, in the spring of 1942, when the United States troops and ships moved into that theatre, she came under the United States Army which, in turn, was under the Navy's Admiral Halsey.'

Mrs Boye sent her reports over short-wave radio, either by voice or by 'CW'. This is a communicator's short term for Morse code. The men at the receivers at an island in the New Hebrides, which was a headquarters of the coastwatchers, paid Mrs Boye a compliment. It was a tradesman's compliment. Mrs Boye, they said, could use the key – for sending Morse code messages – as fast as almost any male operator.

Mrs Boye and her husband, Skov Boye, were living on Vanikoro when Japan commenced the war in the Pacific. Mr Boye was engaged in the lumber business – kauri timber, a product of the Santa Cruz Islands. Many of the white settlers on South Pacific islands, particularly those with families, withdrew before the onrushing Japanese forces. The Boyes decided not to hurry to the Australian mainland, and, as it turned out, the Santa Cruz Islands marked the approximate geographic limit of Japanese sea power in the South Pacific. The Battle of Santa Cruz in October 1942, prevented the Japanese Navy from cutting off the flow of supplies from Espiritu Santo in the New Hebrides to Guadalcanal at a crucial time.

Though she had been given an honorary commission in the WRANS to give her enlisted status – thus protecting her from the danger of being treated as a spy in the event of her being captured – Mrs Boye seldom wore the uniform. Usually, there was no occasion to do so. Vanikoro, being in an advanced area, had few visitors in wartime. Admiral Halsey is said once to have flown to the island in a Catalina flying boat to shake hands with the Boyes.

It was a lonely existence in a part of the world which Radio Tokyo used to call 'the great nowhere'. In the intervals between exciting events, the coastwatchers would count the days to the next arrival of the little schooner, the *Echo*. Their most frequent visitor was this supply ship, which periodically brought food, arms, radio equipment, and other supplies to the coastwatchers from the New Hebrides. On some trips the *Echo* would bring back allied air crews who, forced down, had made their way by rubber boat to one of the islands where the local coastwatcher provided food and shelter.

In all its South Pacific missions, the *Echo* worked closely with the coastwatchers; and on all its trips into the islands it never failed to stop at Vanikoro and visit Mr and Mrs Boye. Names of coastwatchers seldom, if ever, appeared in the *Echo*'s log – Mrs Boye's name is not there – but in the permanent files of the United States Army are numerous despatches and reports from her.

Brenda Kaarlund (Qld) joined as Leading WRANS Driver in November 1942. She had been in the Women's National Emergency Legion, in its Motor Cycle Squad. 'But when I joined the navy it was very different. Oh yes! "Swing your bloody arms!" the Petty Officer bawled as we drilled, "What do you think this is? A bloody corroboree?" And we'd whisper to one another, "Who the bloody hell does he think he is?" We were issued with PKs, "Passion Killers" (bloomers), 2 pairs navy, 2 pairs khaki. Wow! They had a waistband with a button fastener.'

Brenda had never been away from home. Under the instruction of a Petty Officer she got her driver's licence. 'The next day I took the Oldsmobile out, "The Pride of the Navy" as the sailors called it, and promptly hooked it onto the side of a tram on the corner of Queen and Creek Streets.

'But things could be worse for a young girl straight from home. Driving past the Red Light area of Margaret Street once, one officer in the back of the car said to the other, "Business as usual tonight do you think?" I was aged only 20 and driving like mad to get out of it. Mostly the officers we drove were great. We drivers were on 24 hour watch then 24 hours off. You got used to it. I had to go to Boggo Road Gaol for a prisoner one day. Wondered what to say to him. "Got a fag, WRAN?" he greeted me.

'Then there was the Battle of Bellevue when a sailor was killed. The RAN were kept to barracks for a bit and then let loose. Wow! But I loved every minute of the life. Although I didn't think the war would last that long. The WRANS were taken off the cars that night when the war ended. Airmen were opening doors and hopping in; it was crazy.'

Betsy Avery spent her war at HMAS *Leeuwin* (WA). 'It was 1942. We had no uniforms. For seven months I wore civilian dress with a crown and anchor on my arm band. We were under the sea-eagle eye of the disapproving male naval officers and this rig did nothing to help our morale. We had to dredge up every bit of courage, right up from our boots, to survive, let alone prevail at the beginning.

'I'd been brought up on a farm. My brother was at the war and I'd been running the farm for 18 months. All was going well when suddenly all was devastated by a cock-eyed-Bob [cyclone]. There were no men available to help get things ship-shape again, so I leased the farm, and when I reached the city I learnt they were recruiting for the navy so I joined as a transport driver. It was September 1942.'

She was sent to Flinders Naval Depot (Vic.) and her self-sufficiency had her marked out for 'regulating'. 'So, I went from Leading Transport Driver to Leading Regulating WRAN – a type of policewoman.' She was eventually promoted to Chief Petty Officer Regulating WRAN. 'I now learn that girls were dead scared of me. If only they knew how dead scared I was of them! It was a far cry from the farm!

'The male regulators were masters-at-arms. The girls called them "crushers".' Betsy was one of the servicewomen who found it difficult to adjust when war ended. 'The navy had been the whole of our life. We lived, slept and dreamt it. You couldn't expect to find such fulfilment in civilian life.'

Kathleen 'Peg' King (WA) left for England in September 1939 to continue her studies, after completing her honours degree in French, German and Italian. Her sister went with her and the war had begun when they arrived in England. Peg assisted with her fluent German at the German-Jewish Aid Society where her sister worked, attempting to bring people under threat into England. Then she was given a one-week indoctrination course of terminology, cipher and code, two weeks on radio direction finding, 'and then I was taken to Ventnor as Chief Petty Officer Special Duties Linguist. To intercept U-Boats. When they were sending in plain language, I translated, then it was telephoned in to Intelligence. I had majored in German so it was not difficult.'

These Special Duties Linguists were always only in small groups and wore the English WRENS' uniform only to go on duty. 'Two planes, George and Margaret, would patrol all the time, and there were commandos training along the beach.' Later, she was sent to do wireless telegraphy morse. 'Near Portland Bill, living at a coastguard cottage. Not a tree for miles.'

Then 'they asked me to go to North Africa, "a three-way-stretcher", referring to the three languages I was proficient in apart from my own. I landed at Algiers. Wore tin helmet ashore, only to see British soldiers stripped to the waist. We set up in an ex-tourist hotel in the Atlas Mountains, had the top floor with the roof for watch post. There was a water problem. One cup of water a day to wash all over.

'The work was not so intense as the English coast, where German U-Boats were thick in the Channel. Here, the Italians pulled out shortly after we arrived and German boats were heading off to the newer war scene.

'Then the African Coastal Flotilla moved; the war was now in Italy. Me too. I was ordered to report to the Naval Office in Algiers and there was told I would be going with the Admiral's staff to Naples. The only WREN. Arrived there 24 February 1944. The landings on Anzio had already begun, the front line was 30 miles away from us. We watched the troops moving out each morning. The dock-yard was bombed regularly, lots of ships sunk. I was living in an old block of flats, a YWCA run by an Australian woman. Then several WREN cipher officers arrived.

'Naples was an arena of violent differences. We could see Capri across the Bay, Vesuvius erupted in March; visited the grand homes of marquises; but the poverty and dirt were appalling. A woman searching rubbish bins for food for her two-year-old child, vans each night gathering up the people who died in ditches. Our only great hardship on board was having no meat for six weeks.'

Long hours passed in routine listening to the medley of voices coming from U-Boats, from planes, from shore. Boredom interspersed with the odd tense moment. 'I unscrambled a message from Latin America. Later I was informed that because of this message a spy ring had been split up.

But one doesn't get too much of this drama. At Ventnor we picked up only German U-Boats, Algiers we got French and Italian, here there was little intercept work.'

She was sent to officers' training school in January 1945 and, from there, was joined to the Flag Officer of the Fleet and thus sent off to forward areas. The war in Europe ended; it was now ending in the East. She went to Malaya, Singapore.

'The Japs having done nothing at all about sanitation, there were rats everywhere. I had not had leave for a long while and was ready for it, when SS *Gorgon* arrived from Australia with sheep. The Admiral gave me leave to go home for two weeks on her. Mountbatten was visiting Brisbane. I felt more at ease with English naval officers than with my own countrymen by now, but it was nice when a shopkeeper wouldn't charge me for a milkshake. I hadn't had one since 1938.'

She returned to Singapore via Darwin on a RAAF plane. 'You must remember long-distance flights in those days were a series of short-distance hops. We over-nighted at Indonesia. "Passengers need not worry", I was told, "not about personal safety. Camp is guarded."'

The war was over. She returned to England and left the WREN at Devonport. 'Yes, it had a certain feeling about it, the ending, that is. But to get home to Perth in 1947 was good too.'

Peg King's happiest memory of those years is being invited to launch a small ship at Castellammare di Stabia, south Naples. 'My Admiral had given the local shipyard permission to build a tug, the first activity for this war-poor area since Italy collapsed.' The Admiral suggested Peg be honoured because of her being the first WREN to be stationed in Italy. 'It was flowers, wine, me preceding the Admiral ashore, he walking behind me – he insisted this was the way it must be done – cheers, and the tug, *Lady Jane*, slid down to the sea. The foreman had made a model of the tug and a gold bracelet for me. It was nice to see the happiness these men got from working again after their terrible war.'

HMAS *Herman* will always stand for something special in the memories of the WRANS, for it was to this station, on 28 April 1941, that the 14 apprehensive young women in the uniform of the Women's Emergency Signalling Corps, trained by Mrs Mac, came as the vanguard of the Service.

Here they worked with RAN, RN and (after Pearl Harbor) USN Communications ratings, keeping in touch with W/T Stations in all parts of the world. To these girls, the tragic post-Pearl Harbor events were all too vivid and real. Gradually, they piled up messages for overseas stations which could never be transmitted because the stations were no longer in friendly hands. In particular, there were the W/T links with Cavite, Singapore, Batavia, *Coonawarra* (Darwin) and Canberra. As the priority outward signals mounted, WRANS took down the final message from each of the first three stations, wondering as each closed how soon this would also be the lot of *Coonawarra*. Then, as time went on, and the tide turned slowly in our favour, theirs was the privilege of again contacting places and people so long cut off from civilisation.

In mid-1945, WRANS were sent to HMAS *Coonawarra*, Darwin, then a total garrison town without civilians or civilian amenities. They had earlier been at HMAS *Magnetic*, Townsville, during the 1942–43 period of frenetic activity while the Japanese were being pushed northwards island by island; and they were at HMAS *Kuranda*, when Cairns was the hub of war activity and planning, and there, too, when it ended.

'WRANS see death of a Port' wrote Third Officer Mollie Westhoven for the Melbourne *Argus* in March 1943. 'As the war in the Pacific moves north at an increasingly rapid pace, bases once forward areas are fast becoming backwaters.' Like gold-mining towns last century, flourishing wartime centres overnight resembled ghost towns. 'Once almost the focal point of the sea was in the Pacific, now it is almost back to peace-time routine.'

At HMAS *Rushcutter*, Sydney, WRANS worked in the anti-submarine school – a school that is famous far beyond Australia, because of its students who contributed materially to the war against enemy underwater craft. Also at Sydney was HMAS *Mindari*, the gunnery school, with a group of WRANS.

In NSW also was the War Port Signal Station HMAS *Weston* and, the War Port WRANS knew what it was like to stand at their shelterless eyrie, while waves battered the Heads, as they conned the entrance to one of the world's most famous harbours. Here, the girls built up a reputation for sharp lookout, as they identified and 'spoke' the famous and relatively unknown ships alike seeking entry to the harbour.

There was HMAS *Penguin* looking more like a county seat among gum trees than Australia's only service post office staffed entirely by women; HMAS *Kuttabul*, known as the Wrannery, was quarters for the girls working on the many naval projects around Sydney. A popular ditty among young sailors went:

*Never heard of jaunties*
*Never heard of rounds*
*Never knew the Wrannery*
*Was bloody out of bounds.*

The girls at HMAS *Cerberus* (Vic.) received the compliment, 'The WRANS have never let me down', signalled by Vice-Admiral T. B. Drew as he returned to England after his years as Naval Officer-in-Charge. At this station, WRANS all lived in and, because of this, their quarters wore a homely, loved look. They worked on the small arms range – travelling there by boat, muffled in oilskins and sea-boots – in sail lofts, and in the huge galleys where food was cooked for the whole of the self-contained city that is HMAS *Cerberus*. WRANS also completely staffed the RAN hospital galley, the most modern in the Australian Navy.

WRANS from *Cerberus* were in great demand for wartime city marches and, in 1945, the Melbourne *Herald* said: 'Special cheers were given to the two companies of WRANS, who many believe give the finest exhibition in a city parade'. As in Sydney, Victorian WRANS were spread far and wide, and those at HMAS *Lonsdale* travelled 96 kilometres to the War Port Signal Station at Queenscliff daily.

Tasmania's HMAS *Huon* rivalled Western Australia's HMAS *Leeuwin* for beauty of setting. Only one block from the GPO in the centre of Hobart, the WRANS worked on the waterfront where the largest ships afloat could tie up, including the great *Queen Elizabeth* and *Queen Mary*. Here, Petty Officer Messenger Bessie Lachlan made history as the WRANS' only post-woman. She handled, posted and delivered mail twice a day to ships in port, up to 60 bags of mail to two ships at a time. 'Nor was it unknown for the mail for half a dozen ships to be mixed up together in one mad mélange.'

HMAS *Torrens* (SA) was a compact depot, quarters, offices, parade ground and mess-deck encompassed in a small space. 'There was the constant atmosphere of bustling activity with the incessant shrilling of the bosun's pipe. From Wakey-Wakey to Lights Out the voice of authority was heard over the land, piping for this or that WRAN to report to the gangway, for Hands to dinner, for Evening Quarters, for Out Pipes or even – an endearing custom – bringing to the attention of all ranks the fact that the paper boy was aboard.'

HMAS *Leeuwin* was home station to WRANS who served a scattered area from Rottnest Island to Silo Signal Station at Fremantle (where they must climb 211 steps each time they went on watch); there was also the Kings Park Tennis Club, the members' room, no less, having been requisitioned for Communication Branch when WRANS worked with RAN, USN and Dutch personnel. The Western Australian WRANS were for a few months joined by Tasmanian WRANS on board the Depot Ship of the 8th Submarine Flotilla, HMS *Maidstone* and HMS *Adamant*. One WRAN, Writer Coral Ribe, served up north at Geraldton. She was Writer to the naval officer-in-charge there and lived with the local customs officer and his wife.

When the time came that their services were no longer required, these girls, like those of the other women's services, went home. Their newsletter, *DIT*, wrote in October 1945: 'If, in the future, small children should demand to know, "What did you do in the Second World War Grandma?" there are worse replies than the simple statement, "I was a WRAN." '

CHAPTER 22

# *They Keep them Flying*

Clare G. Stevenson didn't learn to knit. 'I can't do anything with my hands except lay bricks and that sort of thing. During World War I my elder sisters were knitting and I had to do the dishes, wash-up for our family of 12. They said that was fair, as I didn't knit socks for soldiers.'

During World War II she made up for it. She was the Director of the Women's Auxiliary Australian Air Force, the service that many believe had the highest morale of all the women's services. 'We were the first, apart from the women in medical services. You could say we paved the way.'

Colonel Sybil Irving, Controller of the Australian Women's Army Service, said just that. 'Of all of us, it was Clare Stevenson who did the most pertinent pioneering work.'

When asked 43 years later if she had to fight for conditions and for her girls, Clare says, 'I fought for four years, nine months. WAAAF policy differed from that of AWAS. The army policy was to keep the girls in their own home state where possible. The WAAAF enlisted to go to war and that meant to go wherever you were sent, wherever you were most needed. The morale was high. The girls knew what a good job they were doing. They were mustered on parade with the men, the RAAF.'

Clare had been one of the first women executives in the Berlei company. She had completed a Diploma of Education at Melbourne University and Fred Burley, the founder of the Berlei company who believed in giving women executives power, was looking for a trained person, preferably one with teaching qualifications, a person who could get along well with non-academics. They met, and Clare joined the company with a position involving public relations, sales training and research. Her company was among the first Australian companies to open a United Kingdom branch and 'Berlei's Miss Stevenson' was sent to England as a saleswoman-executive. 'But I missed Australia.' She returned as World War II broke out. On 9 June 1941 she was appointed by the Chief of Air Staff to become Director of the WAAAF with the rank of Squadron Officer, later to be Wing Officer and finally, Group Officer. She referred to herself, and all members of the WAAAF referred to her, as D/WAAAF.

This arm of the RAAF, the first of the women's services (apart from nursing services) was a long time in the making. The Women's Air Training Corps and the equivalent body in New South Wales, the Australian Women's Flying Club (which had such figures at its head as the famous England to Australia solo flyer, Nancy Bird) suggested using their well-trained members as early as November 1939. They were informed that a Women's Auxiliary Air Force would not be formed. However, within ten months, signals musterings in the RAAF were not able to keep up with the manpower shortage and, in September 1940, the Chief of Air Staff directed that a War Cabinet Agendum be prepared, requesting permission for a Women's Auxiliary section for signals duties as well as domestics for nurses' quarters.

Slow though they were, by 4 February 1941, the RAAF nevertheless had War Cabinet approve the recommendation of the Minister for Air to enlist 320 women for service in the RAAF, 'to meet the temporary deficiency of male wireless telegraphy operators until such time as men became available.' Approval was also given to establish a training depot and accommodation for the women, to be made at air force stations.

The Acting Prime Minister emphasised the necessity of 'the strictest control and discipline at stations'. Strangely, such a unique injunction was not seen as offensive by the women. 'We just wanted to get in there and serve'.

Victoria Buick says her brother John was at sea in the RAN. 'My sister Margaret and I joined up. We didn't fuss about the nonsense the old grey beards went on with. We wanted to help our brother. It was as simple as that.'

On 11 March 1941 the War Cabinet stated that, in the event of their being taken prisoner, members of the WAAAF would be entitled to treatment as prisoners of war. These first girls were not *enlisted*, but *enrolled* for 12 months. 'This legal opinion has been given, although WAAAFs are actually civilians in uniform, they constitute an active auxiliary of the armed forces and cannot be regarded in the same category as civilians or guerillas, whom the enemy would treat as spies.'

Compensation of WAAAFs for injury during service would come under the provisions of the Commonwealth Workers' Compensation Act. 'These benefits rise according to the degree of incapacity, to a maximum payment of 750 pounds.'

On 15 March 1941 (the date they regard as their 'birthday'), 37 women teleprinter operators and telegraphists arrived at No. 1 Training Depot,

Malvern, Victoria. These young women had studied in their own time and could send and receive at 20 words per minute in code and plain language to qualify for entry to Signals.

In June 1941, press statements were released calling for 'qualified wireless telegraphists' to enrol. 'Successful applicants will receive approximately two-thirds of the pay received by airmen in related RAAF trade groups.' In July, it was reported, 'over 2000 applications have been received for these positions'. As well as W/T operators there was a call for girls for administrative, cipher and domestic duties. Then came August, and with a change of government, the recruiting of women met with disfavour.

By October recruiting had ceased. Labor members of the Advisory War Council had originally agreed to the enrolment of WAAAFs on the understanding that the arrangements would not necessarily be permanent, and that women auxiliaries would be displaced by men as they became available. The next Government said it 'wanted to use men and women as effectively as possible'. But it had to make sure 'there were no call-ups without proper provision being made for everything involved'.

By 28 October of that year, 1941, enlistment had been stopped. The *Western Australian* reported: 'This [cessation of enrolment] affects hundreds of women whose names are on the waiting list. They have been undergoing instructions and have spent a great deal of spare time in recent months preparing for national service ... to release fit young men for more active and dangerous duties.' Young girls wrote to newspapers telling of their S/T training four nights a week after finishing their day's work.

For almost all of that year the authorities – and Government – had been frustrating the women's attempts to serve and put their training into practice, but now time was running out. Some call-ups were resumed in November, but by 7 December all choice was gone. As Prime Minister Curtin was to announce to the nation, 'The honeymoon is over'. Five days after the Japanese attacked in the Pacific, War Cabinet approved on 12 December 1941, the recommendations of the three Chiefs of Staff of the fighting services that maximum use be made of woman power.

By the end of December, 1583 women had been enrolled in the WAAAF, the nucleus of the 18 038 they would reach by 1944. By 1942 the WAAAF were serving in almost 200 stations throughout Australia, including Townsville during the bombing, and in 1943 further north in areas closer to the actual fighting than the girls were to their southern homes. For all that, the Minister for Air steadfastly refused to permit the girls to be sent to 'advanced' areas, even to the north-western area where the RAAF was having difficulty finding men to relieve the male signals' staff.

General Douglas MacArthur proposed that WAAAF serving with Central Bureau (Intelligence) at Allied General Headquarters (then in Australia) should move with the Bureau to the Philippines. The Minister for Air rejected the move – and all Australian women on MacArthur's staff were left behind. MacArthur had to request American WACs to be sent to the islands to fill the places vacated by the Australians.

As Colonel Groover Brown, the officer in Command of the American women, was to tell me in 1974, 'It was a disgraceful thing for a government to do to its own brave girls. I made sure my girls knew that they were replacing girls who had been equally anxious as they to do whatever was necessary to save their country.'

Two years were to pass before, on 24 March 1943, regulations were gazetted covering women's auxiliaries enlisted under the Defence Act. From April 1942 the WAAAF had been enrolled 'for the duration and 12 months thereafter'. Now girls who had been serving for between one and two years were *enlisted* to 'well and truly serve the King' and went on doing what they had done so well for so long, holding the same rank. But there was now an important difference: they were assured of receiving deferred pay.

Margaret Curtis-Otter applauds WAAAF Director Clare Stevenson in this. 'After the Japs came into the war and things got a bit tiresome, the powers-that-be at last decided yes, they did need women. Clare Stevenson insisted on her women, on volunteering, being enlisted to deferred pay and all the benefits to which RAAF was entitled. The old men blew through their whiskers, but she was adamant: either the women got the same benefits as the men or she would tell her enrolled girls not to enlist.'

By that time, WAAAFs were on actual operational duties side by side with Australian and American airmen and soldiers, 'guarding the nation's outer defence perimeter' as a journalist from an 'Undisclosed Operational Base' reported. (It was actually Townsville.) 'This WAAAF establishment already has become the largest women's operational centre in Australia and the girls attached to it are the first to go on active service. Much of the work done by the girls is secret. Many are being trained to become expert operators of new devices.

'In this area, a fighter squadron base, in the event of Japanese air raids, fighter planes will take off to intercept the enemy. The girls are on operational duty 24 hours a day maintaining a ceaseless vigil along Australia's northern defences.' Yet until now, they had not been considered permanent, as had men. 'In the fighter sector the girls maintain four six-hour watches a day. In the event of raids, or other enemy action, they will remain at their posts. They are not permitted to be armed, but receive training in unarmed defence, and are already expert at ju jitsu.'

These women, working as radio location operators (the forerunner of radar) on the operational as opposed to the administrative side of the air force, were mustered by May 1942. They were trained in using the new secret and technical equipment that gave fighters warning of the approach of enemy aircraft. 'It will be their duty to pick up the sounds that result in the word "Go!" being given to our fighter pilots. The saving of many lives and property will be partly in their hands.'

Strangely, of all musterings, this one did not refuse enlistment to women who had no trade qualification or experience. Even cooks must have cooked for more than a family or undergone some trade training in order to be posted, but this new work was special. A knowledge of Morse code was not required. 'The qualifications for radio location are based more on character and intelligence than experience and only women of unquestionable integrity will be enrolled, steady types, reliable and not highly strung. They must be bright and alert, intelligent. Importance is placed on speech which must be clear and distinct with no trace of dialect and no impediment. The voice should be clearly audible over ordinary telephone, and applicants must be able to read printed matter without faltering.'

Contrary to expectations, it was found that the WAAAF learned to drill more quickly than their male counterparts, they swiftly assimilated the air force atmosphere and were 'rapidly transformed from a motley collection of young women from different backgrounds (be it country or town) into an efficient, disciplined body, able to carry out orders without confusion.'

The coastline of Australia was screened by radar, keeping WAAAF operators on duty 24 hours a day. The RAAF communications systems depended a great deal on the women W/T. (Almost 800 women signallers were in one station alone, the Melbourne W/T station in Balwyn.) Women staffed Radio Direction Finding Stations to guide aircraft home; large numbers were radio-telephone operators; and most of the telephone and teleprinter operators were WAAAF. The women drove aircraft refuelling trucks, oil tankers and the small sedans transporting senior officers. It is said that in their 73 musterings the WAAAF did everything but fly.

The lull in recruiting following the threat of disbandment which accompanied the change of Government in November 1941 made for difficulties when the Japanese entered the war in December. The rush of enrolments taxed the existing resources, and proved particularly embarrassing to the WAAAF, in view of the previous slow rate of development. Until this crisis, No. 1 WAAAF Training Depot had trained one course per month of up to 90 recruits; but in December courses were speeded up to release clerical staff who were urgently required, and in January, at Geelong Grammar School (Vic.), 462 recruits were put through. These recruits were scattered far and wide throughout the Commonwealth, but had to go without equipment, and to units as yet ill prepared to receive them.

The period of rapid expansion lasted throughout 1942, and was accompanied for WAAAF, as for RAAF, by a shortage of barrack accommodation. Overcrowding of barracks and shortage of latrines, ablutions and laundry facilities were quite common, while the building programme lagged behind demand. Hygiene difficulties slowly but steadily were eliminated, and during 1943 the standard of living conditions gradually rose, and reached a level of 'Spartan comfort'.

'The provision of good living and working conditions was a primary aim of Group Officer Stevenson, the Director WAAAF,' says the official history of the WAAAF, 'and the high standards which were attained, though brought about by the work of innumerable RAAF and WAAAF officers of all ranks in various spheres of activity, were due in large part to her efforts to achieve her ideal. Apart from this sustained policy, D/WAAAF made it her business to interview each WAAAF officer trainee, and to brief as many of her officers as possible before sending them to a new job; she thus kept her high standards well in the minds of both her junior and senior officers.'

Officers in the WAAAF were 25 years of age or over, and were almost entirely drawn from the ranks. In most cases they were women who in their previous work had mixed with the ordinary type of girl found in offices, factories and shops, and who therefore understood them. Efforts were made to select officers with good intelligence quotient; in fact, a statistical analysis, made in 1943, showing the distribution of intellectual standard throughout the WAAAF was of a standard any private school of the time would be happy to have among its staff.

Realising that a man's life depended on their work being efficiently done, the WAAAF fabric workers folding parachutes worked under enormous pressure – even though self-imposed. Each parachute had to be aired and given a complete overhaul every two months.

For several months, the girls were trained under close observation and with assistance to air, inspect and fully maintain the parachutes. Then a final course lasting two months qualified them to prepare, alone, a parachute ready for use, in 30 minutes.

The fabric workers' parachute section was a pretty sight for a woman in those coupon-scrimping days. Gleaming white silk canopies stretched out on the long tables, white-overalled WAAAFs patched and folded the chutes into their canvas cases, and others repaired parachutes, stitching away at sewing machines with yards of the white silk billowing out around them.

The WAAAFs, as did the airmen, worked with aircraft roaring overhead, the noise no longer deafening as it had been when they were rookies.

There was the 'keeper of the rings', going about her duties with several fingers of her left hand covered in jewels. A flight-sergeant in charge of WAAAF fabric workers at the flying-boat repair depot at Lake Boga had this responsibility. Nearly all the girls in that section were engaged or married, and when they were 'doping' they gave Betsy rings to mind.

All the WAAAF fabric workers underwent a training course in the repair and maintenance of rubber dinghies, treatment of self-sealing petrol tanks, spraying and doping of aircraft fabric, the use of a spray gun, and the repair of drogues – or towing targets – after practice.

Their great thrill was being taken up in the aircraft which they had reconditioned. 'These fabric workers knew to an inch or a yard the amount of material covering their aircraft. An Anson took 190 yards of cloth,' Margaret Buick recalls.

The girls also folded parachutes for the paratroopers. 'The boys sang songs, terrible, bloody songs, supposedly funny but really terrible. Just before they went up for a jump. I suppose by naming the thing they were afraid of they hoped to overcome the fear.'

> O! They wiped me off the tarmac like a pound of strawberry jam.
> They wiped me off the tarmac like a pound of strawberry jam.
> They wiped me off the tarmac like a pound of strawberry jam.
> And I ain't gonna jump no more.
>
> Glory, glory what a helluva way to go
> Glory, glory what a helluva way to go
> Glory, glory what a helluva way to go
> And he ain't gonna jump no more.

'A parachute that had been improperly packed and so failed to open was called a "Roman Candle". Mostly the boys just called them "candles".'

> *O come sit by my side if you love me*
> *Do not hasten to bid me adieu*
> *But remember the poor paratrooper*
> *And the job he was trying to do.*

The urgency of the times took its toll on these young girls, particularly among telegraphists and other signals personnel, who worked long and difficult hours. The 'wastage' from sickness, particularly fatigue, was reported to the DGMS with the following as two examples.

'1 An A.C.W. was admitted to No. 1 WAAAF Hospital suffering from frequent headaches. The Medical Officer had tried various methods of treatment and asked that she be admitted for investigation. This airwoman slept for three days and nights, waking only for meals, and dozing again. On the fourth day, she woke up, and said, "I'm better now doctor, can I go back today?"

'2 An airwoman who had been serving 15 months as a W.T. Operator took two days A.W.L., and spent the two days in bed, sleeping. She said afterwards that she just seemed to have reached the end of her tether.'

The length of time that the war was now expected to continue, the time taken to train each telegraphist, and the acute shortage of man and woman power, made it essential that each member should be employed to the best possible advantage. 'The maximum amount of work will be obtained if we demand, not the longest working hours which can be endured for a short time, but the longest working hours which can be maintained over an indefinite period.'

A quotation from a thesis, 'The Health and Efficiency of Munition Workers' by H. M. Vernon, is a pertinent reminder to us that women – at that period at any rate – did not yet understand the 'go slow' mentality men had learnt over the years if they were to survive. 'It is therefore rather remarkable that the very strenuous conditions under which most of the men were working did not react more unfavourably on health than their medical examination suggested. Probably it was because a long pre-war experience had taught the men how to look after themselves, and avoid the futility of incurring excessive fatigue. When, in wartime, very long hours of work were imposed on them by their employers, they soon learnt that they must "go slow" if they were to avoid sickness ... This plan of long hours coupled with a slow rate of work was much less efficient than one of shorter hours coupled with a quicker rate of work.'

The quick change of shifts which were in operation in many units were not those compatible with continued vigorous work. The effects of overworking are insidious, and result in a lower standard of work, particularly an inability to cope with high speed jobs. It is comparable with the oxygen lack experienced by aircrews at high altitudes, resulting in the gradual loss of skill, as health and vigour are impaired.

A vital task in any war is the gathering of data about enemy movements. In the air war in the Pacific, quick and correct recording of Japanese movements was of great importance if their planes were to be intercepted and destroyed. WAAAFs did 'hush hush' work recording the approach of enemy aircraft and tracing their movements, and they were on duty when Japanese raiders visited Australia.

During the Townsville bombings, they remained calm, and efficient. Those on duty stayed there. Though the building shook and trembled with the explosion of nearby ack-ack guns, the girls carried on, and the plotters kept plotting. One airwoman even had to lie on her stomach on the plotting table to keep her balance while she completed her job. The others marched in orderly fashion to slit trenches within two minutes of sounding the alert, in their overalls and tin hats. They carried haversacks with emergency rations, a rug, change of clothing, toothpaste.

There was so much to learn. How could you test for a sense of humour? And if an officer didn't have a highly developed sense of humour, even a sense of the ridiculous, she could never understand girls. A WAAAF officer wrote, in 1943, her diary for a day:

'0600 "Madam, madam come quick! Daisy's passed out in the Abluts!" Agitated little stewardess bursts unceremoniously into nine by ten compartment. Dive into dressing-gown and scoot down duck-boards to Abluts. It was, of course, only a slight faint. Sgt Bull, D.I., and I have hectic few minutes coping with clammy corpse of A.C.W. Bender, while helpfuls 'phone for ambulance.

'0730–0815 C.O.'s Parade. As officers march on to parade ground, roar from W.O.D.: "Stand still in No. 5 Flight!" See out of tail of my eye that it is Skippy (sheep-dog who trots round and round squadrons as he used to trot round and round sheep before he joined the RAAF) trying to attract attention of A.C.W. Crabapple, who magnetically attracts cats, dogs, fish and reptiles.

'Strong sea-wind blowing and we cannot hear Unit Band. Not surprised when, on arrival at office, Adjutant 'phones: "C.O.'s compliments, madam – and have the WAAAFs the music to 'Waltzing Matilda'?"

'0815–0945  Sgt Bull, dark-haired, affectionately known to WAAAFs as "Fair Cow", has letters ready stacked for censoring. "A.C.W. Scrivener's written ten again, Madam," she announces cheerfully, "and how do you think A.C.W. Crabapple's father will react to this?" Holds out gingerly loathsome envelope which looks as though Skippy has used it as his bathmat. "Return it with my compliments," I say. "And add that Skippy is to be tied up before next C.O.'s parade."

'In spite of an incredible diversity of calligraphy and orthography, five 'phone calls, queue of airwomen with garments to U/S, and Sgt Bull's voice on 'phone plaintively compiling the parade state: "Did you say 'dead' or 'in bed'? Look, all I want is ...", am through the censoring by 0945, when Sgt Bull whisks letters off to Unit Censor's office. '1000–1100. C.O.'s Inspection, divided into:

(1) 1000–1041  Sgt Bull and I stand, at alert, in sun at compound gate, exhorting mess staff coming off duty not to dishevel their immaculate hut and to keep out of lats. "just a moment longer".

(2) 1041–1059  C.O., Adjutant, M.O., Orderly Officer, Barracks Officer, W.O. and I, led by Sgt Bull as chief thrower-open of doors, proceed at brisk trot round compound, pace set by C.O.'s long legs. WAAAFs complimented on state of compound except for (a) dump of Skippy's bones in one of drains (Barrack Officer to ascertain whether murder has been committed), (b) Mrs Perkins (WAAAF cat) and two kittens on A.C.W. Crabapple's blankets (M.O. to investigate unhygienic possibilities of). One small messwoman scuttling out of lats. apparently not seen by C.O.

'1100–1115  Private blitz conducted by Sgt Bull and myself. Trail of ants, which mercifully escaped visitors' eyes, heading into A.C.W. Sweet's locker.

'1115–1200  Accumulated odd jobs in office, including compressing vast telegraphist into jacket to prove it is too small for her, and dealing with weeping A.C.W. Smart, who has received long-overdue ticking off from her sergeant, and wants to be posted.

'1200–1215  Rounds of WAAAF mess.

"Madam, must we always have melon-and-lemon?"

"A.C.W. Pye, you are not to take the butter from the next table." "Oh, but, Madam, someone's taken ours!"

"A.C.W. Gapper, why don't you eat your crusts?" Blushes, and giggles from table-companions. "New teeth, Madam!"

'1215–1245  Late and blissful lunch at re-set table in officers' mess. F/Lt Butcher, very earnest, comes and talks shop into cheese and biscuits.

'1245  Sgt Hansom to assure me that whatever A.C.W. Smart had said about him was untrue and he hoped I knew him better than that.

'1300–1405  Welfare committee meeting in Gym. Get a fiver for WAAAF library without any fuss and sit back while football representative hotly denies that team damaged bus in which it travelled to Crossbar on Saturday and that anyway, if it did, bus was in such a state that a little more damage wouldn't matter.

'1410–1430  Sign leave passes.

'1430–1550  Proceed to Maintenance Wing on section cycle, nearly being mown down en route by A.C.W. Trundle, Office Orderly, very unsafe on RAAF cycle. Discuss remusters of aircraft hands comfortably over cup of tea with Adjutant. No disciplinary troubles in Wing, thank heavens. Visit maintenance squadron and workshops.

'1600–1630  Visit Station Sick Quarters. A.C.W. Smith, Mona, has been on M.I. for fourth time in ten days. "If that little so-and-so comes again," threatens M.O., "I'll give her a dose of castor oil, and that'll fix her!" A.C.W. Legge, who fell down a slit trench and broke two ribs, highly delighted because she can walk. A.C.W. Bender, overgrown youngster of 18, wan but smiling.

'1635  Dash over to hockey in time to settle argument as to who is to play left inner and who right on Saturday. Sgt Bull chanting: "Left – and up! Right – and up!" to P.T. class.

'1715  Waylaid on way to showers by A.C.W. Smart with leave pass and beaming smile: "Madam, Sgt Hansom has just rung up and asked me to go the pictures with him. Could I have my leave pass signed?" "All right," I grumble. "But Sgt Hansom is a bigger fool than I thought. You can tell him so from me." "Oh Madam!" Sgt Bull passes along Rec. Hut inspecting windows polished by A.C.W.s Crabapple and Sweet: "They still look as though the flies have been playing hopscotch all over 'em – but you may have your passes."

'1800–1930  Noisy peace at Officers' Mess, broken only by one 'phone call from Cpl Chatterton, Orderly N.C.O.: "Madam, four postings came in on the tender instead of two. Sgt Bull's at the Sergeants' Mess. Where shall I put them?"

'1930–2315  At pictures in village. Seats uncomfortably near Sgt Hansom and A.C.W. Smart.

'2330  RAAF officer walking away from Compound with arm round airwoman. Am about to pursue when Cpl Chatterton pops out of Compound gate: "A.C.W. Gapper's got toothache, Madam, and she's been crying all night, so I rang F/Lt Pullar and he's taking her down to Dental. There was a bit of mucking up in Hut 23, Madam, but they're all right now. A.C.W. Crabapple's got Skippy under her bed and Mrs Perkins and the kittens on top. Sgt Bull told me to tell you she's moved A.C.W. Stout down the other end of the hut, so you won't be able to hear her snoring. Like a cup of tea, Madam? Gee, I bet you feel like calling it a day!"'

A.C.W. Bette Wright joined when she was 18 years old. 'I first went to join the WRANS and was told to come back in six months time. Right! Down to the army, I thought, but the WAAAF was nearer. I've always been glad of that. It was beautiful, lovely. At first we were in the Aspro Nicholas mansion in Toorak. We put polish on the floor and dragged one another on blankets round and round to make the parquet shine.

'Many girls joined to escape home – not unhappy, really, but just wanted a change and the wartime services were heaven-sent. I was in Sydney when the war ended. We were to help with the returning prisoners of war. They were to be reunited with their parents, but it seemed unreal to them. They didn't want to get off the buses when we got them to the meeting place. It was very traumatic.

'But it was a great life, lovely.'

Aircraftwoman Imelda Blake (WA) wrote in 1982: 'One of the nicest memories I have of my WAAAF service days was the time I spent at the cooks' training school at Perth. Our Sgt cook and instructor was the late Herbert Sache, who is remembered for his creation of that popular and delicious dessert – the Pavlova. I consider it an honour to have been one of his pupils. Often we would have the privilege to assist him as he transformed a basic simple dish into a gourmet's delight for a special officers' dinner party. He was a kindly, courteous man, and a wonderful teacher. His melt and mix method of making scones was new at that time, and the greatest compliment I ever had was when he ate five scones I had just baked for morning tea.

'At that time, Perth City Council decided to have a war bond drive, and a grand parade of armed forces was arranged to march through the main streets. A mobile army kitchen was the main attraction with Sgt Sache, A.C.W. Curedale and myself, in our white cooks' outfits, baking biscuits as we moved along the terrace, putting them in small paper bags and tossing them into the crowd. Needless to say, the war bond drive was a great success and lots of money was raised for the war effort. I look back with pride and affection for a very happy memory and the chance to work with one of W.A.'s finest chefs and a wonderful human being.'

The great fear of the Tasmanian girls was that they would be pushed 'north'. 'We were afraid of the heat. We didn't think we would be able to take it.' Gwen D'Emden now laughs about the isolation of many areas of Australia at that time. She lived in the southern part of the island state and had not been as far north as Launceston.

'It was a rude awakening when you got to Melbourne the first time. All those skyscrapers! We wrote pages home about it and described it on our leave back to quiet Tassie.'

Gwen was homesick. 'I just wanted to go home. From the moment of arriving over the Strait I couldn't forget home.'

Crossing Bass Strait is always rough, but the crowded wartime ships added another dimension. 'Storms, a rolling ship, no lights, trying to feel your way round the deck, looking for the girls in the dark. Searching everywhere, even in the life-boats.'

Gwen, like most WAAAFs, is very proud of her service – and of the spirit of the WAAAF girls. 'We went on strike once. For food. It was bad, meat walking off the plate, the lot, no one with spirit would tolerate it. It was necessary to strike to draw attention to the conditions. Complaining got us nowhere. It merely had to be brought forcibly to the attention of people who could eradicate the problem.

'We worked hard. But we had a lot of fun. Liquor was forbidden at our dances, but of course there always was some. One night the police raided us and the boys passed bottles to me and I pushed them one by one behind a big green curtain on stage and a helpful hand behind the curtain took each bottle. When the raid was over I went behind the curtain to retrieve the bottles and – there was the policeman whose hand had taken the bottles from mine!'

Mary Grant, cousin of Gwen D'Emden, sailed off to Melbourne 'to the unknown'. She was mustered as pay clerk in Finance Section. 'There were Canadian Air Force, RNZAF, Dutch Air Force including those in the Indonesian Air Force. And what a business it was trying to convert to the various currencies. We scarcely had time to breathe.'

On home leave, Mary set off on a RAAF plane at 4.30 a.m. 'No seats, sitting on our kit bags, no lining in the body of the plane, cold. We took off, landed again, took off again, and finally landed on a property in northern Tasmania. An awful flight. There were two sailors on board and when we bumped to a landing on Tassie they knelt down and kissed the ground and said in unison, "As God is my witness I will never fly in one of those things again". On this property we waited and waited. Airmen just back from overseas were with us. It was miserable for them. It's the way a war is run. The army controlled all troop movements between Victoria and Tasmania and you came and went as they dictated, army, navy, or air force. They just had to move service people as best they could.'

Vi Davis was one of the earliest girls. 'It was 1941 when we were enrolled, not enlisted then, for 12 months only. We didn't get full uniforms for a year or so, but we worked full time and a half.' Vi worked on recruiting programmes.

Betty Dell was another Tasmanian enlistment. 'It all seems so long ago,' she said in 1983. 'Like another life.'

Clare Stevenson is outrageously lavish in her admiration of the contribution of the WAAAF to the war effort and to the lasting effect of their years of training. 'Take the 1981 gathering of ex-WAAAFs. One thousand and four women arriving from all states, New Zealand and overseas. They organised it so well you could see their training and the encouragement in self dependence had stood them well. It was brilliantly done.'

She was against the Vietnam War. 'Totally opposed to it.' But World War II was different. 'You get angry when you have relatives prisoners of war. You don't like the thought of another nation, determined to conquer or take over a region. Japan had stated she would do that, take the Pacific. You get angry – if you've got any spirit at all that is.

'As for young people coming forward to enlist again, I know they would. If the call came again, if the enemy were approaching our shores tomorrow, the young women would come forward as willingly, determinedly, as they did in 1941.'

## CHAPTER 23

# *The True Glory*

*There must be a beginning of any great matter but the continuying untyl the end, untyl it is thoroughly ffynyshed, yields the true glory.*

When Sybil Irving had Sir Francis Drake's words sent to her troops in 1942, she already knew that it was the continuing, not the beginning of any great matter that was the real test.

Sybil Howy Irving was born at Victoria Barracks, Melbourne, on 25 February 1897, and she lived in all states of Australia through the army appointments of her father, Brigadier-General G. G. H. Irving.

For twenty-four years she was Victorian State Secretary of the Girl Guides' Association. This was undoubtedly the most significant of her life's experiences which helped her to form and administer the AWAS. She had taught the sufferers during the poliomyelitis epidemics of the 1920s and 1930s and hers was one of the two original signatures on the Articles of Association when the Victorian Society for Crippled Children was formed. For this work she was made a Member of the Order of the British Empire (MBE) in 1939.

In the earliest years of the war, she was Assistant Secretary to the Australian Red Cross Society (Vic. Division), and it was from this posting that she was led to the task that did not end until 1947. 'I had no doubt I could do what was expected of me,' she told me, when we sat beside the stream in Vita Sackville-West's beautiful garden of Sissinghurst shortly before Sybil's death in 1973. 'It was the quality of the endeavour that mattered.

'I had always been moved by the prayer of Sir Francis Drake before he went into the Battle of Cadiz, and this stayed me then. "Oh Lord God, when thou givest to thy servants to endeavour any great matter, grant us to know that it is not the beginning, but the continuing of the same until it be thoroughly finished which yieldest the true glory." I repeated it often. I believed in it.'

She was a sincerely religious person, honest and devout, but '. . . there were times when I needed that prayer to remind me that the main thing was to finish the task . . .

'Early on, when we were first getting organised and were at Royal Park, the few girls we had hung their washing to dry on a line they'd rigged up. Over came a runner from the Brigadier. He would not have his men exposed to such sights! What sights? I went out to see. Four pairs of decidedly plain, army-style, white bloomers hanging to dry. I told the girls that as they were already dry to take them inside. And bided my time. A day or so later I had my own runner ready and sent her off to the Brigadier with the memo that if I were to complain this day of the male long-johns on the soldiers' line we would never get on with the war.

'Then there was the problem with the unmentionables. The girls, being in the army, were issued with only 36 clothing coupons per year, scarcely enough to cover the purchase of brassière, corset, petticoat, singlet and pyjamas and handkerchief. Now they told me that Modess sanitary pads were eating up their few coupons. I had to go to the Brigadier. When I told him the problem, he said "You can't speak to me about such a matter! You are not to come to me with these things!" I asked to whom should I speak if not to him? He hurrumphed for a bit and then asked, all right, "How many coupons a packet?" "One," I said. "Very well then, one packet." "No. Very few could manage with one packet a month." The whole affair seemed effrontery to him and it was disagreeable to me but I must be firm. "Two, sir." "One and a half," he said. I bowed out. I couldn't haggle like an Arab toffee maker.

'There were absurd things such as that, but they were of no import. Really, all I must do was bend my mind to getting this vast number of girls working in the army as I had been commanded to do.'

When Sybil Irving was called to be interviewed in September 1941, Major General Stancke, Adjutant-General, Victoria Barracks, Melbourne, wrote to the Minister for the Army recommending that she be accepted as Controller of the about-to-be-formed Australian Women's Army Service.

'Her appearance is smart, and her manner excellent. Being a good administrator and able to deal equally with all classes and ranks, she will, I have no doubt, be thoroughly capable of controlling the Women's Service. She has been strongly recommended by Lady Chauvel, Dr Newman Morris of the Red Cross, and Mr Medley, Vice-Chancellor of the Melbourne University.'

He ended the recommendation with, 'an added advantage is that she has lived in a military atmosphere, as she is the daughter of the late Brigadier-General Godfrey Irving.' This recommendation was approved on 29 September 1941.

Purists today might scent a certain elitism in the selection, especially when it is known that this woman's academic and experience record consisted only of her two years of administration with the Red Cross and eighteen years as Victorian State Secretary of the Girl Guides' Association. Women who would enter the service with the rank of major – many whose names had already been put forward to Army Headquarters – had far superior qualifications. Some were university graduates, lawyers, solicitors, teachers; others were administrators, farmers, air pilots. Yet, with hindsight, one wonders if any woman could have done so well for so long as did this woman. For whatever reason she was chosen, she was chosen well. She was the first to admit to having 'no qualifications at all', yet, in a fashion, she had trained all her life as if these next five years were to be her *raison d'être*.

Her work in the establishment of the AWAS, breaking, as it did, entirely new ground in the history of the Australian Army, was as great a pioneering feat as has been undertaken in Australia by any woman.

War Cabinet approved the formation of the AWAS on 13 August 1941, Sybil Irving was appointed in October that year and recruiting began the same month. 'The urgent thing to do was to find suitable women for possible officers. Recruiting of other ranks could not get under way until we had officers to take charge and school the recruits.

'Each state had to be visited, and quickly.'

The principal object of the Service was 'to release men from certain military duties for employment with fighting units'. It was made clear that the girls were *not* merely being enlisted to be used *in addition* to the men.

The AWAS had amazingly rapid growth. In two years it grew from nothing to a strength of over 20 000. Recruits were called up and enlistments began early in January 1942, and recruit training schools were established in all states. As anticipated, the first authorisation of 1600 personnel was absorbed by the middle of March 1942, and approval was sought and given for recruiting to be continued in accordance with requirements. On 3 August 1942, the War Cabinet agreed that women's Services were to be established as part of the forces enlisted under the Defence Act. The total enlisted to the end of December 1942 was 11 699; to the end of December 1943, 21 934; and to the end of July 1944, 22 803.

Wastage in the Service was approximately 4000, so that at October

1944, the total strength of the AWAS was between 18 000 and 19 000. First enlistments of AWAS personnel were for postings as clerks, typists, stenographers, cooks and motor transport drivers; but other occupations were soon required.

There was no precedent to be followed and important decisions had to be made as to what work women could and should undertake in a hitherto entirely male sphere, where they should serve, and what the required standards of conditions for them should be.

Uniforms had to be designed (Sybil Irving's own simple, classic felt was chosen by consensus for the hat), the confidence of the public had to be won and maintained, and the co-operation of women's voluntary organisations throughout Australia had to be engaged and maintained.

Tact had to be shown in guiding officers in their adaptation to army rules, regulations and conditions, and in dealing with male officers, some of whom were, at first, antagonistic and doubtful of the value of a women's army service.

It says much for the pioneering work of the Controller and her first group of officers, that any such antagonism and doubt quickly ceased to exist and that the AWAS won for itself, both with the army and the general public, a reputation for high standards of efficiency, discipline and behaviour. She was responsible for the initial selection, for final approval by the Adjutant-General, of the original AWAS officer group, the nucleus of the Service which attended the first officers' school at Yarra Junction, Victoria, from 24 November to 12 December, 1941.

Including the Controller, 29 officers attended this school, among them the original assistant controllers for the various states. Nominations for these officers had been made through the women's voluntary national register and 'representatives of all sections of the community'. Of the 29, there was Miss Irving as Lieutenant-Colonel, 6 majors, 13 captains and 9 lieutenants. Senior officers for each state were approved by the Minister hurriedly, 'as he understands it is essential that they should immediately leave for Victoria to attend a training course'.

Sybil Irving was the oldest among them, being born in 1897. One 'admirably suitable woman' was vetoed as being 'too young'. She was aged 30. Most of the officers chosen were close to 40.

At the beginning, none of it was easy. Even at the end, when the girls had proved their value in a way that can never again be doubted, there were still pin-pricks. 'Sometimes', Sybil Irving told me, 'they were more like crowbars.'

One of the earliest problems was one of the worst. 'We had scarcely got the green light to begin recruiting when the light suddenly changed to red. There were doubts that the women would be needed. There was a lot of subversive comment flying around – the sort of thing to which a reply is so difficult. Letters to the papers suggested women were being enlisted for all sorts of nefarious purposes. They would be wearing trousers and would become mannish, would be exposed to moral danger, would be so changed they could not settle down after the war and become wives and mothers.

'I read some of this in the morning paper the day I was to go to Perth to select the first officers there and begin enlistment. No, one never despaired, one merely tried harder and hung on longer.'

A signal from Colonel Sybil Irving's office to the Quartermaster-General, dated 23 October 1941, asked that the Controller be given air travel to Perth to enable her to choose her officers there so that she could return to Melbourne, via Adelaide (where she also would choose officers), in time to direct the AWAS officers' training course in November. Railways had already told her that there was no accommodation available to enable her to return in time, but we find in further signals she is travelling by train; no sleepers were available so she sat up the entire journey. The strain of compressing her programmes, selecting her officers who would represent her in a state as far away from her headquarters as Moscow is from London, and the weariness of steam-train travel over the long desert miles, was a terrible thing to do to her. No male colonel forming a battalion of 1000 men would be expected to do this, yet Colonel Irving would set up a framework into which 24 000 women soldiers would be enlisted.

Among the officers she chose was Major Lorna Byrne, who became Assistant Controller, AWAS. Before the war this woman, a graduate in rural science, had charge of rural women's education in New South Wales through the Government Agricultural Bureau. In 1936, she won the Carnegie Travel Grant and visited England, Canada, the USA and the principal countries of Europe, including Russia. She made a close study of women's movements and education in all these countries and, for these reasons, Sybil Irving asked the government to release her to assist with the women's army.

Major Kathleen Deasey, who later became liaison officer between the Chaplain-General's department and the three army women's services – AANS, AWAS and AAMWS – graduated from Melbourne University with an MA and Diploma of Education. She had taken out her BA and Honours (in the Theological Tripos Part 1) at Cambridge. Later she had studied in Paris and at universities in New York and Boston, attended the International Conference of University Women in Poland in 1936 and worked with groups of British students.

Her appointment as liaison officer was to ensure that enlisted girls would not be deprived of any of the contacts they had known in civilian life with their own churches. Her own belief was that the welfare of the 30 000 members of the army women's services would have an important effect during the post-war years.

Major Jean Woods, Secretary of the Girl Guides' Association in Adelaide, was working in the Guides Quartermaster Branch in November 1941 when Sybil Irving approached her to come to the AWAS. 'Father said, "You must go. We have no sons to send." I thought I would be able to stay in South Australia but Colonel Irving said, "No, you won't be here. You'll be coming to Melbourne. I want you."

'We worked, really worked. The hours and pace were heavy. For me, it was a constant attempt to relieve the Colonel of some of the pressures and to carry out her commands so well that she could be assured that anything she gave me to do would be done as well as I could do it and she could leave it to me. When the pressure was intense she would relax for half an hour, striding over the Botanic Gardens at lunchtime, with me, a foot shorter than her, hitching the side of my skirt up trying to stay in step with her.

'She was held in high regard in Victoria Barracks. Some of the old generals and brigadiers would say, "I remember her as a dot on the lawn," a reference to the sight of a small baby on a blanket on the lawns of the quadrangle. Sometimes she was called "milady", other times "madam".

'We saluted everything we passed,' Jean says now. 'Those few of us in before the Japanese attacked in 1941 were green. I was not sent to a training school – most of us 29 early officers were not, there just wasn't time. But I was sent off to lead a group of training marches. It was awful. One day we set off and suddenly, a well-trained platoon of soldiers rounded a bend coming towards us. I gave the order to turn and headed off down a side lane. Cowards. Every one of us.

'In the beginning, it was very hard to impress men that we would be of any use at all, let alone become a valuable arm of the military body. Sybil was, of course, impressive. She could be abrupt, decisive and self-assured in the public arena in a way women were not expected – or trained – to be in those days, and this stood her in good stead. She went from state to state selecting her officers (except that the Minister for the Army selected the Queensland Group), travelling hard all the time, but always cool and assured.

'Few of us could match that. Apart from everything else, there was the matter of appearance. For early parades, before uniforms were issued, girls who had been in guiding wore Girl Guide uniforms. Sybil and the rest of us early officers wore arm bands – you can see how difficult it was to impress the male army of our eventual efficiency. Major Dora Madden (Vic.) had not been through training school, but was sent off to lead the girls on a marching exercise in the country and, suddenly, "Halt!" (not too loudly from gentle Dora) and she went off to pick a wild-flower.'

Some ex-officers of the AWAS are critical of the 'over-emphasis of Girl Guiding as the nucleus of the service', but Jean Woods and Colonel May Douglas (SA) are adamant it was this that got the service so quickly established. 'The Girl Guide movement was a world-wide organisation with a structure so sound that it had become established firmly in the past fifty years,' May Douglas says. 'Many Guide leaders had been well trained and in turn had trained other troops. The framework was such that the transition from Guides to the army was made simpler for those early officers.'

Major Jean Michelmore (SA) was an exception. 'When I went for interview in those early days (November 1941), Sybil Irving and May Douglas were interviewing me – Sybil with a light at the back of her, of course, me facing the light! "Are you a member of the Girl Guides?" "No", I said, "I was one but left after 18 months." "Oh."

'I was aware of the silence, May Douglas, in the background, standing very still. The two exchanged a look. Then, an interrogatory "Oh?" "Yes," I said, "my mother wouldn't let me go. She said they were very rough girls and I was not to mix with them."

'Another silent exchange between Sybil and May. Then, "Where?" I told them the name of the area where I had been with Guides. "Oh yes. Well." Evidently that troop was not one of which the Girl Guides were greatly proud, so they passed on to other questions.'

The bringing together of some of the most talented, innovative women in the nation was a catalyst for the release of the best in all women in contact in the Service. Elizabeth Lucas, an 'original' officer and one of the last to be demobilised, knew them all. 'Anthropology was scarcely known. Not taught out here. Then we got Camilla Wedgwood who came to us with great knowledge. We called her "our resident officer of anthropology". Brilliant Kathleen Deasey had a mind that went from the abstract to the commonplace, the complex to the simple. Her nativity plays put on in the gardens were so exquisite people still speak of them today. And one met and observed women of great strength of character, such as Dora Madden, whom Sybil Irving called "my right-hand man". She was offered commands of her own with advancement, but she would never accept. She believed she enlisted to do her best to end the war and knew that at Sybil's right hand she worked best for the Service.

'We had officers in Intelligence, that part of the army which is a law unto itself. Their minds were interesting, especially then, when we had not been bombarded by the media on this subject as we are today . . .

'You'd be accosted by AWAS drivers angry because they had been allotted to Americans, not because they had anything personal against the "Yanks", but "they won't let us do our own servicing of our vehicles!" The girls were so well trained that they resented being treated as drivers who couldn't possibly know what was under any bonnet except their own.

'Then you would be with May Douglas whose interests were on another plane altogether.' May Douglas had been a VAD before the war and enlisted wanting to go overseas, but was told she was too old. (She later did do a tour of New Guinea.) She is the only woman to have been a member of all four of the Women's Army Services, the VADs, AAMWS, AWAS, then, after the war, the newly formed WRAAC.'

Jean Woods found 'there was a little that could surprise one in the service. I was detailed off to "train an officer to cross the parade ground without letting her disgrace the service". I'd merely been told she was a war artist, the daughter of Hans Heysen. Now that was an exercise. I totally understood her wonderfully free spirit wanting to be untrammelled by discipline of any sort but – well, it's difficult to explain what she looked like in uniform. This is perhaps the greatest argument against either men or women belonging to a disciplined force: their individuality must be controlled, not tamed, just trained to control it for the good of the whole. War is total. If we are in we are in to win. The quicker we do that, the quicker we get back to living in the way that best suits us. I don't believe any one need lose one jot of their private persona, of their personality or freedom . . . most of us officers . . . were not conscious when on parade that we suppressed our individual selves in the exercise of belonging to a team. It happens in football, cricket, yachting, bushwalking. But for an artist, ah, it is different. That different drum that an artist marches to; I had to march this artist to our drum. Up and down the barracks we went.

We got along fine, laughed a lot, but eventually she could "cross the parade ground" without disgracing the service!'

An extra burden on those early officers was the fact that they were being examined under the microscope of established male army tradition. 'When we were eventually able to get the odd seat on an army plane, we sat in ricketty aircraft – no seats, sometimes on the floor, sometimes on forms lengthwise along the sides of the plane, not fastened down. When it was rough, the whole lot of us rolled off. Then we tumbled off the plane at journey's end and had to appear smart, as became officers, yet womanly, as became ladies – because you must remember that, in the beginning, there had been much criticism to the effect that army life would take the lady out of women. It was very stupid, but it was the age, the period . . .

'We just did our best . . . to get the service going, and once it was on its way we then did not need to do anything, because the results were so magnificent that all talk of "ladies in trousers" and the rest of it stopped when we were able to report – during the dark days of the war – that, in some cases, as AWAS marched into a camp, the men they were to relieve were marching out. At one barracks they arrived to a very warm welcome. Soldiers had unpacked their crockery, washed and polished the dishes, and prepared lunch for them. In time we were accepted for what we were.'

Mona 'Bill' Hornsby (WA) 'went in as a captain, came out as a captain. I was teaching at Claremont, the phone rang, it was Sybil. "You have been recommended to me," she said. "I want you to be an officer." I rushed in during my lunch hour, to the barracks, the next thing I knew I was heading east to Yarra Junction, to officers' school. Went over and back in civvies.

'We were camped at the WACA ground in the grandstand. Had our bunks up on the grandstand, showers below. Toilets – a dirty big rat in one when we arrived, so I got a lump of wood and killed it.' Mona had a reputation for expecting a clean camp. 'If you live in a place you want it to be right.'

She didn't believe in Orderly Rooms. 'Any girl in strife I brought her in and had a good talk to her and told her what a spot she was putting me in. Very few girls didn't respond to a good talking to. There were precautions taken, but things could come unstuck.

'Thousands and thousands of Yanks [were] always trying to get in, but we demanded names etc. at the gate and verified that this visitor was expected before letting a man in. And we checked each man out before lights out. But one night I was doing the lights out round and I said to my sergeant, "Do you see what I see?" "Yanks!" she gasped. "Hordes of them. How did they get in?" It took us a while but we found out: they crept in through the trenches dug as air raid shelters.

'Girls found their own level, sorted themselves out. Rookies, poor little devils, arrived tired, bewildered, had to fill their palliasse with straw for a bed. By the end of the week homesick, awful. I expected sabotage, so many parcels of cakes arrived from their homes to cheer them up. "All right! It's a party," I said, and they put them on the table and became a family. Blasted kids used to fill my bed with things – flour and stuff – the hounds.

'We had nothing to make it homely at WACA, so I took my piano out and my lounge suite. The cook there had been a shearers' cook. I tell you, those girls had a lot to put up with.' Barbara Clinton was set to work "scrubbing slabs". Regularly scrubbing the cement slab floor in the kitchen.'

Mona had to take her first batch of girls out training dressed in their civvies, 'Sitting for lunch on the side of the track eating blasted cold sausages. Aborigines gathering around waiting for left-overs.

'Our uniforms etcetera began to arrive. First of the witches' britches we'd seen. Waist to knee. The girls on heavy artillery were issued with men's knee-length breeches and shearers' thick shirts to protect them from the cold.'

Captain Hornsby served in Western Australia for 18 months, then New South Wales and Queensland. 'All of us from the West got used to that blasted rail journey, day after day of it. Single track. Our train shunted into sidings to let others go by. Usually one girl would have a guitar and we'd have a sing-song.'

Dorothea Skov (Qld) saw an advertisement for girls interested in becoming army officers in 1941. 'I didn't "work" in one sense, but I was secretary of sporting bodies, vigaro, ladies' basketball, suburban church groups, very interested in YWCA.

'At first, it was a total battle to get men to accept us as workers. They were very hostile . . . Articles in the press didn't help. "Servicewomen keep their femininity" and "Girls don't lose their femininity in barracks". This type of article abounded. The soldiers saw us as playing at war. But that broke down. Women had gone into the services with such a load of enthusiasm; they'd go from dawn to next daylight. Soon officers said, "The morale and behaviour of men have lifted since women joined the Service."

'The men back from the Middle East were surprised to see us. "Gawd! The bleedin' women have even got rank!" one said, as I went by with my pips up. They used to turn in the street and stare at us women in uniform. The Yanks were scared of rank. Thousands of US troops were let loose here in Brisbane, back from the islands on leave. Us women officers only had to speak to them and they scared off and let the girls alone.

'Prisoners of war when they returned at the end of 1945 were not scared of rank, but they now turned and stared in amazement as we passed by. Every girl who enlisted expected to release a man for active service. The returned men appreciated this when they got used to seeing us around.

'We didn't think much of politicians. Forde, the Minister for the Army, visited the first Officers' Training School at Brisbane and the jackasses drowned him out. He wouldn't let servicewomen out of Australia. We were glad the kookaburras laughed at him.'

With the exception of the original group of 29 officers, specially selected to get the Service going, every recruit had to enlist in the ranks and do her full Recruit Training Course before receiving commissioned rank, even if she was being enlisted for a specialist job. Even Sybil Irving's sister, Freda, came up that way. Of course, countless silly things were said about the women's services and the women in them. How could it be otherwise in that age and climate, when these services were such a new concept? Some comments Sybil Irving ignored, some she attacked publicly.

On 27 June 1942, she made a press statement refuting a report published in Sydney papers that the first court martial of an AWAS was to be held soon. 'Our regulations do not provide for any member being brought before a court martial.' Colonel Irving made no other comment regarding the young woman in question and, having known her until her death in 1973, I know no journalist who could have successfully leant on Sybil Irving. She was a woman whom it is difficult to describe. Those who met her fleetingly might, and rightly, describe her as aloof, cold and clipped. That was her public persona. Privately she was quiet, tactful, witty to the point, very loving to friends, loyal and supportive. She suggested, never ordered; could not bully. Most of her officers and girls knew this.

Some newspaper columnists attempted to dub the girls with a 'pet-name'. They began heading stories of AWAS as 'Waussies' do this or 'A-Waussies' do that. 'I prefer just AWAS,' Sybil said to journalists. 'It's a bit of a mouthful,' they said, to which she replied, 'No more than AAMC or other generally used military terms. I like it best, because it keeps the W for Women before us. Our aim is always to remember that we are women though we are in the services.'

Sybil wrote, 'Wise men have never doubted feminine courage, but never until this war have women of the Commonwealth been able to show that they can be as brave as men when the country needs their services. The courage and loyalty of our women are impressive and complete. There is among them a quiet, firm, steadfast resolution to play a part in bringing victory to us.'

Although enlistment continued apace, the army was slow to outfit the girls. A letter to the *Telegraph* of 29 May 1942 states, 'Why is it that the WAAAF are fully equipped even to respirators, while the young women of the AWAS are so badly lacking in most equipment? Some have uniforms, no shoes, others shoes and no uniforms, some have underwear, toothbrush and overcoat, while others have not even an armband to distinguish them from their civilian sisters.' (A reply from 'mother of a WAAAF' said her daughter had been in the air force three months and supplies were so bad she was still sleeping 'on the floor in a cold climate. Instead of getting a shirt she got 2 collars. She has to pay full fare on trams because she has only bits of uniforms.'

Women must, of course, be ladies: 'Army girls must act like ladies,' the *Courier-Mail* headlined an article. 'Rules for ladylike behaviour in the women's army and air force are calculated to discourage any wartime abandon. They are permitted to smoke in restaurants, but on no account in trams, trains or on the streets. Girls in both organisations are permitted to drink "in moderation". Any excesses to be reported and certain hotels near country camps are out of bounds.

'Make-up must be discreet, as must nail polish, while hair must be short or rolled up clear of the collar. They must wear their hats straight and wear greatcoats buttoned up, not flapping. Neither organisation permits jewellery except wedding and engagement rings. Each woman must, by the way she is turned out, indicate her acceptance of service regulations. AWAS must endeavour to attract as little attention to themselves as possible.'

They must have done this, because by the middle of the year General Sir Thomas Blamey, GOC Land Forces in Australia, said the army was happy to welcome the AWAS. 'You are part of the army, you have earned the right to serve,' he pontificated. He added that, although the allies were being pushed back 'all over the place', there were signs that the worst period was passing. It is hard to believe, remembering June 1942, that any allied leader would have imagined women to be so gullible, particularly as in the AWAS, two-fifths of those enlisted had at least one member of the family overseas. Sybil Irving believed that this laid the foundation of their sober, hard work, but it also kept them well aware of how and where the battle was going.

In many arms of the AMF, AWAS formed the greater percentage of personnel in units, and in some cases the total personnel. In many of the Car Companies and Ambulance Car Companies all the drivers were AWAS.

In just the same way as the rank and file, AWAS officers undertook duties formerly done by male officers. Both officers and other ranks did highly specialised jobs and secret work which had an important and direct bearing on the safety of the fighting soldier and the successful outcome of battle operations – 'hush hush' work, such as compiling operational maps, and specialised jobs, such as testing 'walkie talkie' radios after they had been tropic-proofed, army food supplies, and collating and mathematically checking scientific and technical problems being handled by the Operational Research Section.

Lorna Byrne (NSW), one of the first officers to be commissioned in this service, was also one of the most popular. She is still 'proud of the girls. Members of the AWAS were not posted only to Base areas; they served all over Australia, wherever they were needed, from Gun and Searchlight Stations and Sig. Ops Sections on lonely islands and in isolated parts of the continent, to the operational areas of the Northern Territory and, eventually, New Guinea. They were, of course, all volunteers. Many of these girls had never been away from home before, and being sent hundreds of miles away meant they had to readjust to this new phase in their lives amid an excitement, fear and responsibility they could never have anticipated – an adjustment that their daughters in the 1980s have not had to make. Their tasks were not easy. They lived and worked under the same conditions as the men whom they had released for overseas service. Many jobs were menial and monotonous. Postings in some of the isolated areas took them to all sorts of unpleasant conditions – life on lonely islands with mosquitoes and sandflies as companions, and to sandhills and the edges of swamps.'

One of the most unusual jobs in all the varied activities of the Australian Women's Army Service was that of Corporal Georgette Boxall, of Brisbane. She was a marine draughtsman in a watercraft workshop operated by the Corps of Electrical and Mechanical Engineers.

Cpl Boxall, wearing khaki 'battle dress', working suit and a black beret, was called aboard any small ship which came into the Brisbane River workshop for repair. Her job was to examine the damage and to transfer plans for repair to paper. In doing this, she also prepared estimates of material required. All the craftsmen worked to the plans and blueprints prepared by her. Motor launches, tugs, barges large and small and landing craft were all familiar to her. 'When I came into this job I didn't know the front from the back of a ship.'

Her oddest job was to inspect the damaged propeller shaft of a 200-tonne motor barge. Carrying a flashlight, she had to crawl 6 metres along the greasy shaft tube before she could see what work was to be done.

Her biggest job was one of which she and the whole workshops were proud. The workshops were given an old 20-metre barge which had been lying abandoned for years on a mudbank. Could the army do anything with it?

Small vessels were in great demand. The CO had a look, and said they could. He roughed out his ideas in chalk and Cpl Boxall went to work with pencils and drawing board, producing side and bird's eye elevations of the proposed rebuilding.

The workshops set to work. In a few weeks, the army had a neat 125 hp diesel motor vessel capable of taking almost 25 tonnes of cargo. The former mudbank shell became a trim ship with quarters for a crew of six, besides her master. Superstructure, bunks, galley – every part of the rebuilt ship – grew from the blueprints of this 24-year-old AWAS.

Lieutenant C. E. Mountjoy was the only woman to hold the position of OC of one of the sub-sections of LHQ, Victoria Army Directorate of Armament, dealing with munitions.

By her appointment, she released an A class officer for service in the field. She had four men and an AWAS under her control and was responsible for administering her sub-section, including the ordering of all ammunition and explosives requirements from overseas and local sources. She was responsible for collating and recording all technical developments in ammunition, both allied and enemy, for passing all claims for costs of ammunition, and for keeping statistics on the ammunition supply position of the Australian land forces.

She visited ammunition depots to gain knowledge to assist her in the work and took part in shoots from landing craft and observed the building of these craft.

Women such as Corporal Boxall, Lieutenant Mountjoy and the thousands of other AWAS provided the power behind the army machine in the forward areas and, in every phase of their multifarious activities, they did much to solve the army's manpower problems.

The AWAS equivalent of the military police were the supervisory personnel who were involved in any matters affecting the welfare of the Service.

One of their meetings addressed the problem of the entry of AWAS into the Royal Australian Artillery.

When the rapid approach of the Japanese called for anti-aircraft, searchlight and coast defences, the total enlisted in the RAA for these duties up to December 1943 was 17 officers and 3577 OR. Many Searchlight Stations were manned completely by AWAS personnel, doing their own guard in all weathers, and on the anti-aircraft gun sites, AWAS did everything but load and fire the guns. Sybil Irving believed girls should not do the latter. 'These girls will be the mothers of the children who will rebuild Australia. They must not have the death of another mother's son on their hands.'

Women's Service policy was always directed towards members being engaged on duties of a non-combatant nature; but if AWAS were to take guard duties and completely man searchlight detachments, they must have some means of defending themselves and their equipment.

It was suggested that guard duty at night was a severe strain on the nerves; in a medical survey taken over three months, of 430 personnel in hospital, 139 were gunners. Tests showed that the same girls were being admitted constantly to hospital.

After much discussion, it was decided that women required to carry rifles in the course of their duty should be trained to fire from any position and to have confidence in the use of their weapons; any member judged as not temperamentally suited for such duty should be immediately relieved without any adverse effect on their service record.

As the operational theatre of war moved away from Australia in 1944, there was a considerable re-organisation of the RAA, and most of the anti-aircraft and searchlight defences were then manned by VDC personnel. AWAS of the RAA were then re-allocated to other arms and services of the AMF.

From the first day of their enlistment, the women had worked to serve in forward areas. Now, in November 1944, a War Cabinet decision announced that 500 AWAS were to be permitted to take up signals and clerical duties in New Guinea. Ten officers were to lead 52 women who included 12 NCOs, 'typistes', stenographers, clerks, draughtswomen, cooks and a hairdresser.

An example of the attitude of the colonial times (of which New Guinea was still a part, being mandated territory of Australia) was given at a conference of senior officers before the AWAS left for New Guinea, when Lieutenant-Colonel Wedgwood spoke of her experience of life in New Guinea prior to and during the present war. She felt that it was 'tremendously important' that officers posted there should remember the great importance of keeping up the dignity of the Service.

'There was a temptation to relax too much in a tropical climate. From the point of view of contact with the natives it was most important that the white women should keep up their standards. The natives should not be too friendly with them. One must bear in mind that white women will have to live in New Guinea after the war and what happens now is going to affect their future. With regard to our own and the American men, it is for the servicewomen to set the standard.'

Personnel going to New Guinea were warned against using up too much energy when they first arrived. After the first two or three months, one paid for this with exhaustion, she said, and because work being done by servicewomen in New Guinea appeared to her to be very heavy for the tropics, Lt-Colonel Wedgwood thought it might be necessary to place some limitations on their free-time activities.

In 1945, Captain Hornsby found she was off to Lae, in charge of the first group of AWAS. 'Signallers and clerical staff. Couldn't go out alone, must be in pairs with escorts. There was an officers' club but nowhere for the kids to go, so we got permission for them to go to the OR club. The first time the kids were out, the punch was laced with jungle juice. My poor little sergeant was upset, she'd been in charge of the kids. I told the men, "It's the last time my girls come to your mess." The men wrote home saying stupid things like, "AWAS are officers' playthings." There was a big hullaballoo about it. Yes, we did have more to put up with through being women.' The girls were all on Atabrin. 'I was brilliant yellow. Then I had dengue fever. Gracie Fields visited and sang, "Wish me Luck" and I thought, I'll need it.'

Mona came home to a job in Post-war Reconstruction, 'But I wanted more. I went into advertising in Melbourne, then bought a catering service and got a good team of girls around me. Then I bought a pub – I'd managed several pubs, getting my funds together. The night I moved into my pub I went to bed not knowing how to get past the debt collectors the next day. But I managed in the long run.

'The army did me a great deal of good. I've always mixed well, but there were so many girls – they write to me. When I was in hospital, oh, they made the time go easier.' The captain lost her legs with diabetes, a breast with cancer. 'Those blasted kids and the things they got up to! They keep me going, thinking of them.'

## CHAPTER 24

# *'Sigs'*

In May 1942, 1000 young women were called up as signallers. The signals corps was one field into which women moved soon after women's services were enlisted. The 3600 AWAS who eventually served in signals were a part of the team formed in June 1942 as 1st and 2nd Australian Signals Training Battalions (AWAS). The first training centres were at Ivanhoe Grammar School, Melbourne, where all women from states other than New South Wales and Queensland were trained; signallers from these two states were trained at Ingleburn (NSW).

Forty young Tasmanians were chosen with great care to go to Ivanhoe. Melva Martin was one. 'After all medicals etc., we were instructed to report to Hobart for swearing in and spent five hours in a steam train covering the 125 miles from Launceston to Hobart. That night we took the oath and were given some instructions. The following morning we again boarded a very slow train, taking all day to reach Burnie to board the *Taroona* for Melbourne.

'Because of the presence in Bass Strait of Japanese submarines, the ship was in almost total darkness, the sea was rough, the ship took a zig-zag course which was a protection against attack . . .

'Next morning, very seedily, we went on deck to have a look at the shores of Port Phillip, feeling like John Batman must have after his crossing in his tiny ship, only to find we were enveloped in a thick shroud of fog . . . When the ship finally tied up, we were bustled into trucks and ferried to Ivanhoe Grammar School . . . We were besieged by photographers who were anxious to see what had arrived. I have a very battered photo which was published in the *Sun* of 1 July 1942, showing five Tasmanians learning to make up their beds, still wearing overcoats as it was freezing.

'Our huts weren't properly finished, so we had to clean them out, fill our palliasses with straw, and make up our iron beds with two blankets in the depths of Melbourne's winter. There were many tears shed that night. We were already homesick, very tired, cold and beginning to wonder what we had let ourselves in for.'

The huts, showers, cook houses and mess-halls, being erected to accommodate 500 girls were still under construction when the Tasmanians arrived and the class-rooms were still being wired for buzzer and sounder practice.

The commanding officers were Lieutenant-Colonel R. C. V. Humphery and Lieutenant-Colonel T. J. Farrow, the AWAS administrative officers Jean Woods and Joyce Whitworth (NSW).

The No. 1 Companies consisted of sounder, wireless and line telegraphy operating sections, the No. 2 Companies, cipher, keyboard and signals clerk sections, while the third companies trained switchboard operators. The various courses lasted between six weeks and three months, and in this time, the girls reached Morse speed of 20 words per minute.

All students after joining the units had to complete a three-week general signals course, which included squad drill, saluting, badges of rank and general military subjects. Each member of the Signals staffs and units of the Australian Corps of Signals had a double responsibility: first, there was the necessity to operate always with the maximum efficiency; and, secondly, character of the highest integrity was called for. The integrity of the individual is an essential factor in these security-sensitive information areas, which deal with the transmission and reception of secret messages passed over the army signals communication channels. At all times, the security and success of both present and future operations rest with these operators.

The first course for potential officers commenced in September, only three months after the first training school began. Twenty-five cadets from all states were called up to study the comprehensive syllabus which included, in addition to signals subjects, military law, administration, organisation, map reading and practical work in the field. It was decided to transfer as many male officers as possible from the units to the forward areas and, consequently, many of the students spent the first part of their commissioned service as instructors in the ensuing courses both for NCO and officer candidates.

'The work was constant, solid on the nerves, so to relieve this, weekly competitions were introduced. Squad-drill competitions were held every Saturday afternoon and the winning sections were granted additional night leave,' remembers Melva Martin.

'As well as our sports, our male instructors at that first school formed two teams and played football each Saturday, and us "sigs" rookies crowded around the oval and cheered as it if were a VFL Grand Final.

'Competition was earnest, you might even say savage. It was a great scheme to allay the boredom of the repetitive, concentrated work. Our course leader, Lieutenant-Colonel Humphery, who guided and trained all of us who were at Ivanhoe in the early days, was a splendid organiser of study and system. The women who became officers – and immediately began training others – were able to do that within three months because of his brilliant method of teaching and his faith in us. After the first batch moved out as reinforcements, he transferred from the army to the mercantile marine and was appointed senior wireless officer on a passenger steamer that was eventually sunk and Lieutenant-Colonel Humphery lost his life at sea. We were devastated.'

On 24 November, the Melbourne unit moved to Bonegilla, as did the Ingleburn unit early in the New Year of 1943. Huts were wired up for buzzer practice, telephones were installed and loudspeaker systems were put into operation.

As the operators became fully trained, they were sent out on exercises in the field, where they gained practical experience in operating wireless and telegraph instruments. By this time, all the company commanders were women.

'Many of our instructors hated the job,' Alice O'Toole (WA) says. 'They were men rushed home from the Middle East expecting to be sent to New Guinea to stop the Japs' advance, and then to find themselves coaching a school of rookies was very disappointing for them. Some gave us larrydooley. Eventually, they bucked up and were our greatest admirers.

'Throughout the war years, the Sigs were mainly shift workers, as all the overseas messages came in during the night. In the various camps I was in, our main hours were three days of shift from midnight until 0800, three days from 0800 until 1700, then three days from 1700 until midnight. That would be followed by a three-day break. Sometimes we even had to do 12 hours on and 12 hours off, depending on the number we had. For the night shift we had to collect our rations for a 3 a.m. meal – loaf of bread, tins of pilchards or baked beans, tin of jam, which for one month would be apple jelly, then the next four weeks plum.'

The troops in World War I had a song which tells us they, too, had the same boring jam.

> *Plum and apple, apple and plum,*
> *Plum and apple, there is always some,*
> *The Officers get strawberry jam,* NCOs *get beer,*
> *But we poor boys in the Signal Corps get apple and plum!*

'In 1944, a small contingent of Sigs manned a Sig. Office in Atherton in the centre of the Atherton Tablelands in Northern Queensland. Here we had to work 12 hours on and 12 hours off, then change over. At this time, the three AIF Divisions were gathering up there prior to embarkation for the forward push north through the islands which had been in Japanese hands since 1942. There was plenty of work, but very little entertainment available. There was a picture show in the local theatre every Saturday night and it was a case of first come, first served . . .

'On the way back to Brisbane, I was put in charge of a whole carriage of men – much to my horror. Whoever did the organisation of the travel arrangements failed to notice that my Army number contained an F, denoting female.* The AIF men were TX, and militia had simply 'T' for Tasmanians. Needless to say, I soon got out of that detail, as it was a three-day trip from Townsville to Brisbane.

'It was a hard life in many ways. Long hours of solid work – shifts – lack of sleep during the heat of the day when on night shift. Being so far from home, we only got leave once in six months or from Queensland, 12 months.

'When we worked the 1700 till midnight shift, we had to be on parade at 0800 and then do all the camp duties during the day, which tired us out and didn't give us much rest and, in one camp, led to a mutiny. All leave was cancelled, but so many went AWL one particular night that many NCOs lost their stripes the following day. Still, it got results, and the girls on the night shift were relieved of some of the latrine cleaning, painting of bricks in the camp grounds, and climbing light poles to clean the globes.'

Privates Alice O'Toole and Pat McCarthy were (still are) friends who joined in Western Australia. 'I came from a big Irish Catholic family,' Pat says. 'All our men were in the war so of course I went. My sister was a VAD/AAMWS.'

Alice also came from a serving family. 'My father had his twenty-first birthday on Gallipoli. We were patriotic. Flag raising, saluting the flag, all that. When I asked Dad to give permission for me to join up he said, "Don't come crying to me to get you out if you don't like it. It's the Army, you're in to stay." It's 40 years on Tuesday since I took the oath,' she said, like someone remembering a birthday or an anniversary.

---

*Army numbers of both sexes were prefixed by initials denoting state (i.e. V for Victoria); if enlisted for overseas (X). Female personnel also had F, e.g. VFX 124737.

Pat: 'The Japs were in the war when we joined the Signals Corps in 1942. Mostly older men and very young boys in it and we went in to release any who were fit to go to the front . . . we'd go to Sigs on transfer and the men would be packing to leave.'

Elsie Solly from a saw-milling family deep in the forests of Western Australia looked in the Orderly Room and said to the CO, 'There's three men in that room who could be sent off. We three girls can take their place.' Next week they were gone.

Alice and Pat 'went over the other side' together. 'I thought we were off to win the war.' But Pat's boyfriend returned from the Middle East, they married, 'and I was pregnant within two weeks. Alice and I had done our Sigs training. Now I was out on my own. My husband was sent off immediately to the islands and I didn't see him until the baby was 18 months old. I missed the girls and the service terribly.'

Alice missed her. 'I was sent back on the troop train, back West, five days travel, eight carriage-loads of us sitting up all the way. But we were better than the boys. They were in terrible cattle trucks. Got out with the flies to eat. Army people would get off the train and light fires and set up cooking gear and get a meal going. There would be a big tub of water for us to wash our plates in. A billy of water was carried round and you wet your washer in it and washed your face. The dust, heat and flies always won out, though. The engine broke down twice on the way over. Worn out. Hot boxes, boiler.

'We were given a route march across the Nullarbor to get us away from the men – cat calls, wolf whistles followed us across the sand.' Alice married a serviceman. 'We've been lucky.' Pat had six children, her husband lay for eight years crippled, speechless, before his death in 1981. 'All the AWAS stuck to me. They were real mates. Took me out, looked after things for me.'

## CHAPTER 25

# The Petal and the Bee

*B*efore the discovery of penicillin and the wide spectrum of antibiotics, venereal diseases were difficult to treat; the results of infection could mean death or crippling among both adults and children.

Although venereal diseases are traditionally associated with war, the peace-time figures have always been high, even if social niceties have prevented their being published. This must be recognised if we are to correctly assess the wartime casualties from these most ancient diseases.

Indeed, at the Tenth Australasian Medical Congress held in Auckland, New Zealand, in early 1914, a percentage figure was stated that was later to be almost the same as that given for men in the armed forces. 'It is fairly certain that 10 to 15 per cent of the population of London, Berlin and Paris are syphilitic and a much larger number are gonorrhoeic. There is good reason for thinking that Australian cities are affected to much the same extent.' The Congress produced figures to show that 7189 deaths in Australia in 1914 were attributed to syphilis, and this did not take into account naturally aborted or stillbirths.

In 1915 night clinics for venereal diseases were opened at the Royal Prince Alfred Hospital, Sydney, and during this first year 2279 patients attended and 34 children under the age of one year were admitted for treatment.

Earlier still, in 1908, it was claimed that 25 per cent of sick children in Melbourne were 'tainted' with syphilis and 10 per cent of *all* children in that city were 'syphilised'. Of 100 consecutive child mortalities at the Children's Hospital, Melbourne, post mortems showed that 44 infants who died in their first year of life were diagnosed as syphilitic.

Throughout the depression years, the 1920s and 1930s, enamel plaques containing warnings were placed in both men's and women's lavatories on all railway stations. There was a large trade in proprietary medical 'cures' and chemists advertised openly that they could 'cure' the disease.

Up until the 1930s, war had little effect on the prevalence of the disease in Australia, because of our isolation. The men who went to World War I were infected 19 000 kilometres from home and the majority did not return for the duration of hostilities.

If the above figures were the norm in peace-time Australia, how much more danger was there, when almost the whole of Australia's armed forces were rushed home in 1942 to defend their homeland and were joined by an army of American servicemen?

In 1941, when only a handful of girls were enlisted, the risk was not apparent. By 1942, when thousands of fit, young women were pouring into camps, and often serving in areas where the ratio of girls to equally fit, young men was one to five, it would have been dilatory for the services to ignore the imminent danger.

The WAAAF Administration, perhaps the most efficient and modern in the sense of recognising that society's then taboos would not fit the conditions in which Australian women now found themselves, had a 'set' lecture prepared. Female doctors or nursing sisters lectured on 'Sex Hygiene'; this was the first time most girls had heard the term. If, today, this lecture sounds both simplistic and sanctimonious, we must realise that it was the most startlingly frank document for its time that any service girl had been exposed to. (Even though it did go on so long as to bore most into inattention.) So dramatic was its broader impact that, when word leaked out to *Truth*, the issue was beaten around in print, with the supposed shock and disgust at this 'slight' to our 'gallant women' covering the salacious innuendos.

The prepared lecture began: 'I have been asked to discuss with you the subject of Sex Hygiene. At the outset I will explain exactly what is meant by Sex Hygiene. Then, as I proceed, I am sure you will realise (if you don't do so already) how important this subject is to . . . you, both as individuals and as members of society in general.' The lecturer then was to list the venereal diseases, syphilis, gonorrhoea, soft sore, lymphogranuloma venereum, granuloma inguinale – hastily pointing out that the last two 'are fortunately rather rare in Australia. They occur mostly in tropical countries (e.g. Asia).' (Of course, we were already there – and liable to go there in far greater numbers.)

After explaining the derivation of the word 'venereal', the tutor was to continue: 'I do not propose to deal with this topic on religious or moral grounds, but simply from a practical medical point of view. Most doctors, in the course of their work, come across enough examples of unhappiness, disability and death caused by venereal disease to convince them of the seriousness of these diseases and the need for preventing them.'

A spirochaete was drawn and the word was written on the blackboard, then the speaker continued: 'Almost all people who contract syphilis do so as the result of having sexual intercourse with a person already infected by the disease [or] . . . it is possible to get it as a result of being kissed by a person with syphilis or by drinking from a contaminated vessel of some kind. (Emphasise rarity of accidental or innocent infection – kissing commonest of all innocent methods of transmission. Story of young man and five dancing partners in Roxburgh's *Common Skin Diseases*).'

Those of us serving in military hospitals flew to the bookshelves to read Roxburgh on this interesting deviation.

Gonorrhoea, we learned – or were told – results after intercourse 'with an already infected person,' as does soft sore. 'The only absolutely sure way to avoid venereal infection is to avoid sexual intercourse outside marriage . . . All persons who neglect this principle become infected in the long run if not in the short.'

What followed, after being informed that 'there are 2½ million sperms in each ejaculation of human semen', quite surprised many girls of that generation, whose sole instruction before marriage was, 'some things happen when you marry, but don't worry about it, it's over quite quickly if you don't make a fuss.'

'In order to make sure that her purpose will be fulfilled often enough . . . nature gave us a sense of attraction to the opposite sex and pleasurable satisfaction in the fulfilment of the sexual act. These emotions serve as a lure and an enticement.'

No one had told us that before. But we had heard, or sensed: 'Behind them is the purpose – reproduction.' Now came the part we all waited for: how is it done? We were told. It was 1942, in Brisbane, and there was an estimated quarter of a million servicemen in and around that city, almost equal to its pre-war population. All these were fit young men, all were in uniform and either back from the jaws of death (the cliché that we suddenly learnt was a reality) or about to face sudden, unexpected, unwanted death, a combination that is the greatest aphrodisiac known to mankind.

We listened and heard the sexual act likened to the pollination of flowers by birds or bees, described with such phrases as 'bright petals' and 'honey sacks'!

But what did this have to do with women dressed in the uniforms Australia's armed services provided? Surely no petals were less attractive than these lumpy costumes? Freda Irving (AWAS) says, 'I was always conscious that in uniform I looked like a sack of potatoes tied in the middle.'

The lecture continued: 'If every woman realised the reason for her sexual endowment and the emotional impulses she experiences as a result of it, she must know that marriage supplies the only satisfactory solution to her need for sex fulfilment.' We were told that marriage offered sexual satisfaction, companionship, emotional security and 'it minimises the risk of venereal disease'. On the other hand, sex outside marriage 'inevitably, in the case of a woman, will bring disaster and unhappiness . . . in the form of venereal infection and/or illegitimate pregnancy. Remember that you are the mothers of the next generation. You owe it to your children-to-be to avoid these risks and dangers. Remember, too, that moral standards are set by the women . . . *not* by the men.'

So what was new? We had been told before of our primal sin and our shameful luring of innocent men . . .

The 3500 word lecture went on . . . and on . . . with a score of organisms and female organs drawn on a blackboard. Many of the girls had scarcely left school, blackboards were anathema. The whole, over-long message cannot be said to have left a lasting impression on us, or succeeded in assuring us of its relevance in our present lives.

As for the final . . . sermon? It was interesting, inasmuch as it was somewhat frank for the era, in that it stated openly that sex was sex, but the information it conveyed was scarcely needed. Without words having ever been spoken to us, most of that generation of girls was already instinctively imbued with an unnamed, vaguely understood fear of 'going too far'. The danger of venereal disease, 'whatever that was', was small, compared with the virtual social death of becoming pregnant outside marriage. But the lecture given to the WAAAF (and with little change to the other women's services) had added the extra taboo that would most assuredly result from this 'going too far'.

Contraceptives were given a few hundred words, as were 'illegal operations'. Most of us knew nothing about the first, but much about the second, gained in a whispered, behind-the-hand method of spreading information aimed at creating straight-down-the-line terror of the results of 'going too far'. Contraceptives were useless, according to the lecturer: 'The only way to avoid pregnancy is to avoid sexual intercourse.'

'Illegal operations' are mentioned only to be condemned. 'A great many women who undergo such operations die annually in the septic blocks attached to our general hospitals from damage and infection. Most of the percentage who survive are so damaged or infected that they never again enjoy good health.'

Well then, we wondered, what if a girl does 'go too far'?

'It is far better for a woman with an unwanted pregnancy to see it through and have her child adopted. In doing this she will ensure her own safety and wellbeing, and as well she gives the community another, and potentially useful, citizen. Between eleven hundred to fourteen hundred adoptions take place every year in the state of New South Wales alone. There are always waiting lists of prospective foster parents.'

This necessity may have been considered by some of us, even in those days of hypocritical double-standards, as an immorality equally as disgusting as that same social disapproval that caused girls to risk their lives 'in the septic block of our general hospitals'. But such radical ideas would not be understood, let alone be considered, by the arbiters of women's social behaviour.

Of course, this was not the lecture given to men. We swiftly learned that their lectures began on a rather jokey note: 'Excuse me doctor, but is it true that one can catch VD from a lavatory seat?' 'Oh yes,' replies the doctor, 'that is possible, but it's a dirty place to take a woman, isn't it?' And the one about the young soldier who was attending Army Education classes in literacy – his tutor asked him if he had learnt enough to now be able to write home to his parents and the lad replied, 'Well, no, I only want to write one letter home and I guess it will be a long time before I learn to spell spirochaete.'

We got no such humorosities. Women have spoken to me since about their reactions. 'I no longer can remember why, but I do remember that at the time I thought it had nothing to do with me. I don't think I understood much of it.'

The hospitalisation of patients suffering with venereal disease was assigned to the army by the War Cabinet. Accordingly, in each capital city, a special ward was allocated for treatment of VD in servicewomen. Separate hospitals for VD and gynaecology were unfortunate, as a stigma came to be attached to admission. 'I was sent to 105 AGH, Dawes Road. My mail was redirected there, so I knew the postal clerk in my muster knew where I was and, because I guessed that if *anyone* knew where I was *everyone* knew, I felt awful. We were treated well enough there, but, well . . .'

There were 14 women medical officers in the WAAAF. 'Everyone said they were all great but I must have struck the only rotten one in the barrel. When I reported first to her she said, "You've got yourself in a pretty pickle now haven't you miss!" I didn't need to be told that. I'm older now and I think about it sometimes. And I think, they were beautiful times but terribly cruel times. You'd go to a dance, you might have taken the signal that afternoon that a navigator you liked a lot was shot down, missing, and now you were dancing with another navigator. You knew when he was next due in ops room. There was ... madness I suppose. Then, if we'd waited to think, it was another kind of madness, it was the war.

'We were sitting in the chapel one Sunday morning in Townsville and the minister was preaching: "Almighty and most merciful father: We have erred and strayed from thy ways like lost sheep." As if on cue, the just-returned air-crews swept by on bicycles, singing at the top of their lungs:

> *We are poor little lambs that have lost our way*
> *Baa Baa Baa!*
> *We are little black sheep that have gone astray*
> *Baa Baa Baa!*
> *Gentlemen songsters out on a spree*
> *Damned from here to eternity*
> *God have mercy on such as we*
> *Baa Baa Baa!*

'We laughed. But really, we cried inside. We all knew those boys, and watched to count them when they came back after a strike.'

CHAPTER 26

# *That Branch of Physiology*

Cyesiology may well be a word that is unfamiliar to most people, even to those whom it most closely affects. Yet many servicewomen were discharged for this cause. The *Oxford Dictionary* defines cyesiology as: that branch of physiology which treats of pregnancy.

The word is Greek for pregnancy and was doubtless chosen to confuse those with salacious interest. Cyesis returns in the AWAS for the six months for January to June 1945 were 457; of these, 108 were single girls. (There were 16 000 AWAS.) Prior to this, in 1944, of 1328 pregnancies, 263 were of single girls out of an enlisted 22 800, and in 1943 the ratio was 666 to 168, from 21 700 enlisted in the Service.

This incidence of 'unwanted pregnancies', as they continued to be called, was little greater than occurred in the civilian population, but because these women were in uniform there was greater comment. (There was also a much greater chance of being detected and far less opportunity for concealment.) 'Sometimes I felt that all through the time we served, much of the civilian population and *all* the newspapers had only one interest in us, and that was our transgressions. From smoking in public to doing what everyone else did and having the same number of babies other women did, our actions were commented on. Sometimes it got on your goat,' remarked one woman to me.

In this women in World War II were only being treated in the same way as women in the previous war. As early as March 1915, before Australian troops went to Gallipoli, scurrilous stories about the behaviour of nursing sisters in Egypt appeared in Australian newspapers. The main thrust of the complaint was that nurses were seen 'out', publicly, with Australian troops. As one nurse tartly replied, 'The Australian population should be glad that there were Australian girls to go out with the boys. The effect of alternative companionship for the men in the Cairo of that day was already causing special hospitals and isolation compounds to be set up.' One would have thought that the next generation would have learnt from this, but they did not.

There were plenty of scandalous tales told of the girls. It would be strange if there were not, given the claustrophobic lives many civilian women lived at that time. Male soldiers have been damned since time immemorial, why shouldn't females suffer the same penalty? It was when newspapers made mileage with the stories that leaders stepped in. 'I am growing tired of listening to stay-at-homes slandering the youth of this country who are prepared to lay down their lives in its defence,' Queensland's Acting Premier protested in August 1942. 'The same campaign of slander is being carried out against the young women of our country who are serving in the Naval, Army and Air forces. These young women, in the vast majority of cases, are a credit to Australia and a credit to their parents. The fact that exceptions to the rule exist to my mind is proof of the rule, and the conduct of the young men and women of the fighting forces should not be judged by the lapses of a few whom we have always had with us, in war or peace.

'The people of this country should thank God for the high standards of physical and moral courage possessed by the youth of Australia. Without it, we should all be lost.'

It was good newspaper stuff. *Truth* newspaper came out with headlines on 20 September 1942: 'Filthy Fifth Column Slanders Servicewomen.' Purporting to be a denouncement of the slanderers, the paper spread a story over three columns. It was 'fifth columnists, attempting to wreck the Australians' war effort, to lose the war for the allies'. 'The splendid women of the WAAAF have been the main target for these insidious Fifth Column Attacks,' said the captions to photographs of WAAAF spread over their pages.

'This is an air war. Everyone recognises that air power is a terrific force which more than likely will mean the winning or losing of this war. Is there any significance to you that about 99 per cent of the rumours you hear — and perhaps help to spread — are attacks on the morality of the WAAAF?

'A pet malicious rumour is that mass abortions for women in the services are going on in Adelaide's General Hospital. Think about that one. The statement is preposterous, but it is a rumour going about, embellished as it travels.'

*Truth* told all the gossip, the dirty talk of grubby, stunted minds. 'Just recently 150 pregnant WAAAF girls were brought down secretly to Adelaide by train from "up north". Where did they hide the train in the days it took to come south?' asked the newspaper.

They asked rhetorical questions. 'And where, does anyone know, is situated the birth control clinic and maternity hospital for the WAAAF? The story is that much more important defence work had to be stopped so that these phantom establishments could be rushed to completion, so great was the need for them.

'Officials are completely satisfied that women in the services are as moral as they are in civil life, and they don't propose to say anything at all to deny or investigate the rumours. This policy, *Truth* believes, is unsound. Churchill's Committee produced facts and figures to deny immorality charges against women war workers in Britain. We could do the same.'

We didn't. We just let the rumour-mongers run until they tired of it and turned to something else – the Americans (we girls felt the Americans could look after themselves). We all had friends or relations in the WAAAF; I had two cousins. One had always been called my 'better-half' because, as young girls, we were inseparable. I wrote to her, furious. 'Ah well,' she replied, 'while they're having a go at us they're leaving the AWAS alone.' Being in the VADs I was safe. There were too few of us to give zest to such slander.

The army had military police, the women's services had Supervisory Personnel. Established in late 1943, they were as much of a help and confidante to girls as they were the law with power of arrest. A special school for training personnel was established in Melbourne in 1944 and military regulations amended to accommodate their role as provosts.

One of their tasks was to investigate applications for discharge. Many of these applications stated compassionate grounds such as needs of family. Another constant duty was to maintain a high standard of discipline and deportment. Working in pairs, they patrolled the streets, visited dance halls and other public amusements and 'supervised' the girls.

Occasionally, the civilian police warned the AWAS Controller that patrols should enter certain parks at night. Queensland police constantly made this request in the form of a warning, and rightly so, given the ferment in that state in 1942–43, when Brisbane had a greater proportion of servicemen to civilian population than any other city in the world and a greater density of young servicewomen than any other place in Australia.

In the early days of 'the phony war', the nurses and VADs required impeccable references from their home community to be admitted to the services. As 'the real war' hit, and the cry went out for tens of thousands of young women, it was natural that such qualifications must be waived.

For 'incorrigible' girls, the senior officers suggested that instead of 'by reason of numerous convictions she is deemed incorrigible', a girls' discharge certificate merely stated, 'services no longer required'. (Some areas had discharged girls as 'considered unsuitable for any further military service' and endorsed the papers 'Disciplinary'.)

Many civilian women's organisations and the churches were both damnatory and damaging to the servicewomen. The Moderator of the Church of Scotland, Professor John Baillie, stated that 'a coarsening of the fibre of the nation's girlhood was threatened by their life in the services'.

Speaking for the WAAAF, Squadron Officer Audrey Herring, Deputy Director, WAAAF, said that communal life had developed qualities of thoughtfulness, unselfishness and practical commonsense. 'WAAAF are noted for making their quarters home-like. They are permitted to wear civilian clothes when on leave, and encouraged in their leisure time to take up feminine activities and handicrafts.' She wisely quashed the rumours by speaking of the advantages of the Service.

Army chaplains for some time sent back to local clergy in a girl's civilian parish the name of discharged personnel 'including those of single cyesis cases.' An order, LHQ 181208, was sent out on 30 December 1944 entitled 'Rehabilitation – Spiritual Welfare of Discharged Personnel', stating that senior chaplains were to be advised of any cases which the assistant controllers did *not* want interviewed by the chaplain. Until that time a girl was unable to conceal her discharge from prying or unkind eyes in her home area.

'Single Cyesis Cases', that is, single girls who were pregnant, were automatically given tests for VD in Victoria and Queensland. 'We were considered to be filthy,' a Dandenong woman told me.

In 1944, the War Cabinet directed that 'when it is ascertained that a member of the Army Women's Services is pregnant, she will be discharged, and that in cases where a discharged member is unable to make her own arrangements for accommodation and maintenance, the Department of Social Services will arrange for her accommodation and, where necessary, her maintenance.' The head of each women's service in each area was required 'to forward a weekly list of pregnant members of her service to the Deputy Commissioner of Pensions'.

Because of the shortage of trained social workers available for the army, a course was organised in 1944. Almoners had already been inducted into the service and now were joined by welfare workers who could assist in many ways, including investigating problems in relation to the soldier's family or home life.

Clare Stevenson, D/WAAAF as she always signed her correspondence, took a strictly practical, firm view. 'We were at war. Whatever people wished to do, believe, or make-believe in peace-time was now no longer pertinent. From the beginning, I had my girls in barracks in the same areas as were RAAF men. It was the first time many, or most, of the girls had worked close to men. I realised to protect them I must have them quickly strike up a relationship with the men that would prevent as much as possible the over-interest that dividing the sexes may excite. And it worked. There was a camaraderie between the WAAAF and RAAF that was admirable. Of course there were romances, there were weddings, there were problems, as there are all of these things in civilian life. But, per head of enlistment, we still had lower pregnancy figures and less with VD than other services of comparable size to ours.'

Clare, then in her eighties, was still a vigorous, untrammelled thinker. 'We were very down to earth in the WAAAF,' she claimed. 'To us, preggos were preggos. Contraceptives were available to the RAAF – openly, not in the rather sleazy by-application method of the older services. The first time I saw an airman reach to the top of a cabinet and take out a pack of the almost-only contraceptive device of the day, I recognised the sense of it. As well, we, the officers of the WAAAF, talked to the girls, not only officially, but just running into a girl an officer can make comments on remarks made by a girl and in this way settle her down. History will not change young girls or their needs or their attraction to men. But we could in a small way, protect them'

Sheila McClemans, Director of the WRANS, says, 'All women were unsophisticated by today's standards. A naval officer took a shine to one of our girls and swept her off her feet. Male naval officers knew this man was ill with psychological problems and had been put ashore for this reason, but no one spoke of it. That girl should have been taken aside and told. One could not expect a girl of that period to recognise what this man could and could not be capable of.

'There was no social security. Churches would hide girls. There is no other word for it. The Salvos had a large deal table with oil-cloth on it and hard wooden chairs. 'They have to be taught their lesson,' I was told. The Church of England had a shabby house in Melbourne. A few were well ahead of their time, even encouraged girls to wash themselves at night and put make-up on. It doesn't sound much today, but that was really forward thinking then. Clare Stevenson and I decided to do something about it. We saw a chance when they were having trouble with women in munitions. The Social Welfare Director extended assistance to girls who had been scorned previously. At least it was a beginning to the end of a sorry period that scarred numberless young girls.'

Sybil Irving, Controller, AWAS, stressed on her officers that it was their responsibility to assist girls. 'The majority of the officers did try. It depended, of course, on the personality of the officer concerned, but many went out of their way to help the girls under them.' Dr Phyllis (later, Lady) Cilento gave lectures on sex. This was astounding for those days, even if the contents would not be acceptable in the 1980s.

Major Dorothea Skov says, 'Today's young can't go back that far. They can't appreciate how innocent – or how restricted – women had been. Nor can they appreciate Brisbane in wartime. I've seen US sailors en masse charging down the road in Yeerongpilly, young, free from the war for one night. I tell you, the life of an officer in the women's services had its problems!'

The incidence of venereal disease, 'unwanted pregnancy' and 'illegal operations' among servicewomen was, of course, recorded. Much was made of it at the time. Jokes, the most insidious form of denigration flew around. 'There was this WAAAF on night duty at the camp gate and she points her rifle at this RAAF fellow coming in late and shouts, "Halt! who goes there?" "Don't do that," answers the fictional male, "you scared six months growth out of me." "Really?" says the WAAAF. "How about you taking the rifle and doing the same for me?"'

These things stick. They were meant to. Women were invading that most sacrosanct of male bastions, the armed forces, and the resistance, often unconscious and instinctive, was to the death. 'Unwanted pregnancy' – *any* pregnancy outside marriage – was punished by dismissal from the service. The girl went from a closer-bonded group of girls in her own age than any family circle could know, to total isolation in a society that shunned her. Those I spoke to readily commented. 'She was a fallen woman. We forget that, in this day and age, but that is what a pregnant girl was then, and she knew no one would take her in, so she never asked.' Another said 'It was awfully sad, but you were so scared it might happen to you that you hardly had time to worry about girls who "got caught".'

They remember their feelings at the time: 'I'd run a mile rather than "go to bed" with a boy. I was terrified of "getting into trouble". I was very fond of a Seventh Divvy boy once and I was sorry for him going back to the battle. He begged me. But I told him I wasn't a girl like that. I felt awful after he'd gone overseas again. I wished I'd been able to make him feel better. But if you got "in the family way" in those days, in or out of the services, no one, including the boy, wanted to know you. You were "fast", no better than you ought to be, loose, immoral and bad.'

'My uncle tried to handle me when I was a little girl, but I never told my mother, because she would have blamed me and I would have got a thrashing for having in some way, unknown to me, tempted that awful man. When I joined up, the lecture on VD didn't alarm me at all. I already knew my place in the scheme of things, and if I'd been silly enough to let a man have his way with me and I got into trouble I'd have killed myself. I don't think that this was only *my* way of thinking, I think most girls would have faced death rather than be sent away to hide your face behind a high wall at the Salvation Army or one of the convents for fallen women until the baby was born.'

Others wondered about girls who 'disappeared'. 'After a girl had the baby what happened to her then? None of us knew. I've wondered since about one girl I knew. She was my age, 22. She just went. Years after the war I asked for her in her home town and they said, "she disappeared in the war".'

One reflected, 'I bet there are some girls who spent the best years of their lives in the services and yet feel they can't come to the reunions.'

Like most officers, Dorothea Skov had total sympathy with the girls. Dorothea was Officer-in-Charge at Brisbane. 'There was so little one could do. No girl wanted her family to know. If a girl was very young and her family had shown interest in her we encouraged her, firmly, to get in touch and tell them of her problem. But that was not always conducive to results. Families mostly wanted nothing to do with the girl "until it was all over" so she could return home in such a manner that family and friends would not know . . .

'We could not force the older girls, 20 and over, and they mostly went off alone. There was no social security for such girls then, no maternity leave, no benefits, nothing but charity, which at its best left a lot to be desired. We had a small fund with which to help any girl, but it was little enough. We could get them civvy clothes, for instance. But, of course, there was not time to visit them or even learn how they got on. They never contacted us again. It was war. But it was shameful for young girls to be so treated. I thought so then, and I think so now.'

'In my arms' the frightened young soldier sang in a popular song in 1943. 'In my arms . . .'

*In my arms, In my arms*
*Ain't I never gonna get a girl in my arms?*
*In my arms, In my arms*
*Ain't I never gonna hold a bundle of charms?*
*Comes the dawn, I'll be gone*
*And I long to have a sweetie holding me tight*
*In my mind I've got a crazy notion*
*If I'm a'gonna cross that ocean*
*I need a girl in my arms tonight.*

# CHAPTER 27

# *A Boy from Alabama*

For the first time in its history, Australia had the reassurance of a great ally on her own soil. The presence of the hundreds of thousands of Americans in our time of peril should have been a constant delight to us. Instead, almost from the outset, it was a festering sore.

The USA was committed to the defence of Australia, which should have been enough to assure their servicemen of welcome, but mankind does not behave with such simple, uncomplicated responses. We had not seen our own fighting men since they sailed away to war in 1939. Many were now dead; many more were in the limbo-land of women's minds: men reported missing – over 30 000 were thought to be prisoners.

This last figure, if translated into percentage of population, would mean that if the same percentage of US men were prisoners approximately 500 000 Americans would have been incarcerated. But of course they were not. In 1942, they had just come to the scene of battle. This was the way beleaguered Australians thought in that bewildering year. Great Britain could send us no men or arms; her Royal Navy, that 'Pride of the Ocean', had not protected us since 1913, when we gathered our own small navy together to try to defend a coastline so immense that the whole coastline of Great Britain itself could be rolled over and over in it.

We were, in truth, in need of a great ally. And it came to our aid. 'Only after they were bloody well goaded into it by the Japs attacking,' was the constant reply to news of their entry into the war.

It was not until the actual arrival of American troops that we recognised that Australia was only one of the smaller nations in a world-wide struggle. We hated admitting it. We hated even more recognising that the conduct of this war, in which we had already lost sons, brothers, husbands and friends, was determined by three great powers: America (who had lost little to date), Britain and Russia could dictate to us. Being only a part of the British Empire, we had no direct representation: where our men or our materials were sent was, to a degree, outside our control. We were now standing in the greatest danger Australia had faced: we were preparing for invasion.

That the United States of America was now our ally was fine, but in the way little things rankle and are apt to divert attention from the main matter ... in this case survival ... we loathed the American propaganda machine. Hollywood hit us, and we retaliated blindly against the only ambassadors we could see ... the young, unscarred men so composedly taking over our cities. Humphrey Bogart, John Wayne and their like, winning the celluloid battles, were as much to blame as any other factor for our unspoken resistance to the American invasion of our homeland.

It was always unspoken. When our proud 9th Division arrived home, and we saw them for the first time since they sailed in 1939 and won fame through the Siege of Tobruk, the streets of our cities were thronged with 'Yanks', most with an Australian girl on their arm.

'What do you think of us stealing your girls?' the Americans asked the battle-toughened diggers. 'Aw, you didn't steal them,' a digger is said to have replied. 'You just sorted them out for us.'

For civilian women, the distinction seemed not to be too onerous, but woe betide servicewomen if they were seen out with a 'Yank'. Unit newsletters commented openly on girls seen out with 'Yanks'. In the Christmas 1943 issue of *Signals* 'a Journal compiled by the Signalwomen', a mock Dorothy Dix column put it plainly.

'*Question* I have an American boyfriend who is very charming, and has been taking me around a lot. Now he has gone back to his unit, but no Australian boys seem to want to go out with me. Can you advise me? I have done nothing wrong. (Signed) Worried, West Aussie.

'*Answer* Unfortunately, your case, innocent as you say it is, is being judged by others which our boys have noticed. You may remember the remark that the Yanks were "not stealing our girls, only sorting them out". You seem to be suffering ... maybe unjustly ... for the sins of others. My advice is to wait till you get back to WA and hope that nobody there knows of your friendships. There you may find someone who will believe your story when you eventually decide to tell him ... as you should.'

All these years later it seems petty. We were fighting for our own survival and contributing with our allies to the common cause, yet our pride was daily being undermined. Taxis, always short in wartime and now few and far between because of petrol rationing, were disdainful of Australians in a queue and would drive straight past us to an American. 'Bloody Yanks!' some diggers said. Others spoke with their fists. Both American and Australian military police were hard pressed. Wartime emotions are fierce.

By September 1943 there were 120 000 US Army personnel actually in Australia, and an unknown number of air corps. They were concentrated in only a few centres and were most visible. Yet the 863 000 Americans in the South-West Pacific area were the greater problem. In addition to supplying her own army, there was the economic challenge for Australia to assist with supplying many of the needs of these servicemen. The American demands were heavy; as well, men and materials must be found for building roads, aerodromes, camps and hostels for those Americans within Australia.

On top of all this, the civilian population found it had to share the limited wartime facilities of its cities with these men, the taxis, cinema tickets, cafés, rationed food, telephone services, office staff and local supplies. And the returning Australian soldier found he must share the always limited supply of girls as companions. Americans of all ranks had about twice the spending allowance of Australian servicemen. An Australian Army private received 6s 0d per day, £9 15s 0d a month. The American private received £17 0s 0d a month. The official history of World War II states: 'Their reputation as free spenders often won the Americans more than their share of the available amenities and this was frequently the cause of resentment.'

The doughboys had everything going for them: splendid, well-fitted uniforms of fine material, good quality shoes and, above all, money.

Many girls succumbed to the novelty of it all. Jack O'Hagen wrote the catchy song, 'When a boy from Alabama meets a girl from Gundagai'. In its way, it was charming and should have lived, but it died. The common description of our allies, 'over-paid, over-sexed and over here', was heard openly in the streets. Of such disruptions is war made.

If there ever was a time when Australian servicewomen felt they had been badly treated – cheated, in fact – it was when the American WACs arrived in 1944. The American Women's Army Corps arrived in Sydney in May to a glorious welcome from thousands in Sydney Harbour. Lieutenant-Colonel Mary Agnes Groover Brown recalled that day when I tape-recorded her in 1974. 'Little boats sailed out to meet us, hooters sounded, wharf labourers cheered, bands played, everyone waved.' The WACs were lined up in battle order on the deck of the ship wearing steel helmets and raincoats the same as the GI soldiers. 'There was a dance at the Sydney Town Hall that night – thousands of GIs were turned away as they had no invitations ... There were just too many wanting to get in. It was the first all-American dance held in Sydney. Scores of the girls met boys they had not seen for years.'

The newspapermen loved them – why wouldn't they? 'Many items of women's attire which are unprocurable here are provided in the WACs kit. Besides two uniforms including dainty underwear, eight pairs of rayon stockings and sockettes, they can purchase brassieres, girdles and suspender belts at their store.

'The WACs are frank, natural and easy to talk with. They said Australian girls were "awfully sweet" and "such lovely English complexions",' reported the *Daily Telegraph* of 13 May 1944. (One wonders just how many Australian women's services' messes displayed this news item. Certainly it was stuck on the notice board at the 1st Australian Orthopaedic Unit and the bonegraft boys gave the nurses hell about it for days.)

But what really rankled with Australians was this: the American WACs had been brought out to replace Australian girls. Colonel Groover Brown quite sympathises with them. 'Because your girls were not permitted to enlist for overseas, those who staffed General MacArthur's Headquarters in Australia could not go with his force when he moved up through the islands. He wanted the Australian girls to go, they wanted to go, but your government refused. So – I had to come out with WACs who were enlisted for overseas service.'

The Australian Women's Army Service watched the American girls sail off to their posts in the South-west Pacific and New Guinea.

'We were coldly furious,' Colonel Sybil Irving told me. 'I was determined that this unfair restriction must be lifted. They may have taught the WACs to say "bonzer" but we were not amused.'

Colonel Irving was referring to a card handed to each WAC at the dance on their arrival in Sydney, explaining Australian slang.

> *Fair dinkum – okay; good-o – fine; cobber – buddy;*
> *ta-ta – goodbye; ta – thanks; bonzer – very good;*
> *sheila – girl; good on you Yank – congratulations;*
> *give 'er a go – take a chance; what's the strength*
> *of you, mate – want a fight?*

Colonel Irving made her move immediately. It was not easy; from the beginning of enlistment of women, the all-male government was adamant that the women's services would not, under any circumstances, go overseas. It is a comment on this remarkable woman's persistence that by 1945 permission had been dragged out of the powers-that-be and AWAS were on their way to New Guinea.

Some of the things that happened appear ludicrous 30 years later. In September 1944, the Federated Women's Club of Virginia (USA) launched a project to send wedding gowns for Australian brides. Mrs William Murray, the club's Vice-President, said: 'At least 20 bridal gowns will be sent to Australia and placed at the disposal of any Australian servicewoman who wishes to be married in the traditional wedding dress instead of in uniform.

'Money for the first bridal outfit was contributed by 42 junior women's clubs throughout Virginia.'

It was no doubt well meant, but to many of us it smacked of condescension and charity.

There were those of us who declared that the only thing the USA had given us was – *The Wizard of Oz*. Judy Garland, Frank Morgan, Ray Bolger, Billie Burke and all of them danced and sang until, for a short time, we could forget the present and the grey dreariness descending on us.

We went skipping along the yellow brick road with Dorothy and Tinman, Scarecrow and Cowardly Lion. We only had to hear the songs and we brightened; we saw the movie over and over again. Judy Garland went straight to our hearts, men and women, and we kept her there. She reminded us of home. 'There's no place like home,' she said at the end of the film. 'I'll never leave home again.' We cried, the men cried. The forces of evil had been conquered, the good, the laughing and the friendly faces were around us once more, and we were reminded of the verities. Hollywood gave us a great deal with that film.

CHAPTER 28

# Down on the Farm

*The earth is yours and the fullness thereof.*
*Enter upon your inheritance*
*and accept your responsibilities ...*

The praises of members of the fourth Women's Auxiliary Service, the Australian Women's Land Army, were relatively unsung. Working far from the areas where they could parade their uniforms through city streets, they toiled in unglamorous surroundings, at sometimes unpleasant and almost always heavy physical work, usually for longer hours than the 48-hour week then prevailing. Sometimes they lived in large camps in the bush with cooks and often they camped, a few together on the edge of farmlands, and cooked for themselves. They went where they were sent. At their peak enrolment, in October 1944, there were 3068 of these labourers in the field, keeping food up to the vast armies then being provisioned by Australia.

The Australian Women's Land Army as a national organisation was established on 27 July 1942 under the jurisdiction of the Director-General of Manpower, with a view to offsetting, in some measure, the serious depletion in the strength of the rural labour force due to service enlistments and transfers to munitions and other war factories. Before this date, privately sponsored land armies, modelled on the Women's Land Army in Great Britain, were operating in some of the Australian states. Notable among these were the land armies controlled by the Women's Australian National Services in New South Wales and Western Australia and the Women's Auxiliary Transport Service in Queensland.

The variety of climatic and geographical conditions, as well as the different agricultural problems in Australia and the varying extent and nature of the demands for women for rural work, tended to increase the complexity of organisational difficulties, making it necessary that there should be flexible administrative control.

An officer was appointed in each state, under the control of the Deputy Director-General of Manpower, as Superintendent of the Land Army, to supervise the selection, enrolment, discipline and welfare of members.

The Land Army was planned to function in two divisions: full time members and auxiliary members. Full time members enrolled for continuous service for 12 months (with the option of renewal) or for the duration; such members were to receive appropriate badges, a distinctive dress uniform, working clothes and equipment. Auxiliary members were those who were available for periods, each of not less than four weeks, at nominated times of the year. These members were to be used for seasonal rural operations and to receive a badge, working clothes and essential equipment on loan.

Practically all members of the private land armies were enrolled with the official organisation, and an intensive recruiting campaign began. Because the principal objective in the foundation of the Land Army was to provide some accretion to the depleted rural labour force, the policy was to refuse enrolment to women currently engaged in work on the land, either self-employed, or as employees or relatives of landholders. In this, the Australian Women's Land Army differed from the New Zealand organisation, in which girls normally working on the land were eligible for enrolment. The decision meant that recruits would be chiefly drawn from the metropolitan areas and larger provincial towns and, in any event, that they would be mostly quite unskilled.

It was realised that objections would be raised by potential employers of Land Army labour, firstly to being offered females to replace males, and secondly, because unskilled females would be quite out of the question. So, along with the recruiting campaign, an intensive drive was undertaken to induce farmers to use the new type of labour. The responses ranged from opposition, through scepticism, to qualified and unconditional support. It was therefore decided to concentrate attention on utilising members in those industries where support was strongest – in horticulture, vegetable and fruit growing, pig and poultry raising. Later, members did sheep and wool work, dairying, flax work, dehydration of vegetables – in fact, almost every type of work done on the land.

One initial handicap was the lack of suitable accommodation. 'A certain amount of opposition was also encountered from farmers' wives who feared they would be involved in additional housework,' reported the Director-General of Manpower.

In January 1943, Cabinet approved of an establishment for the Australian Women's Land Army at 6000 members, of which 3500 were to be enrolled by 30 June 1943, and of the formation of an Australian

Women's Land Army Auxiliary comprising casual workers. Both the Australian Women's Land Army and Auxiliary were to be formally constituted by means of National Security Regulations, and the Australian Women's Land Army was to be accorded a status akin to that of a Fourth National Women's Auxiliary, but a final draft of the National Security (Australian Women's Land Army) Regulations was not completed until 1945, when the war was over. The actual peak of enrolment was in October 1944, with 3068 members – 2565 Permanent, 503 Auxiliary, far short of the target.

Members had to go where directed and perform whatever land work might reasonably be required of them; they should receive a minimum of 30s 0d per week, plus keep, or 50s 0d per week if no keep were provided; and trainees at Australian Women's Land Army Training Establishments or with approved farmers under controlled conditions should receive an allowance of 20s 0d per week, plus keep.

In most states, employers voluntarily agreed to a higher minimum of £2 0s 0d per week, plus keep. In practice, due to the operation of Awards in some sections of the industry and piece-work rates in others, the weekly wage of many land girls exceeded even that minimum.

In some states, employers preferred women who had received elementary training, rather than raw recruits. They showed little or no inclination to take advantage of the reduced rate of pay applicable during the initial training period of four weeks.

Training establishments were set up in Victoria, Queensland, Western Australia and Tasmania. In NSW and South Australia the need for such establishments did not arise, though in NSW arrangements were made periodically for the training of AWLA Field Officers at Hawkesbury Agricultural College.

That women, like men, are not immune to the glamour of a uniform was shown in 1943. In this year, when demands for food were persistent and acute, it was decided to offer a work uniform to women who joined as auxiliary (that is, part-time) members. Registrations of auxiliary members throughout the Commonwealth rose from 382 as at 31 July 1943, to 1880 during the peak period in January 1944.

Following the enthusiastic efforts of several prominent New South Wales farmers to recruit local labour, it was decided to form in country centres 'Local Auxiliaries' of the Australian Women's Land Army to include women from nearby towns who were not able to join either the Australian Women's Land Army or the Auxiliary, but who would be capable of giving part-time assistance to local farmers either for a specific period at given times of the year or for several days a week.

The glamour group of the Land Army was the mobile corps, who travelled from district to district and even interstate, performing seasonal work. In New South Wales and Queensland, for instance, seasonal labour demanded the use of the Land Army on the mobile 'shock troop' basis rather than as individually placed members on farms.

For this type of mobility, permanent hostels were established at central points with a number of smaller, satellite hostels spread over surrounding areas, which provided accommodation for the large number of auxiliary members brought in at the peak of the season for short-term assignments. Land girls travelled daily from the hostels to work on local farms.

These shock troops were rushed to wherever crops required them. In 1943 and 1944, contingents of New South Wales members were sent to Queensland to help harvest the cotton crop. A contingent of over 300 NSW Land Army girls left Sydney on 8 February 1945 for South Australia, to work in the Barmera, Berri and Renmark areas picking fruit for the dried fruit harvest. This contingent – the largest to be sent to another state – included many 'three-star' girls with three years' service. A special train, with a 'sick bay' under the supervision of a trained nurse arranged by headquarters, also tea and coffee urns to supply drinks between meals, was provided to take the girls direct to South Australia.

In Tasmania, a 'Land Army Mobile Unit' was established at the request of the Food Control Authorities to ensure that none of the fruit was wasted. The members were not used as ordinary pickers; these shock troops, also, were rushed in wherever the need was urgent.

Permanent camps were established in centres where sufficiently large numbers of members could be centrally accommodated for work all the year round in fairly concentrated farming areas, for instance, at Batlow and on the Murrumbidgee Irrigation Area in New South Wales, and in various parts of Victoria and South Australia engaged in flax production.

Other camps and hostels of varying sizes were also established for housing seasonal workers. In one instance, as many as 300 girls were accommodated in one camp for some months. In Queensland, some seven camps accommodating 240 girls were set up in the Dawson Valley for the harvesting of the cotton crop, while in New South Wales as many as 69 camps were operating at the height of the 1943–44 harvesting season.

Hotels, boarding houses, showground buildings and public halls were among the premises occupied as camps, and in some cases portable huts and hostels were set up; the control and discipline of hostels and camps were placed in the hands of a supervising matron. An interesting insight into the make-up of Land Army girls is a comment by the Director General of Manpower, W. C. Wurth.

'As far as possible, the aim was to recruit officers from the ranks, but many of the members showed a marked disinclination to accept the higher status with its responsibilities. Where only small groups of members were working and living together, the practice of appointing one of the group as Welfare Officer, or leader of the group, proved successful, and an appropriate allowance for the additional duties was made.' (Wages of field staff ranged from £3 15s 0d per week, plus keep, for staff officers responsible for establishment or supervision of large camps, down to £2 15s 0d per week, plus keep, for the lower ranking officers.)

The close of 1943 found members of the Land Army engaged in all types of rural work: in the fruit, vegetable, dairying, flax, tobacco and cotton industries, in mixed farming, in poultry raising and in pastoral industries. In addition, a few members worked in associated industries, such as fruit packing and grading, and wool classing. In Victoria, a number qualified as certified herd testers and were assigned to this work. On the shoulders of these girls and women rested, to a large extent, the responsibility of feeding the navy, army, air force and civilians of Australia and the US servicemen, both in Australia and in the South-west Pacific. They worked from the cotton fields of Queensland to the apple orchards of Tasmania.

From an attitude of scepticism, the farming community passed, wherever farms had experience of the work of Land Army girls, to one of praise and respect: 'This Land Girl is capable and willing to do any duties required. These have included root picking, milking, feeding 100 pigs, tractor driving, attending sheep (mustering, yarding, etc.), killing and skinning sheep for rations, chaff-cutting and corn-crushing.'

'We appreciated so much this AWLA help during the harvest. Her assistance and stay with us has had an unusual and additional value, in that it cheered and inspired us all to further efforts and made happy what could have been a drab, exhausting and anxious time under wartime conditions. She helped put the crop in, driving the tractor. The work which she carried out was very satisfactory and her conduct excellent.'

Helen Ising (SA) writing in August 1944 from the outback, gives an impression of one girl's work on Evelyn Downs Station, Oodnadatta.

'I am enjoying the life up here very much and find continual interests in the different conditions and surroundings. The only other employees are 20-odd blacks. The station is 700 square miles and runs 5000 sheep, as well as goats and lots of good horses. Shearing is in full swing now and my work consists mainly of piece-picking the wool and helping to class it, and yarding sheep.

'I have done all sorts of things I've never done before. For example, riding after horses at full gallop and going on 30- to 40-mile rides after lost horses, leaving home at midday and returning at eight or nine o'clock at night.'

By 31 December 1945, the last of the great army of girls who travelled their homeland helping to feed their own forces and that of the USA was demobilised, and three years of hard, largely unsung service to their country ended.

> *When the Land Army all go home, how sorry the farmers will be,*
>   *When they wave us goodbye with a tear in their eye*
> *It will bring back a memory.*
>   *What a sad day t'will be, for you and for me,*
> *When the Land Army all go home.*
> – from *'Land Army Girls at Benyenda'*

# CHAPTER 29

# *Anything and Everything*

Among the myriad schemes introduced by the Red Cross Society, perhaps the most momentous was the Red Cross Blood Transfusion Service. This was pioneered mainly by a young clinical pathologist, Dr Lucy Bryce, in 1926. Red Cross now conducts this service in 38 countries, but the Australian Red Cross can boast that it is the only service in the world which provides all blood and blood derivatives totally free of charge to the recipient (with the help of federal and state government funding). It was the first service in the world able to provide the precious Anti-RhD Globulin to protect all those mothers and babies who were at risk because of an incompatibility between their own and their baby's blood group.

At first, blood donors were paid – and, it is said, a number of professional people walking round today paid their way through university by selling their blood. During the Depression, young people saw it as an easy way of making some money. By 1938, a group of voluntary donors held a meeting in the YMCA, Melbourne, with Dr John Newman Morris in the chair, and spiritedly denounced 'the acceptance of blood money'. Professional blood selling was ended, and a Voluntary Blood Donors' Association was formed.

In that same year, after Hitler and Chamberlain met at Munich, the International Committee of Red Cross warned Red Cross societies to organise to a wartime level. And so the Red Cross War Book was prepared, with the approval of the army. When war came the following year, no aspect of the problems of sick and wounded servicemen and their families was left untouched, from psychiatric social workers to education in nutrition. Their work for prisoners of war was so successful that many POWs declare they would not be alive today if it had not been for Red Cross parcels.

This care continued. In June 1946, the Supreme Court of Victoria brought down a decision to release unspent POW funds to the general funds of the Red Cross on condition that the Society undertook to care for ex-prisoners of war in need of its help for the rest of their lives. The Society agreed. The sum involved, £3 069 000, has been expended many times over in caring for the needs of ex-service personnel, but the Society 'keeps a special eye' on the welfare of men who spent years of their young lives in foreign prison camps.

During World War II, Red Cross workers collected £13 903 269. A field force of 540 was maintained, including 193 women who served in hospital ships and aircraft carriers in nearly all areas where Australian forces were engaged. A story is told of a digger in a Solomon Islands hospital during World War II. He complained to the medical officer that all he had received from Red Cross was cigarettes and barley sugar. The MO called an orderly and said, 'Take away this man's pyjamas, pillow-slip, back rest, meal tray, bedside locker, bedside chair and the deck chair he sits on outside. Stop his supply of library books and take away the basins and canvas stands, bedside screens and matting on the floor, the water bag, the grapefruit and lemon cordial, his bath towel, sandals and tinea sox he wears. Take his razor blades, soap, shaving cream or tooth-paste; he need not play draughts, quoits, chess or Monopoly or receive materials to make handcrafts. As for his diet, cut out whitebait, vermicelli, marmite, malt extract, pineapple, lime juice, peanut butter, asparagus – all these things are provided by Red Cross and he complains about them.'

These goods were bought with money primarily raised by this Society, which has been inspired and supported by thousands of Australian women for 70 years. More than 54 000 litres of blood serum and 35 000 litres of whole blood were distributed to fighting men and civilians; convalescent homes were established for servicemen and women; prisoners of war and civilian internees were supplied with food and comforts; and stores were distributed through the field force and other agencies. Overseas civilian relief to the value of £313 300 was provided, and £1 250 000 was contributed to the British Red Cross, mostly for prisoner of war service.

Stories of the women who worked with Red Cross in both the 1914–18 and the 1939–45 wars are scattered throughout this book. They worked at home and abroad, wherever they were called. One women, Gwen Cadd, epitomises the army of women whose great works will never be known. She joined the Junior Red Cross 'as a youngster' and has now received the Distinguished Service Award. During World War II she was appointed Western Australian Director of Hospital Visiting and worked with the influx of evacuees from islands to the north of Australia as well as with Australians from the bombed areas of their own country. After the war, she went on to work with incapacitated travellers and on any other humanitarian matter that came her way.

As recruiting officer for Red Cross, she chose women and sent them off on work and journeys that took as much courage for her to send them as it did for them to go. She does not speak of her own work, but comes forward only to speak of the work of others.

'The girls were attached to the AIF and could be sent anywhere,' she says of the Red Cross Field Force. 'When the war was nearly over there was the transporting of American war brides – the Australian girls married to US servicemen – and their children. We had to see them across to the eastern states to take ship to their new homelands. Instead of bandages and blankets we were now collecting and packing baby food onto the train, things for the children; you never saw anything like it – napkins flapping to dry on the back of the train. What a circus they must have looked, chuffing away across the sandy wastelands. There was no rest for the Field Force on those trips I can tell you.' Gwen saw the war out in Red Cross. 'Probably the greatest day for us all was when the prisoners of war came home. We picked them up from the ship when it came in – all POWs had to report to hospital on arrival home. The hospital was bursting with flowers when we got back: there had been a message on the wireless and everyone stripped their gardens and rushed the flowers into Hollywood Hospital. They were everywhere, up the stairways, everywhere. You couldn't put a cup down on a table for flowers.

'The order of the day was, "Get these men anything they want!" It was just wonderful to have them home.'

Different in some ways from the eastern states because of its isolation across a broad desert, Western Australia nevertheless mirrors all the women who worked for Red Cross.

One of the best-known names among the women in the West during World War II was Vinnie Simper, who became Officer-in-Charge of the Mobile Field Force (Red Cross Transport Drivers). Vinnie owned her first car in 1935 and her brother taught her running repairs. 'I was always mechanically minded. The Vacuum Oil Company had their Mr Russell Haigh put us through a course of elementary mechanics: eight lessons and then an examination. That was in 1940. Mr Haigh then encouraged us to join the Mobile Field Force.'

The army asked for 'unencumbered' drivers to go overseas as a Mobile Field Force, Red Cross, attached to the army. 'But they didn't send us overseas. They sent us to the bush,' Vinnie says wryly.

Like the other women's services, this one languished, unbidden, until the Japanese attacked. Then, with towns in the north of Western Australia being bombed and the threat of invasion imminent, 'drops' had to be made to feed the civilians, who were under instructions that when the invasion began they were to head south through the interior.

On 4 March 1942, Vinnie entered in her diary: 'Appointed OIC Transport, Western Australia.' On 6 March she set off on her first job. 'Left for Geraldton, Mullewa and places en route to arrange for emergency stores to be left at places, some in cellars of the various cattle stations or private homes where they would be ready should Red Cross need them during the evacuation.

'Darwin and Broome had already been bombed. The last plane from Java with women and children on board had to travel south and made a forced landing at Mingenew the day before we set off, 5 March. Red Cross attended to their needs but it also proved that medical stores and clothing and comforts had to be stationed at vital and emergency depots for the future.'

Her journeys to the lonely outback were never easy. 'Our unit did 118 580 miles. In forward areas petrol was available for us from the army, but we were on very rough roads and tracks and had to head off into the scrub where four-gallon drums of petrol were left for us. It was nothing to get water in the drums. On one trip north we were stopped thirteen times, which meant cleaning the filter, sometimes in pouring rain because we were in "the Wet" of the north. I got the idea of using silk to cover the filter, as water floats. It was slow, but it worked.

'No written instruction was allowed so drivers had to memorise the mileage from Perth to the various camps, and from there on to get to the RAP or CCS we were bound for. We'd follow bush tracks, hacked through by the army, until we located our destination. It was hard physically and tiring mentally, but we all got through.

'If there were no beds at a hospital for us, we slept in the trucks on top of the Red Cross goods – tea chests were pretty hard, believe me!

'We made three trips in blazing heat in February 1944. It was 125 degrees in the shade and 132 in the driver's cab. We were carrying our own petrol in drums this trip. Bush fires were running for miles on Bindoon Hill. At one stage we had to pull into a bay cut into the side of a cliff. Tops of trees were ablaze half a mile in front of the ground fire, and ashes were falling on the bags we'd thrown over the petrol drums.

'Eventually we moved off, with one driver going ahead on foot while others watched the petrol drums. The howling nor-easterly wind made it dangerous and the heat caused punctures in our old tyres, broken fan belts and other mishaps. This particular job took three weeks, including weekends. An army convoy got trapped and was held up by smouldering logs, but we got through — by exceeding the speed limit.

'Our skirts had to be 14 inches from the ground. Useless for working on a truck. I applied to Red Cross for permission to wear trousers, and as they were more practical (as a horse-rider I was used to trousers), but in those days it was "not the done thing". You've no idea the red tape! They felt it was "infra dig". I replied it was more infra dig showing one's behind when bending over loading or climbing up into or under the truck, to say nothing of changing a wheel. Eventually HQ said yes, we could wear trousers. You'd never believe it today, but the men said they didn't know if we were men or women!

'Once we were asked to take a soldier with us who was AWL. We told him that if the MPs searched the truck, to lie flat and keep quiet. Well, they did search us, but we told them we had dropped our load and were returning empty. One MP looked through the foot-hole of the tail-board but he could see nothing in the darkness under the canopy. Further along, hours later, there was a knock on the back of the cabin to warn us to stop. This lad hopped off and headed into the bush to find his camp and we drove off hoping he could get in undetected.

'The routine of delivering goods was the same for the three years and three months we did it, but the men always appreciated our battling in with deliveries and always had a cup of tea for us and begged us to stay to talk, but we didn't have that sort of time.

'Altogether, there were 45 places we had to visit, 40 metropolitan clubs to deliver the raw material for Red Cross supplies to be made from, interstate goods to be taken to the railways for eastern states and goods to be picked up. The physical demands on the girls were great, very strenuous. But we did what we set out to do, a man's job.'

While Vinnie and the other drivers were off in the trucks, other Red Cross workers were doing the many things they would do for 'the duration', as the saying went. 'Waste products, or rags, was an arduous and filthy job, but we made £13 000 out of it for Red Cross during the war years and that money bought a lot of comforts for the troops.'

Other voluntary helpers were cycle and horse messengers during the years that petrol was stringently rationed. Some women made up the cases that goods were packed in for transport. 'Nailed up old bits of timber for crates, packed them, then nailed old bits of timber to seal the lid.' There were classes to be run and attended — first aid, home nursing, signalling and a score of other skills that would come in handy during war.

Their drivers drove all hours of the day and night, taking ambulances and cars to meet troop ships, hospital ships and naval vessels and planes. 'In the black-out it was sometimes tricky but – that's how things were.' Sometimes transporting patients from ship to hospital had its excitements. 'Each driver was responsible for their passengers. Some managed to get away, "went on the scoot", as we used to say. Then we had to search for them all over the city, even to the red light area. Yes, we always got them back to where they had been originally directed. We had a utility available to pick up the worst cases, but it was never used. We managed without that.'

Barbara Clinton was one of the drivers trained by Vinnie Simper. 'At first I was a cycle messenger. On a push bike. Vinnie had written a splendid report on horse transport – and we were never sure if it would come to that because of the shortage of petrol. Then Vinnie trained us as despatch riders – Don Rs. She did a wonderful job, efficient, thorough, easy to follow when she taught us motor mechanics, sensible and nice to work with. Some people imagined ours was an army force, but it was officially a Red Cross Mobile Field Force, a brilliantly organised and efficient service.'

Barbara herself did a splendid job. She was with the AWAS and later joined Red Cross as a full-time worker. Like others, she went off in charge of trainloads of girls on the east–west railway. 'On my first trip I made sure all the girls got a shower when we called in to Parkes, near Kalgoorlie. It was a crude affair, but the water was wet and clean and we still had the worst of our journey ahead of us. Then, when I'd done the scores of jobs and answered all the queries, I went for a shower myself. Bliss. I washed, began to dry myself, stepped out on to the red earth and saw a cock-eyed-Bob [a whirlwind reaching from the ground to high in the sky] whirling in over the desert at us. I began to run for the train, but it caught me and swept round me, and my tin plates flew up in the air like frisbees and my hat and equipment went after them. The spiral sped onwards and upwards leaving my freshly scrubbed body caked with red dust.

'I was green on that trip . . . We set off from Kalgoorlie on the standard gauge across the Nullarbor and halfway across the train pulled up to allow the cooks to serve a meal; they had it going on the train but we ate on the Nullarbor. The girls got off, had a meal, then they were told to get back on the train. I counted my charges on board: one short. I counted again. Crumbs! One still missing. I looked out over the great, flat plain.

There was nowhere a body could go. I rushed along to the other part of the train, the males' end, to tell the colonel ... into his compartment in my panic and there, in the luggage rack, was this mature woman (her daughter was also a servicewoman on the train). I was young, fresh from the country, naive as they come. "You're not supposed to be here!" I stuttered. They replied in terms equivalent to today's piss off, so I did. But it taught me one thing: make sure to count the girls *off* the train as well as on in future.'

Delcie Lyon had been 43 years in Red Cross and received the Distinguished Service Award. Part of her work in World War II was to escort women from Perth to the eastern states. 'That was towards the end of the war. I went with the *Skaubryn*, the refugee ship that had caught fire in the Indian Ocean. The refugees were taken off at Perth and we set off for Melbourne in a Dutch ship. It was a terribly rough trip. The Great Australian Bight is rarely calm but this was an awful voyage. I was so sorry for the people, and I was kept running, I can tell you.'

Other trips were by train, two of them with the early migrants. 'They couldn't speak English. They needed shoes and brassières. Phew! It was go, go, go.' Another train trip she did was with American war brides. 'After each trip the canteens seemed easy work, the all-night snack bars, coffee stalls, behind Foys, open all night. We'd meet returning soldiers at the malt house, part of Swan Brewery, and there we'd feed the men. In Red Cross we seemed to do anything and everything.'

# Shells, Bombs and Depth Charges

When war was declared in 1939 citizens were required to fill in National Register cards. On these cards were to be listed occupations, qualifications and skills. The object of this registration or 'Identity Card', the people were told, was to ensure that individuals did what they were most suited to do to help the nation in its hour of need. The historian, Paul Hasluck, in writing of this, said of the civilian population, 'They might have expected that in time a hand would reach out to them and a voice say: You are just the man the country needs.' But this did not happen, certainly not to women.

The fighting men were committed and munitions must be kept up to them and stockpiled against attack at home.

Women had been employed in munitions prior to 1941, but in this year increases in the number of women in the industry brought political difficulties, amongst which was the question of pay. In April 1941, after a conference, the trade union view was announced by the ACTU in Melbourne: men and women should receive equal pay for equal work in the services as well as in industry. The conference had decided that it would be unfair to deny female workers full payment for their work and it would be unjust to men, as it exposed male workers to unfair competition from underpaid female workers.

From this arose another pressing consideration: 'the special problems of wartime'. With menfolk absent, young women usually did not have the advantages of sharing the income benefits of their family, therefore it was 'imperative to assure young women of economic independence in order to maintain "normal ethical and social standards".' There was, of course, some opposition to equal pay, because of the affects it was likely to have in 'breaking up the family as the social unit'. There was fear that the displacement of men by lower-paid women would let 'capitalists and profiteers' exploit 'cheap female labour'. Muriel Heagney, Secretary-

Treasurer of the Council for Action for Equal Pay, brought her organisation into action both industrially and politically.

Although preference was to be given to single women, 'married women may be employed if they have superior qualifications'. By 23 July 1941, approval was given to employ married women in 'professional and technical' capacities, the definition including 'factory workers generally'.

The review of manpower requirements prepared for the War Cabinet in July 1941 stated that 10 000 women would be needed for munitions and aircraft production. Most of these were to be 'unskilled trades'. The munitions department believed that, if necessary, half the unskilled work that was still proposed to be done by men could well be undertaken by women. That would mean taking on 35 000 more women in order to release that number of men.

The manufacture of munitions had, of course, been carried out in Australia before this time, but never to the extent now needed. The great amounts required for this war of 1939–45 ran into many millions for some particular items. By war's end, £45 000 000 had been spent on building factories and equipping them with machinery, while the cost of ammunition was £41 000 000. Total expenditure on munitions was 'about £271 000 000'. These materials were made exclusively in government factories.

The government built 11 major factories as well as 106 smaller factories and annexes and employed over 50 000 persons. Small arms ammunition and the cartridge cases of gun ammunition were made first at Footscray (Vic.), where manufacturing techniques for small arms ammunition had been established in 1888, but the true cradle of ammunition making in Australia was the factory at Maribyrnong (Vic.). From here, training was given to the 20 000 workers employed in the various explosives factories in Australian states, since all new hands were totally inexperienced in this precise and dangerous work. The dangers are apparent, even today, when much more is known of the behaviour of the components that make up explosives. On 2 October 1939, A. E. Leighton, Consultant on Explosives for the Commonwealth Department of Supply, had written: 'It is unlikely in my experience that we shall continue to enjoy freedom from accident.'

All objects which could cause a spark were excluded from workplaces: metal objects, cigarettes or matches, watches and buttons. Clothing was joined by tapes and special shoes were provided, the soles of which were held together by wooden pegs in place of the usual metal brads. 'We walked between buildings on raised tracks called "gritless cleanways" made of wood, sometimes asphalt. These were hosed several times a day to keep them free from dirt or grit. As well as friction, sparks could be caused by electrostatic charges,' said Audrey Morphett, one of the women who worked at Salisbury (SA).

'Everything to minimise danger of sparks was done. Heavy door handles were earthed and they closed automatically. Before going into some rooms we had to whistle and wait for an answer from inside, so as not to startle the operator. Some of the explosives were very sensitive. The floor and work-bench were covered with conductive rubber, as was the pot containing the several tonnes of explosive. Our shoes were soled with rubber. All this was essential at Salisbury where electrostatic charges were built up in the dry summer atmosphere.

At Salisbury, the explosives in use were nitro-glycerine, cordite, TNT, tetryl, lead azide, lead styphrate, mercury fulminate. For filling were shells, mortar bombs, detonators, percussion caps, cartridges, fuses, primers, depth charges. 'We had most of it at Salisbury including nitric acid and ammonium nitrate,' Audrey Morphett recalls.

One of the major factories, that at St Mary's (NSW), had air conditioning on account of the humid summer weather. 'We used to say those workers were soft,' munitions worker Mrs Rita McKenna says, 'but we were only joking. We knew the danger.'

Maribyrnong (Vic.) made and filled almost every type of ammunition: shells, bombs, mortar bombs, pyrotechnics, cartridges, grenades, fuses, primers, detonators, depth charges, naval mines and demolition charges. The range and diversity of manufacture and filling at this factory was unapproached by any other factory in the British Commonwealth.

Rita McKenna, who worked at Maribyrnong, believes that few, if any, workers thought of explosion or fire. 'We were most scared of getting poisoned. We got head things, not like an ache, more like migraine, and some got dermatitis.' It was well known that nitro-glycerine when absorbed by the body, either through the skin or by inhaling the vapour, depressed blood pressure and caused violent headache which aspirin and other analgesics did little to relieve.

Many individuals were prone to dermatitis caused by TNT and tetryl. Methods of prevention developed in consultation with the Department of Health did much to reduce the hazard. When dermatitis persisted, whatever the conditions of working, the only remedy was to transfer the victim to another section. The incidence of dermatitis was highest among workers handling tetryl, particularly in the fuse-filling and shell-filling sections where tetryl pellets or tetryl exploders were made. (Exploders were made by putting tetryl into bags about 2.5 cm in diameter and 8 cm long, made of heavy woollen cloth.) 'Machines making these components created a dust which, in spite of the ventilating systems for extracting fume and dust from the air, would settle on the arms, faces and necks of the girls who did this work. Unless the dust was removed efficiently with special soaps, clothing completely changed at the end of a working section, and showers frequently taken, the incidence of dermatitis was high – often high enough to seriously impede the output of explosives. No completely satisfactory answer to the problem was ever found.'*

'A greater menace to health than the dermatitis was poisoning by TNT, which was readily absorbed by the human body; it attacked the liver, causing serious and sometimes fatal illness. During the hot, humid months, when excessive sweating increased the rate of absorption of TNT, the number of workers declared by the medical officer as unfit for duty became a serious embarrassment and led to a great difficulty in maintaining production. At the worst time of the year the turnover of skilled workers in the TNT filling sections at Maribyrnong and Salisbury rose to as high as ten per cent per month and the finding of enough new workers and of employment for those declared unfit for work with TNT was a major problem.'

Perhaps, finally, the most important act in munitions manufacture is filling the ammunition with explosives. At the vast complex at Salisbury (SA), where Audrey Morphett worked as an explosives inspector, one area did only caps and detonators. Very small amounts of explosives were pressed into small metal capsules. These 'initiators' were made in this area because they were too sensitive to transport with safety. Another area handled primers and fuses, a third filled cartridge cases with a propellant and fitted them with primers and filled shell bodies with high explosives.

That third section had to be in a separate area, owing to the large quantities of explosives used in each filling operation. The buildings were set at 50 to 100 metres distance from each other to reduce damage in the event of an explosion.

This factory at Salisbury covered over 20 square kilometres, had 1595 buildings linked to one another, and to the outside world by 66 kilometres of road, 55 kilometres of 'gritless cleanways', 21 kilometres of water mains, 26 kilometres of sewers, 242 kilometres of power lines, 10.5

---

*The Role of Science and Industry*, Chapter 16, 'Ammunition and Explosives' by D. P. Mellor, War Memorial, Canberra, 1958.

kilometres of underground telephone cables and 43.5 kilometres of stormwater drains.

'The whole complex was a city of such fine tuning that we scarcely needed to be told – as we were told every day by posters – not to speak "outside" of our work,' said Audrey Morphett. 'It was so all-enveloping when we entered the gates that we knew we could never convey even a small concept of it to anyone not part of it.' It was the biggest project undertaken in South Australia up to that time and was the largest explosives factory in Australia, where explosives were made and ammunition filled and assembled, eventually costing £10 000 000.

Audrey had volunteered for the AWAS when enlistments were first called for. 'They knocked me back. They said I was too old for the army. [The maximum age for the services was 45.] I didn't know what I could do to serve. I suppose you could say I hadn't really been educated to do anything. My mother taught me at home.'

Audrey's great-grandfather, James Hurtle Fisher, had built Cummins, nine and a half kilometres out of Adelaide, in 1842. 'I'd just lived at Cummins, at home, as some country girls did in those days; rode ponies, took the spare horse for my father to the hunts, that sort of thing. When I was 15 I went to Hermitage for three years. Some girls may leave the Hermitage to marry a prime minister. I just came home and was here when war broke out.'

In fact, she hadn't done so little. In her twenties she had become District Commissioner for Guides for Glenelg, later Divisional Commissioner and, by 1941, she was State Commissioner. She had therefore built up a long association in command of girls and women. 'My war effort until I went to Salisbury was, in the main, for the Guide Thrift Depot.' Then she attempted to enlist. 'I thought, well, that's that. There is no place for me in the war effort, so I re-doubled my efforts to work to earn funds for war charities. Then I was contacted, out of the blue, and asked if I would go to Salisbury munitions factory. Not to *join* the army but actually to *work* for the army.

'The Army Inspection Division called six of us together, me, my friend Judy Whitely, and two other friends of ours as well as another two women. We were promptly sent over to Melbourne – in civvies of course – booked in to the Hotel Windsor, and, each day, taken out to Maribyrnong where we were taught by the inspectors – women – out there to do the job. Because there had been no explosives factories in South Australia until Salisbury was built, Maribyrnong was the only place we could be trained.

The "head serang" took us over, the senior inspector. We studied and studied.

'Back in South Australia we went straight to work on the cap section. As time went on, Judy and I were the head of this work. New girls were coming along all the time and we had to train them.

'The detonation section opened, then the cordite. This took great concentration when observing. You just had to constantly retrain yourself to be acutely observant. Cordite caps had to be very carefully handled. If bumped together they could explode. Girls working there had to wear protective clothes and cover their hair in case of grit or dust setting off an explosion. "Quick!" You'd hear them call to one another, "Miss Morphett's coming!" and there would always be someone with their hair sticking out from their head covering. They hated the shoes and all the fireproof and protective clothing as they padded along the floor, carpeted so as to avoid causing a spark.

'Cordite was bad to work with. Some girls could not tolerate it. They became ill. They would absorb it through their skin. It smelled badly too.

'We inspected explosives only. Caps, detonators, fuses, cordite. We were not involved in making shells, only explosives. One got quite used to it. Outside the actual work rooms we inspectors went on our rounds along "clear areas" or "gritless walkways" built up three feet above ground. Dressed in our protection gear, we were careful to stay on the walkway, as we must not soil our footwear in case we caused sparks.

"There were little rooms sticking out from these pathways where the girls worked filling caps with explosives. Inspecting the detonator work was precise, watching for the height of the filling in the cap as this is the detonator, and if this does not detonate, a weapon has lost its whole explosion. It was all routine work, but with a difference.

'I was walking on the "clearway" towards a room to inspect it and the girl workers when it blew – one woman was among those killed. Their work was very dangerous ... But there was always laughter ...' This modest woman was the senior examiner at Salisbury. Paid by the army, Audrey was a civilian, was awarded no medals, wore no uniform.

Helen Crisp, the first official government social worker in industrial welfare, wrote in September 1941 in the *Australian Quarterly* of women munitions workers in a small arms ammunition factory in Victoria: 'There were nearly 900 and the age limits had been extended to 40 and lowered to 16 for special cases ... the majority of girls [were] drawn from domestic employment.'

Those who had previously worked in factories had tried many different trades, such as paint spraying, biscuit making, fruit cutting, jam and pickle making, assembling radio parts, cotton cloth weaving, printing, egg testing, dry cleaning, etc. Helen Crisp reported that 'The girls were obviously attracted by the higher wages offering in munitions work and the vast majority were prepared to do overtime for the extra pay. They were expected to work six days a week and, eventually, to go on to two shifts. When asked why they were taking up the work, some said that they wanted to do something to help the war effort: but, if questioned directly, the majority admitted that the relatively high wages had also affected their decision. It is unlikely, however, that girls would deliberately give up so much of their leisure and work such inconvenient hours, if they had not felt in return that they were doing a worthwhile job. Munitions work is made more attractive by its aura of respectability and patriotism. Many girls who had not liked to enter factories before, felt no compunction in becoming cogs in Australia's war machine.' During the period of this study, the weekly wage for ordinary adult women workers was 47s 6d, with 18s 0d compulsory overtime for Saturday, making a total of 65s 6d a week. Juniors were paid less, according to age.

In an age when women lived at home and very few were able financially or socially to afford a flat or house of their own, one of the larger problems tackled was that of finding lodging for employees, for many either came from the country or lived too far from the factory to allow them to do shift work. An outside, voluntary committee made a survey of suitable homes and these addresses, with particulars and comments, were then forwarded to the welfare officer for reference to girls seeking lodgings.

During the period of Helen Crisp's study, the main reasons for absence from work included stomach disorders (95), colds, flu, etc. (45), PMT and other gynaecological complaints (32), family ties and worries (19), boils (4).

Many women spoke up bravely for women at this time. Kathleen Fitzpatrick, President of the Council for Women in War Work, wrote in 1943: 'The tendency of this war, as of the others, is to open to women less skilled, less remunerative and less responsible jobs than those of men. We hear much of total war, but in this country the whole direction of the war effort is in the hands of half of the citizens. Women are sometimes permitted to offer advice, but even in matters which so vitally concern them as the rationing of food and clothing, not one woman in the country has been entrusted with a position of real authority and responsibility.

'In wartime, women are eagerly welcomed as workers, but only as workers of inferior status. This is both undemocratic and inefficient, since the country needs people who can do the jobs best, regardless of their sex. Moreover, unless women concern themselves with this matter now, there is every reason to expect that after this war, women workers will continue to form an inferior caste in the community. There are many young women of today who will never marry, because the men they would have married have been, or will be, killed in action. Life is not easy for the woman who must walk alone: need it be made harder by poverty and the humiliation that a semi-dependent status breeds?'

The problems of wartime are linked with those of the days before the war and with those to come. 'Perhaps the war may bring more understanding between women by the violent changes of habits it causes, exposing formerly "sheltered" women to the conditions of the wage-earner, and leaving married women with no husbands to fend for them. The well-being of each woman should be the concern of all women, and the betterment of any one section will tend to improve the status and conditions of all. These injustices are as degrading to men as to women.'

## CHAPTER 31

# The Invisible Crew

'Their lives are in your hands,' the girls were told. 'Nothing but the best is good enough for the men who fly the planes we make.'

The message to the women of the Beaufort Bomber Division of the Department of Aircraft Production was plain. Jean Page, one of the girls who built the bombers, recalls. 'They had to be perfect. You wouldn't let anything but the best pass through your hands. Those men were depending on us. We knew it. It seems funny to think of it now, but we were very earnest.'

Bill Ewarth, manager of the assembly line, knew they were earnest. 'Jean was one of the young girls building bombers. You only needed to tell them once that the men flying the planes took all the risks – they never forgot. They were diligent, painstaking, hard working, accurate, loyal. But one day they said "No", they would not do as ordered. No, they said. It wasn't a strike; they just would not use the screw supplied to them for the fuselage. They knew the work could not proceed without this part being done, but they said no.

'The thing was, the screws sent to us were a fraction small for the hole. They were not the screw threads listed on the specifications. But it was not a vital part of the aircraft, it would have done no damage at all. "No," they said. "If the specifications state one thing, it means that it is the best, the one they believe to be the safest." And so they would not put the screws in.

'I had to ring up and tell the suppliers they would just have to scout around and get the specified screws, and quick, because these girls would not use anything that was not on the specifications. You just had to admire them.'

'Under the spur of war, women have turned their hands to numerous tasks that were formerly regarded as the exclusive prerogative of the male,' stated the brochure put out by the Beaufort Torpedo Bomber factory, appealing for even more workers.

'Of the total 10 000 employees, approximately 34 per cent are women, approximately 80 per cent had no previous factory experience, let alone experience in aircraft production. These women have contributed to a remarkable degree to the defence of Australia.'

The production of these bombers began in an empty office in 1939. Aircraft production was in its infancy before this war. Throughout the next six years, it developed to a stage where they manufactured practically all the 39 000 different types of parts required for each Beaufort. 'We made the complex Twin Row Aero Engines, constant speed propellers, intricate hydraulic landing gear, gun turrets, self-sealing fuel tanks and flying instruments.'

There were enormous difficulties in procuring the materials and also with labour shortages, but these all-Australian-made aircraft came off the assembly line in a steady stream.

The women worked in most sections of the plant, from preparing aircraft parts for the assembly line to the final assembly itself. There were girls as young as 17-year-old Jean Page and as old as their mothers. Some were riveters, others solderers or electricians wiring on the assembly line and engine bulkheads; there were machine operators and milling machinists shaping small castings or forging. There were 'stock chasers' ensuring that the correct articles were delivered to the production floor – these girls needed a thorough knowledge of aircraft parts and nomenclature, as well as the ability to read drawings; others used precision measuring equipment and some, as inspection staff, operated machines for testing the hardness of metals.

'We inspected and checked all parts on arrival and issue from Beaufort Stores,' Jean Page says. 'Some girls were in a viewing room inspecting parts, others were doing laboratory work. Anything, we did anything. Operated drilling machines . . . three girls would work together riveting a rear fuselage or with a power press, or riveting tail plane spares, or the duralium "skin" on tail planes. Some were engravers, numbering the thousands of parts.

'Few of us had been in workshops before. I was straight from school, some were seamstresses as they called them then, office girls, hairdressers, housewives, all sorts.'

Women traced the intricate designs in the engineering department and were draughtsmen and technical artists. Compiling the aircraft parts list was a type of housekeeping no woman could have envisaged before the war – and no man, either. 'They were always happy, that was the great thing,' Bill Ewarth remembers. 'It was an outstanding characteristic of Beaufort women. They had a sense of achievement.'

Every Beaufort that took to the air carried an invisible crew. 'In spirit, the girls were there.'

# CHAPTER 32

# *The String Bag Cometh*

'What did they have in newspapers before the war, mother?' John Moore (later a prominent Melbourne accountant), as a small boy asked his mother.

And well may he have wondered, for by 1942 the papers were full of war; news from the various 'fronts', photographs ranging from men in battle to women queueing for pet food at butchers' shops – the first time there had been such a need in Australia where until now, there had always been ample scraps to be had for the family's pets.

There were photographs of women carrying their own shopping home. 'Because of manpower shortages, home deliveries have been curtailed until after hostilities' end.' Until now, tradesmen such as grocers and butchers had called for orders and delivered them later the same day or on the following morning; for those with a telephone, goods could be ordered and delivered even more promptly. Bakers' carts made their daily rounds; ice carts came twice a week. In 1942, it all ended.

Women, struggling to get their shopping home, found they had no suitable containers in which to carry it. Some brought suitcases with them to the shops. One woman was photographed packing her goods into a pillow slip. With all the stitching and sewing going on for the war effort, it was not long before the ideal carry-all was found and soon every household owned a hand-made string bag. 'A "string bag" is the latest acquisition for the Australian woman shopping for her family!' the papers cried.

Whether inspired by the netted pattern of these bags or not, a similar container immediately appeared, this time christened a 'snood', a netted sack for holding a woman's hair neat and tidy, 'and especially useful for safety in factory work'.

The nation had been catapulted into what John Curtin called 'a season of austerity. Make your habits of life conform to those of the fighting forces,' he said, on 19 August 1942. 'The civilian population can learn to discipline itself, it can learn to go without.' He was as eloquent as was Churchill in time of war. 'Every day you read about some man you knew dying fighting far distant from the places of entertainment ... Let us think of them a little more, or ourselves a little less.' Everything, he said, that in any way resembled a peace-time way of living must be stripped away.

The history of the past three years was that the enemy had gained all the time and still held the initiative. 'Consider our fate, should he be victorious . . . What will we have then? Today Port Moresby and Darwin are the Singapores of Australia. If those two places fall, we are faced with a bloody struggle on our soil when we will be forced to fight grimly, city by city, village by village, until our fair land may become a blackened ruin. We will fight. Our record is proof of that. But what is the cost? The cost must be paid now – not to an invading enemy, but in equipping our fighting men so that they will hold Port Moresby and Darwin, so that they will hold this Australian bastion for democracy, and finally, wrest the initiative from the enemy.'

It was a call no woman – or man – could resist.

'Our fate is in the balance as I speak to you.' The Battle of the Solomons was at that moment being fought.

A series of measures, which in scope and severity transcended any hitherto contemplated, was introduced with a ruthlessness and speed which Government knew would involve individual inequities and arouse much opposition.

Some indication of the acceleration in the war effort can be gauged by the percentage of national income expended on war: 11 per cent in 1940–41; 29 per cent in 1941–42 and 43 per cent in 1942–43. There was a great change in the life of the nation. Apart from those many women entering the labour force for the first time in our history, other women traditionally employed in one type of labour were now directed to transfer to a totally different form of work or a different abode, and to change the habits of a lifetime.

Restrictions were imposed, unaccustomed demands were made on almost all the population, but perhaps on none so severely as the housewife. It is one thing for soldiers to see patriotism in the 'bold and simple characters of warfare', but a totally different matter for those away from the shrill of trumpets and the flutter of flags to trudge and drudge as never before – and all this with no uniform, no badge of valour.

More manpower than ever was required to supply the needs of the allied forces now concentrated in the South-west Pacific. Australia and New Zealand were the only major food producers in this arena and Australia the only major manufacturer where items such as food stuffs, footwear, clothing, rope, soap, tools, blankets, and other items might be obtained.

American and Australian services were building up huge strategic reserves of non-perishable food stuffs – and three months' supply for one million troops and a year's supply for 200 000 troops.

Rationing of clothing began in June 1942 and rationing of food followed. Petrol had been rationed since October 1940 and restrictions were not lifted until February 1950. Beer, in short supply, was rationed, as were cigarettes and tobacco. When either beer or cigarettes were available at shops, long queues formed, hoping to get their ration before the shopkeeper sold out his meagre allowance. Interstate travel by train was banned except by those holding permits.

Cities and large towns had enforced black-outs. In houses, black-out curtains were put up and windows made safe from shattering with adhesive tape. Buckets of sand and little spades were on hand to douse fire bombs, and regular air raid practices were staged, with sirens screaming and air raid precaution officers in tin helmets hurrying citizens to the slit trenches and shelters.

Railway stations looked more like army camps than civilian transport depots. Every city station, and even smaller country centres where there was a refreshments room, resounded to the tread of hundreds of thousands of pairs of boots tramping up and down the platforms. Platforms, waiting-rooms and station approaches looked like the Retreat from Moscow, with bodies in khaki and navy and air force blue lolling or lying everywhere, their kit-bags, tin hats, gas masks and ground sheets lying around or under them.

By January 1942, private boarding-school buildings in the cities were evacuated and the students moved to the country, while the military and air force took over the school buildings. Other buildings were commandeered, often at short notice and with what must have been distress and vast dislocation problems for those who had worked to raise the funds to build and operate them. Among the places I moved into while serving in military hospitals in 1941–44 were first, a brand new, modern ward in what was in those days called a lunatic asylum (the civilian nurses called to us from their antiquated old building, 'Where do you think the money came from to build the palace you've pinched?' while they went on toiling throughout the war in the sub-standard, century-old buildings); second, a children's orthopaedic hospital ('Do you mind if we carry the children out?' the staff snapped at us as we swept in under orders to hurry, because wounded patients would be arriving on the morrow); third, Glennie Girls' School, Toowoomba, where the school mistresses in their own small cars were valiantly attempting to evacuate the girls as our ambulances rolled up the drive and we leapt out; fourth, a district hospital in the country, where we slapped our tent wards down in the middle of their ordered calm and took over their kitchen; and fifth, a totally unoffending little church school into which we tumbled with our beds, blankets and bandages on a Friday afternoon when the unsuspecting schoolboys were getting out their cricket gear.

As well, there was the billeting. All over the land women were opening their doors to military and air force officers who asked (ordered?): 'How many can you billet? We have here information you have three bedrooms, only two of which are in use.' But it was all calmly accepted, because by January 1942 we knew we were in danger; in February we knew our 'island fortress' could no longer protect us. General Douglas MacArthur, driven from the Philippines, announced in Melbourne that Australia would be next to fall. There was the belief that we should draw back to a line north of Brisbane and fight there to the last man.

Mrs Len Scott, evacuated from Darwin to Brisbane, was on a tram when she heard two women discussing the news that Darwin had been bombed. 'That's getting close to Australia, ain't it!' one woman remarked.

Air-raid shelters were being dug in back-yards, mileage and sign posts were being removed across the continent. (The station master at the tiny town of Currabubula NSW took down the name sign at his station and placed it under the seat on the platform where it remained for the duration of the war. He is reported as saying that he 'didn't want them Japs to know where they were'.)

Australian women knew that 'the worst had come to the worst'. They were facing the worst. 'It is an entirely new set of events and there are no pioneer women to look after us, no woman who has been through it all before. We have got to find out the code of conduct proper to the moment and apply it without help,' Sybil Irving wrote.

The women performed an amazing feat of human adjustment to this entirely unpredicted set of circumstances. It must be recorded as one of the great achievements of the war. Until now, women's lives had been arranged for them, but initiative and judgement and a feeling of responsibility to the job, no matter what it cost, had been part of the pioneer woman. 'Women had defended the homeland for almost a century,' Sybil Irving had said. But it is always moving, and amazing, to witness human gallantry. It was the day of the ordinary woman responding to extraordinary times.

For rich and poor, the pleasure of shopping was over. There were no eggs – dried eggs were on the market. Little dried fruit was available. Recipe books from the Depression were hunted out, cakes were made with dripping instead of butter (ready-to-mix cakes were another of the items not yet invented). Shopping became the great leveller. Mrs Kath Bradley remembers: 'Some of the "big knobs" who wouldn't look at you once, now swapped recipes with you as we all waited in the queue.'

The belief that much of the bunyip-aristocracy brand of snobbishness disappeared with the tumult of threatened invasion and hardship during this war is not entirely true. Any diminution in this crass indulgence on the part of the rich had taken place either when the class-distinction in dress had been markedly obliterated by off-the-rack, ready-made dresses. Mass-produced garments had slashed years off the evolution of egalitarianism. The maid and the mistress could no longer be immediately identified by the difference in apparel. For all that, the closeness in that time of peril did do much to mix the classes – at least while the war lasted. Women sewed together, sorted used clothing, ran street stalls, rolled bandages and, side by side, they prayed for their sons.

Women who had lived in the same street for years, but never met, suddenly called on one another. Two such women were Mrs W. A. Elmore and Mrs F. Denholm of Cain Street, Melbourne. Both women had menfolk reported missing: Private Elmore MM, at the battle for Bardia in early 1941, and Ship's Engineer Fred Denholm after the sinking of the *Commissaire Rainel* in September 1940. Then, in late March 1941, came a telegram to Mrs Elmore telling her that 'Bomber', her husband, was safely back with his battalion. 'I didn't know Mrs Denholm, but I knew how she felt when I heard she had a telegram to say her son was safe. So I went up the street to meet her.'

Mrs Elmore's husband was a veteran of World War I. 'I watched and waited for my husband in two wars. I kept busy. You have to.'

All civilians took time to adapt to the changing needs of war in the 1940s; much that was done during the 1914–18 war was repeated immediately this second world war began in the belief that what was needed in one war perforce would suit any war. And so they knitted. Socks by the thousands, woollen socks that reached to the knees, although the 'boys' were not in the trenches of icy Europe, but in the burning deserts surrounding Tobruk and Libya and later in the jungles of New Guinea.

Surely one of the most awful setbacks women war workers received was in February 1941 when the Commissioner of the Australian Comforts

Funds, Eugene Gorman, flew home from Egypt to Australia and announced: 'The women of Australia are wasting their time hand-knitting socks for men overseas.' No doubt Major Gorman had much on his mind, but his statements – resounding almost as a reprimand to these thousands of women who were knitting furiously, in their own time, with wool paid for by themselves – could have been put less bluntly.

'The men are in shorts most of the time,' Major Gorman said. 'What they need are long, machine-made standardised stockings which fit far better than hand-made ones.' No woman who prided herself on her 'well-turned heels', would believe it. 'It is simply useless to load them up with hand-made socks. They can be a jolly nuisance.' Which was little consolation for the good women who had been trying so hard, some knitting a pair of socks a day, in the belief they were needed.

As for comforts for individual battalions or units, this, too, was ridiculous, he said. 'If people have the fantastic idea that we can line the men up every Monday morning and hand out comforts to them, let me explain that this is a *war* we are fighting.

'The best way to help provide comforts was by cash, giving to the Australian Comforts Fund,' he said. The ACF channelled money to most of the organisations working with the troops, including the Salvation Army. But giving in this abstract way was a poor outlet for the pent-up emotions and needs of women at home, needs few men could understand.

In many ways, there was little joy for women. With clothing or cloth being rationed, mothers, even young girls, were reduced to 'making over' curtains for dresses, curtain linings for skirts. Men's cricketing trousers, as well as the unworn parts of discarded trousers, were unpicked and, with the inside turned outside, made into trousers for smaller boys or skirts for little girls. Old blankets were cut up to make dressing gowns, even overcoats and capes. Flowers were appliqued over moth-holes or worn spots. It may be thought that, as a reflection of the times, a certain shabbiness could have become fashionable, but this was not so. Instead, the smartness of one's apparel demonstrated a will to 'carry on regardless', as the new saying went.

Women wore brooches awarded them, with stars representing the number of sons, or a husband, serving abroad. Many regarded these as a symbol of 'doing her bit for her country', and keeping up appearances was just another psychological means of keeping going while hearts were yearning. Baking a fruit cake with part of the house ration and packing it in a Willow Brand cake tin, stitching calico tightly around this and stencilling the soldier's name and unit for an address was another bewildered, hopeful, hopeless act to help mark time and use up time that might otherwise be spent weeping.

Few organisations were not involved in some way. The Girl Guides' Association was a part of the international service helping with rehabilitation of refugees and 'displaced persons' (as those whose countries' borders had altered were now called).

At home in South Australia, the Girl Guide movement earned money to buy, among other things, an ambulance. They collected bottles, newspapers, scrap paper. They were loaned a worn-out truck, 'Sooty', so named because the charcoal-burner, hooked on to provide fuel when their petrol ration tickets ran out, covered the girls, the goods and any onlookers unwise enough to stand too close, with black soot.

'Sooty didn't go too well,' recalls Audrey Morphett, then State Commissioner. 'I hated it most when she gave out in a city street during lunch hour. The times we pushed Sooty . . .'

This Guide Thrift Depot was run as a big business. 'We kept closely co-ordinated lists of the wants of our "customers", as well as of the items offered to us. A day's work-sheet might have read "gas stove here, pipes there, gates somewhere else". It was all run by volunteers.

'When Sooty couldn't get round everywhere we needed her, firms offered to pick up for us. Eventually we were using all of a big old four-storey store-house in Adelaide. We handled ironmongery, curiosity items, engine parts – we were a real clearing house for things in short supply.'

Mr S. Willard, a railway watchman at Quorn (SA) during the war, remembered work done by the women in this tiny railway town: 'The train used to go through Quorn in those days to Alice Springs and the troops going to Darwin and north to the islands went through here, thousands and thousands of them, and the women of Quorn fed them all. This was a remarkable effort . . . there were plenty of railway widows here, wives of train crews that only got home for brief spells during those busy years. The women fed up to 600 troops a day. At first they cooked on their own wood-fired kitchen stoves and kept food fresh in their Coolgardie safes, with water dribbling down strips of cloth to keep the food cool; enlisted the children to peel vegetables and, when their men brought their blacked-out trains in, sent them out to cut more wood to keep the fire going under the coppers out in the back-yard. Later they raised funds and got a refrigerator and things, but right until the end they toiled.

'I know women all over Australia did these things during the war, but

I don't think there were many places where women had to work in this way in the sweltering heat and blinding dust.'

Reports in the daily newspapers told of women appearing in the public transport workforce. '*2 June 1942* "In Melbourne, Yellow Cabs have selected 12 women to work for the company", the Chairman of Directors, Mr M. Shmith said on 2 June. "The women will lease the cabs on terms equal to those of the company's male drivers. They will drive only in daylight and be free to choose their hours between 7 a.m. and 7 p.m."'

The Victorian Railways had taken on girls as porters and the Tramways Authority – rather unwillingly – was also considering it. Melbourne was the first city in Australia to employ women on this work, in fact, eventually having 300 on its payroll.

On 19 June 1944 a press release stated that 'New South Wales women have saved Australia £1 million' and had done valuable work during the critical war period. Members of the Country Women's Association and the National Defence League were being asked to do an 'ever-increasing amount' of war work. Previously, they had made camouflage nets; now the demand was for labour to recondition army clothes, for though 'voluntary women workers are reconditioning many thousands of army overcoats and uniforms, even more help is needed'.

The Acting Prime Minister, F. M. Forde, estimated that in one year alone, New South Wales voluntary workers made more than 500 000 camouflage nets for the army, saving at least £437 000. Even more significant was the saving in manpower, leaving full-time workers free for other war tasks.

These women created a voluntary industry which had never before been attempted. Thousands answered the call for volunteers. Sporting and business organisations, public schools, department stores, churches, hospitals, public bodies and municipal councils co-operated. Off-duty policemen made netting frames and women workers in Newcastle made 10 000 frames and extensions in off-duty hours. As the Japanese swept down through Malaya, Java, Timor, and into New Guinea, an even greater effort was called for. Netting centres spread like cobwebs all over the countryside. The old, the crippled, all helped. Several generations were found working side-by-side. Housewives turned their 'baby room' into a netting centre.

Scores of volunteers went to locations to garnish the nets. Garnishing – or scrimming as it is often called – is the work done to make the net conform to its surroundings, the purpose of a camouflage net.

The CWA organised 144 active country centres which had sub-centres working for them, as well as 162 active metropolitan centres. At one time there were 462 centres. In addition, many people received twine from the CWA and made the nets in their own homes. The National Defence League had 119 netting centres with 10 000 members.

Some of the other tasks people performed included cutting sisalkraft, used in the patching of ordnance stores. They did 'invisible darning' on worn clothing, sewed on buttons, repaired and refurbished clothing to be re-issued, remade old army towels into floor cloths for hospital use and sorted condemned clothing for use as engine-cleaning wipers.

From October 1943 to June 1944, the CWA handled 78 000 jungle green trousers, 19 000 tunics, 9500 greatcoats, 123 bags of cleaning rags, 1050 hand towels; they sized 3340 singlets, 2060 'drawers', and 1480 shirts. 'Without such help,' stated an army report, 'it would have been impossible to keep troops in New Guinea adequately supplied with necessary clothing.'

The National Defence League had ten centres working at similar jobs, but also reconditioning anti-gas equipment, sorting and patching army web equipment, gaiters, forage caps, making up housewifes (sewing kits) and field dressings; 10 000 part-worn army garments were sized weekly, and they reconditioned 223 500 pieces of army clothing and equipment.

Manpower regulations were not impossible to flout, but some effort was made to round up those thought to be avoiding service of one kind or another. On the weekend of 14–15 May 1943, during a city check, 30 women were questioned.

In the first week in March 1944, when the peach crop was ripe, 2000 women were 'telegraphed' their call-up notices to report for interview at National Service offices two days hence. It was one of the 'most sweeping manpower moves for about six months'. By 6 March, most of the women were in canneries, sorting the peaches, washing the halves and pushing them into cans.

The 2000 included women in low-priority and 'possibly many in high-priority employment', but the food was needed for export and for the troops.

Electric light was forbidden in shop window displays and advertising signs. Petrol was rationed to the point where families had to use other means of transport such as bicycles, for their travelling; and, in some cases, horse transport, which had only just disappeared from the roads in most parts of the country, came back into use.

The war threw up all sorts of anomalies. The Women's Auxiliary of the

Australia–Soviet Friendship League organised themselves to send food and clothing to Russia.

During the war, many women lived in the shade of miserable anxiety; every waking moment they feared to be handed a telegram that would bring total desolation to their lives, a changed diet, poorer housing, loss of status in a community, and loneliness.

Other women, placed in positions of authority hitherto sacred to men, were confronted by prejudice and, in some cases, jealousy and opposition which had to be allayed and placated. Had they been men, all that waste of time, thought and energy would have been unnecessary.

Some women believe that members of their own sex were more quarrelsome than men. 'If letters are not answered, or files mislaid, or clerks unpunctual, they become troubled, worried, cross – and that leads to anger. Men take things more easily – especially those in government departments!' they found. As to quarrelsomeness, Bill Ewarth, who worked with women in an aircraft factory during World War II, has told me: 'To tell you the truth, we were all a bit short at times.'

It was still being said that an army marched on its stomach, yet it is impossible to count the varieties of tasks women were called on to perform to keep that same army marching. The Victoria League collected and distributed 15 000 magazines annually to camps spread across the map from Singapore to Darwin and New Guinea, as well as to minesweepers.

Fifty women, working as an independent group, spent every Friday at the Melbourne Showgrounds camp 'patching and pressing' for airmen from other states. The YWCA Rest Hut at the camp set up a sewing room for these women, and there they darned hundreds of pairs of socks, mended uniforms, stitched on stripes, took up trousers, and pressed uniforms crumpled from men having to sleep overnight on troop trains.

Among its many other war activities, the Country Women's Association supplied sheepskin vests for the air force and navy – and coaxed flock owners to donate gifts of pelts to be made up. These women also knitted 'sea-boots', soft, warm thigh boots for the navy, from fine, home-spun wool with the yolk left in; these were practically waterproof.

'The Padres' Few Bob Fund' was given £1000 by the ladies of the Methodist Padres' Auxiliary in Victoria 'to enable them to make the lives of the men more comfortable'. Another service given by these women resulted from a letter from the Middle East from Padre Warfe. 'Fleas are a menace in this part of the world,' he wrote. So the ladies devised flea traps, simply crocheted wool necklets about a metre long which, when worn next to the skin, were said to act as a trap for the vermin!

Dr Ella Stack (the woman who was Mayor of Darwin at the time of Cyclone Tracy) remembers that 'the female surgeons at Rachel Foster Hospital in Sydney only stopped operating during World War II when their gravid state prohibited their reaching the patient'.

There was confusion, some stupidity, ignorance and self-aggrandisement amongst women in a country involved in total war, yet there was greatness too. Another thing was pride, and no one who stood in the crowd in an Australian city in those tumultuous days can forget it. The troops marched by; the 9th Division had been brought home from the Middle East by the Labor Government (and Churchill never forgave them for it). Those men swung by, loose-limbed in a way that set them apart from all other fighting men, fit and confident as were all men who wore the figure '8' on their colour patch as a memento of the years they fought with Montgomery's Eighth Army in the desert and later withstood the Siege of Tobruk. Battalion on battalion loped by. If there were bands, I don't recall them, nor drums, trumpets or banners. All that remains is the heart of the matter, the marriage between these men and the women in the crowd who had fought at home, each knowing the other had been there when the whips were cracking. None of us in that street – wherever that street was – had been tried and found wanting. When that instant in time descended on us and we knew we could lose our homeland, knew we could be lost as a race, we rose up and fought. Not all of us, no. That is as it should be; that is democracy. It was a cord that bound us. We shared the sorrow; after all, we women lost our beloved boys as these men lost their comrades. But equally, we shared the pride. That is what made us weep as the men swung by that day.

Artists gave their time freely. I got off the Regimental Aid Post (RAP) on a troop train in Melbourne one day in 1942 and couldn't push my way through the crowds in Swanston Street to see what was happening. But I could hear. From the back of a truck the great voice of Strella Wilson sang 'Land of Hope and Glory'. A hundred thousand people stood silent, tears running down their cheeks. If a people ever melded into one and knew love and pride and what we could live for and what we would die for it, it was then.

> *Land of Hope and Glory, Mother of the free,*
> *How can we extol them, Who are born of thee?*

It might not have been written for our land, but it was ours in that moment. All ours.

> *Wider still and wider, Let thy bounds be set*
> *God who made thee mighty, Make thee mightier yet!*

When the singer ceased the song, and a second of silence like a mighty hand was lifted from us, a roar filled Swanston Street and we pressed forward until we were compacted like an immovable army.

There are many things, most things, about every war we must condemn, but being a part of the body of one's own people at such a time is an emotion that time can never erase.

# CHAPTER 33

# *War in the Outback*

A southerner visiting Darwin is suddenly conscious of how close we are to Asia. The great centres of population, Sydney and Melbourne are 3000 kilometres away and have no sense of a weight of foreign powers sitting so near. The visitor up north is instantly conscious of island nations 150 kilometres away; the airwaves are choked with foreign languages.

The people of all areas north of the 26th parallel are aware of the vulnerability of Australia, but much more aware that they themselves are twenty times further from Sydney or Melbourne than they are from Asian nations. If this is the case today, how much more so was it in 1939 when the road being built to join Alice Springs and Darwin ended at Adelaide River? The rest was a track. The cyclone of 1937 in that 'outpost of empire' had damaged the city and rebuilding was still not finished. There were few white women.

One of these women, Molly Walsh, a typist with the army in Darwin, wrote: 'Friday 5 December ... a number of soldiers were due to go south on annual leave and had already handed in their equipment and gone on board the troopship *Zealandia* when an order came through cancelling all leave and they were put ashore and returned to their camps. Rumour had it there would be a riot ... but rumour also said there was something more behind the cancellation than mere muddle-headedness.'

Two days later the tropical lethargy was blasted with the news that Pearl Harbor had been bombed.

Molly noted six strange ships in the harbour, the most ocean-going ships she had seen in the bay at the one time. 'While I stood looking out over the dazzling water, truck after truck sped by me, taking barbed wire and working parties from Larrakeyah Barracks to strategic positions.' Already men had been taken from building the road to putting down airstrips.

The historian Barbara James has written: 'Darwin began to take on the air of a town awaiting disaster – hurried weddings, air-raid practices, false alarms, garrisons, barbed wire entanglements, an anti-submarine net across the harbour and a massive evacuation of women and children.

'The evacuation of 1066 women and 900 children between mid-December and mid-February was a mammoth task. One of the most actively involved was former city council alderman and deputy mayor, Ted D'Ambrosio, who was a "zone warden". "My area was from Daly Street to the wharf," he said. "First we had to find out who was in our area and then issue them with two cards, one to be taken off them when they re-evacuated so they could be crossed off the main list.

"Most were given only 24 hours notice or less, and allowed one suitcase weighing 35 pounds ... the biggest problem was coping with irate husbands who didn't want their wives to go, and took it out on us. I had so many bruises by the end of the evacuation it wasn't funny.

"We evacuated them by air, sea, road – whatever was available. My own wife went out by plane on 10 December ... The worst time, though, was for the ones who went out on the *Zealandia*. The conditions were unbelievable," says Ted D'Ambrosio.'

Nancy Eddy, recovering from a 'bout of fever', took her five-year-old and carried her new baby on board '... and the baby had just contracted the fever. I remember my husband coming home on Thursday, 19 December, and telling me to pack and be ready to leave in an hour.

'All I could do was pack baby napkins and a change of clothes for [us] ... There were nine people in my cabin and I had to carry my baby in my arms the entire trip as he was so sick. But I felt especially sorry for the women who had not even seen their husbands before they left – it was very hard on them.'

Both Wendy James and Nancy remember the tense trip down the Western Australian coast with the ship trying to avoid the mines.

Some women were evacuated on the USS *Grant* on 23 December. This cruiser had been in Manila during the Japanese attack and was given orders to head for the nearest friendly port. On arriving in Darwin, the Captain was promptly asked to evacuate a group of women and children to Brisbane. Kath Garton, with her friend Kath Finlay, was on board the *Grant*. She remembers her husband Len giving her a small gun to carry at all times. 'I carried it down my brassière or had it under my pillow,' she says. 'But I was never really sure whether I'd shoot myself or the Japanese if the occasion arose.'

Edna Tambling also went out on the USS *Grant*. Her husband Ern, or 'Tam' was put in charge of the evacuation and travelled with the women. 'We were notified at 7 p.m. one night that we would leave at 8 a.m. the next day. I remember we let the chickens out to run loose and then packed a few clothes,' Edna says. The Tamblings named their next baby Grant in honour of the cruiser.

Among the last of the women to leave was Audrey Kennon, who worked for Captain Gregory in the port, and was responsible for helping take men off the ships and put women on them. As one of the few females around over the Christmas–New Year period, she ended up cooking Christmas dinner for 12 men. She was finally evacuated by plane just a couple of weeks before Darwin was bombed.

Another who held out until the end was Jessie Litchfield, the press correspondent for many Australian and overseas papers, and who had been in the Territory since 1907. It was not until they threatened to carry her out that she finally agreed to go. She later wrote:

'Whether the decision for evacuation was right or wrong is debatable; there is no doubt whatever that the method . . . was crude and cruel in the extreme. Only the barest necessities could be taken . . . but no arrangements were made for the safeguarding of possessions left behind . . . [they] were left to the looter and the despoiler.

'Arrived in the southern states, they were left to fend for themselves. Those who had relatives and friends . . . were the fortunate ones, but there were many whose lives had been spent in the Territory, and who had known no other home. Their plight was pitiful. Can one wonder that some of them gave up the struggle for existence and simply faded out of life, too sick at heart to carry on any longer?'

Poppy Octavia Secrett's husband, Stan, went off with the Civil Works department when the war came to Darwin, and Poppy was evacuated with her children – after a fight. Wendy James remembers it.

'Mother had already moved house a couple of times in Darwin, so she dug her heels in and said she was not going anywhere again. All the women wanted to stay. No one wanted to leave. But the boat was waiting at the wharf. A huge military policeman knocked hard on the door and said to my mother, "You're going!" She refused and he threatened to throw her over his shoulder.

'She stormed up the wharf pushing baby Lorilee in the pusher with John and me at her side. We had a lean time in Perth. Our father was spending his youth and vitality constructing staging camps and air fields and it worried her. She said, "Bugger it. I've had enough. I'm going home!"

'John and I were sent to boarding school and somehow she managed to wangle her way to Alice Springs then to Dumarra, carrying baby Lorilee.

To cover their embarrassment at having her there, the authorities granted her status as housekeeper at Dunmarra Station where Dad was working. She got pregnant again. Then Dad embarrassed the authorities by smuggling her to Alice Springs covered with blankets in a truck so she would be near a hospital for the birth of the twins.'

It was during the Wet that the bombers came. The north was lush and green, soaked from the monsoonal rains. The lovely harbour was dotted with the allied ships Molly Walsh had noted weeks before when the bombers came in on 19 February 1942. The first bombs to be dropped on Australia fell, killing 243 people and injuring around 300. The harbour was ablaze with burning ships, burning men were in the water; the city was rubble.

One of the women who told her story to Barbara James was Winnie Sargent of Stapleton Station at Batchelor, south of Darwin. Winnie had stayed. 'Many [of the evacuees] came to our camp at Stapleton ... and we fed them and directed them on their way, further toward the inland. Dad and I were still carrying on, slaughtering cattle and supplying the army with beef. The air force would fly their planes over almost every day, and drop orders for beef.

'The Japs left us alone for a while, though now and again a reconnaissance plane would fly over for a "look-see".'

She and her father used to guide and direct units on manoeuvres through the country they knew so well. Because of this, they were granted official free passes to travel anywhere between Katherine and Darwin (most civilians were not allowed north of Larrimah).

Darwin was bombed many times during the months that followed, as were areas as far south as Katherine. Along the same parallel, in Western Australia, Wyndham, Port Hedland and Broome were bombed. In between these last two towns is the old property Wallal Downs, an isolated 304 000 hectare sheep station owned by Harley Lacey and his wife Gray.

On 21 February, 63 women and 60 children were evacuated from Broome on the coastal steamer *Koolinda*: just in time. The stream of refugees from islands the Japanese had over-run was increasing; civilian and Dutch Air Force planes were bringing the last of the escapees into the small town. It is estimated that upwards of 8000 refugees from Java, the Dutch East Indies and other islands passed through Broome, the little pearling town where 450 Europeans and approximately 1000 Asians had been involved with luggers and pearl diving. Because there were fewer than 200 houses in this outpost, passengers on the 16 flying-boats waiting to continue their flight south were eating and sleeping on the craft on the lovely, opalescent waters of Roebuck Bay.

On 3 March the enemy struck and machine-gunned the moored flying-boats until all were destroyed. The women and children who escaped death or mortal wounds in the boats leapt into the water, but some were killed by the bullets ripping across the bay as they attempted to reach safety.

The official figure was given as 70 dead and about 30 wounded. All aircraft on the water were destroyed, as were eight on land.

Mrs Harley Lacy and her family on Wallal Downs had been ordered to head off across the desert to the south, should Broome be attacked. When the feared-for event happened, however, the third of the big 'blows' (cyclones) for that year had left the route a quagmire. The long letters she wrote at this time give an unparalleled picture of life in the outback.

Every tree was down, but the cables tying the roofs had held. The wireless mast bent in two and they had '28 inches of rain in six weeks ... 29 windmills are out of action ... the hospital staff and doctor have gone to Marble Bar, and the wireless station is moving there soon. There's not a woman left in Hedland and no bread in the town and no staffs in the hotels, just the manager ...

'Harley started to urge me to pack up. We'd got the drums of stores out, so I packed a personal drum, with stores of all sorts, the kids' special foods, change of clothes for the family, medicines, books, toys, etc. Then Broome was bombed and Harley got me to promise to pack all my own things ... next morning two strange but warlike planes came together, circled round the house, then one went in the direction of Broome and one went into the sea. Harley left me reporting this to Hedland, and went down to investigate, but came pelting back and said, "Get Annabel, get the cases into the car, there's a huge seaplane landed and a boatload of men almost to shore".

'He took over the [pedal] wireless, and we got the things in ... a boy reported men coming over the plain, so off we went. Harley got off at the stockyards and said he'd wait and see, and to go two miles then he'd put one smoke up if wrong, two if right ... we waited for what seemed ages before we saw the smokes.

'When we got home, it was after ten ... At 11 the mob of women and children, crew etc. arrived, 19 altogether. There were seven women and five children. They'd left Java the night before, and had run out of petrol. They thought it was a RAAF station. Three came. The other one we saw went back to Anna Plains, and landed there, but they couldn't get any petrol, so dismantled the ship and set it on fire. The other was shot down by Japanese near Beagle Bay, we heard them report it on the wireless. Natives found them ... My refugees ... were awfully nice women, all young, but helpless, used to millions of servants. The men seemed a very fine type too. They couldn't get petrol anywhere ... then at about 9 a.m. a large plane circled overhead and landed ... a Dutch transport plane with more refugees, also out of petrol. There were three women on this, one dying of cancer, with a small boy of three. One with a baby of four weeks and one other. Two could speak English. This lot made 30 in all, without us, so we gave up trying to sit at meals and had a buffet, much to Ada's relief ...

'The men hadn't had a proper sleep for some time, as they'd come straight from the fight in Java. One Group-Captain said his sixth and last plane was shot down, so he just got his wife and son and boarded the plane for Australia. It was hard to believe. The transport plane transferred the flying ship's petrol to herself and went to Hedland, taking the women and children, and brought out petrol and lovely fresh vegetables ... and lots of fancy tinned stuff ... We haven't had a truck since New Year. That afternoon she took off again with her own crew and the remaining women, and bread and eggs from me, as there was none in Hedland – next morning at 4.30 the seaplane went off ... I felt completely exhausted ...

'Mrs Spry arrived ... looking like you'd imagine the people in *The Grapes of Wrath* looked. In an ancient truck with one hard seat facing front, one back, occupied by Gran Ogilvie and Margaret, miscellaneous gear roped on behind, and a piece of calico over the frame of the hood, which waved in the breeze as they went along. Poor old thing was in floods of tears. She was going to Miningarra till they could get south to her brother Jack in Wagin. Mary said they had to get out and crank twice, before they got out of sight, and sure enough they returned at 3.30, having only gone five miles. Alec Kempton, the driver, got a new carburettor from Harley, and they left next afternoon ... Mrs Spry did up the piano in calico for me ...

'The next arrivals were the engineer from the NW and his off-sider – forerunners of the evacuees from Broome. They're still here waiting for instructions. They were making an aerodrome in Broome, but the contractor and all his men left them. Two days ago five huge transport trucks packed with men and with a tractor to pull them through bog, came through and boiled their billies here for lunch.

'The Archdeacon was with them. He was in Broome for the bombing.

It's simply remarkable the way he is always in the thick of everything. He was even on the *Lusitania* when she sank ...

'... We're leaving in the morning, I'm driving Ted's car ... and Sabre is driving the utility and trailer. We're taking an awful lot of stuff but ... Callawa will be glad of the stores ... Mrs Darlington says it will be weeks before we can get to Warrawagine, unless we're pulled over by donkeys.'

In 1942, two-thirds of the land-mass of Australia still relied for transport on camels or donkey teams as it had done for seventy years. From Callawa, she described the trip.

'We had Annabel's cot, my bridge table (for school) and sundry luggage, on the trailer, a 40-gallon drum of petrol, also a case, six tins (kerosene) of water, a 40-gallon drum packed with stores etc. A 40-gallon drum of bedding, extra tyres and tubes, a tin of kerosene, a box of tinned stores, a box of 24 bottles of Flytox, the machine and the petrol iron, on the truck. And the back seat of the V8 crammed with luggage. Mary's saddle and bridle was on board, needless to say.

'The road surface was quite good as far as the desert bore, but it was overgrown with trees to such an extent that I was driving blind a lot of the time. After the bore the ... road gets awful, great washaways and half a dozen very steep little creeks ... I stuck in the first creek. The back of the car sank to rest in the bank and had to be dug out. After that I got Sabre to dig each bank before I went in. They all seemed steep on my side and shelving on the far one, so they were easy to get out of once we got in safely. Mrs Darlington informs me I'm the first woman to drive across the desert, so I've done a bit of pioneering.

'We arrived here just at dusk and my hands were sore and blistered with pulling on the wheel through the ruts. We only meant to stay a couple of weeks on our way to Warrawagine, but ... the river is a banker again, and everyone's stuck.

'Two days after we arrived here Kit Gugeri and Leo [worked on Anna Plains] appeared ... and we heard all Kit's news. The seaplane, a Dornier, same as ours, which landed there, wasn't discovered for three days ... Kit says she never saw such poor things as they looked when they got to Anna Plains. She had 40 people there for 10 days. There were several families escaping from Broome as well. They couldn't get on for bog. Eventually they were all taken off by several planes. Stanley rushed into Broome for extra stores and was there for the first bombing of the town.

'Kit and Leo left here next morning and Mr Darlington pulled them across the river with the donkey team . . . Leo has not been seen since. He waited for the camel team to be collected at Warrawagine to pull him back, then the Blow caught him, so he'll be there for weeks.

'The Blow did a lot of damage in the Marble Bar district. The Jeffries lost everything, house and all, only one wall left standing . . . Coongan lost most of their mills and the roof off part of the house. The Sprys are stuck there on their way south, and Mrs Spry said they felt in danger of their lives. They all spent the night in the kitchen. We talk to all these places on the wireless.

'Very shortly they are having an all-day service on Marble Bar wireless, and all pedal stations have been issued with pictures of all Japanese, Dutch, American and Australian air-craft and give a code to describe them, and we have to report anything immediately. As a matter of fact we've done nothing else but report at Wallal since January.'

Forty years after they returned, Wendy James told me: 'In November 1944, John and I joined our parents and went home to Darwin to join the other four civilian families already back in town. There were acres and acres of army camps.

'Life was exciting because others were coming back and it was like a big family reunion as all the women met one another again and us kids tried to recognise the other kids . . . It made for a great closeness between our mothers. As each woman returned, they put their arms around one another.'

## CHAPTER 34

# *What Did You Do in the War, Grandma?*

On 15 August 1945 the bells had been rung all over Australia as they were being rung in Europe. We called it VE day, Victory in Europe. Germany had capitulated, Hitler had taken his own life, the doors of the extermination camps had been flung open by the Russians and Americans and revealed that the reasons we went to this war (as opposed to the sordid trade wars of the past) were indeed vindicated for all time. For the first time we knew exactly what had happened to the Jews of Europe, to the Gypsies and any others who did not fit the mould claimed to be superior to all others.

Our airmen would come home, those crews of groups such as Bomber Command, whose numbers had been so grievously decimated; we would at last see the sailors, still on every ocean of the globe, the boys who had scarcely seen home since 1939.

The following month, on 3 September, the bells rang out once more but with such fervour this time that even in distant suburbs and in tiny country towns, the sound was joyous. Women queued with men to toll the glad tidings on every little church bell. It had ended; it was VJ day; the war the Japanese had begun had finished. The whole war was done with; the living would come home, the lights would go on again all over the world.

The time had come for the women's services, along with the men's, to take their discharge – with one important difference: Controllers of the women's services had been told as early as June 1944 'that as the war was de-escalating', their members should be given discharges, on request, in areas where their work was not absolutely essential. So that they would not be occupying a place that could be filled by a man. 'All wives of returning POWs should be given discharge and fiancée's leave.'

By mid-1945 women were being discharged at a rate of 150 a day and this soon rose to 190 a day. Discharge orders were as follows: X-ray, medical board, civilian forms to be issued – identity card, food ration card, clothing coupons, etc.; then we must hand in equipment and clothing. Over the counter went the tin hat, gas mask, the ugly groundsheet/cape and the khaki uniform. Lastly we were told what leave and pay were due to us.

Standing there in the – to us – foreign army headquarters in the city, over-dressed in the new civvies we had splurged our deferred pay on, we suddenly realised the clerk had moved from us to someone else and we were alone. There were no farewells.

There was no one any longer to tell us what to do, where to go, what time to return, how to behave, when to put the lights out. There was no one to tell us to get our truck out of the way; to scream down to Brisbane with our ambulance because a hospital ship was due in. No tent-mate would comfort you when you cried at night for the young boy whose foot was amputated that day; no one would discuss the vagaries of W/T or the art of recognising someone 300 kilometres away by the way they used their Morse key. Now there was no one to whinge to (a slightly different meaning in the services – more a sort of disgruntled discussion with your peers), no place where we knew we would find others of our kind.

Tottering out on your new-bought high-heeled shoes (the first you'd worn for four years), as bewildered as when you entered all those long young years before, you are confronted by a line of fresh-faced, new, young, laughing soldier recruits marching by. Thinking that you, in your civvies, have come to enlist, they shout in chorus 'You'll be sorry!' – the old army cry to the novice. You don't reply, you just totter on down to the tram and places and people and a life you have not known since you left school so long ago and a whole world away.

There were women who had worked long hours in factories, on farms and in a hundred and more jobs that had not been available to women before this war. Never before had Australia's women been so emancipated from the tyranny of the home, family and conventional society. What would they tell their children and their grandchildren when asked, 'What did you do in the war, Mummy?' Did belonging to the armed services make a difference to the future lives of women, change them, or change the way life had treated them prior to the war?

On the surface, the answers are inconclusive. In the RAAF magazine *Wings* dated 22 June 1943, when the war was still unwon but the danger to Australia had receded, there is an article about rehabilitation of WAAAFs by S/O Betty Rapke.

'With the men who are being discharged, there are two great factors.

The rehab. officer tries to get them placed in jobs that will be for life, and will suit any medical disability they may have. Neither of these points affect WAAAF so much, for most girls marry and few are discharged for medical reasons.'

By this, we would believe the years of service had altered little women's personal lives. It should be noted that this service, the WAAAF, gave women every opportunity to emancipate themselves. Even the rehab. officer, Betty Rapke, could not have been better chosen. Before the war, she had been in the Women's Army Training Corps and secretary of the Girls' Employment Movement. Her father was a JP, her mother a social worker and her brother a solicitor.

An indication that their years of life in the AWAS may have had little effect on them as women of their times, is given in the figures for reconstruction and rehabilitation classes when one girl did wool classing, one electric motor mechanics, 32 cooking, 28 shorthand and 19 typing. Overall, very few women showed any interest in the re-establishment proposals offered. Kathleen Deasey said, 'About 75 per cent of servicewomen gave the reason that they intended to marry. This apathy regarding training was probably due to the security given by the service. Our of one draft of 1500 women being discharged, only 135 desired full-time training. Of this 1500 women, 40 per cent had enlisted under the age of 21; 431 said they needed jobs; 130 had jobs kept open for them.

'Readjustment will not be easy in the demobilisation period,' she warned. 'Everyone will be trying for jobs and there will still be a sense of loneliness.' She believed that many women were unaware that 'courses taken up in the army for post-war employment are not as valuable as outside courses as these have a higher status than army ones.'

Sybil Irving and her AWAS assistant controllers were concerned. 'The situation is serious, as many girls enlisted straight from school and have no training; stenographers will have lost their speed; juniors will have become seniors and employers will not be willing to take them unless they are efficient.'

The following gives an indication of some of the pressures being brought to bear on girls who had been away from the 'real' world for several years. When the war was drawing to a close the servicewomen were bombarded with advice on the *one* career they were now expected to follow. The League of Soldiers' Friends (Church of England) in conjunction with the Fellowship of Marriage of the Mothers' Union, prepared a brochure on 'Spiritual Parenthood'.

'Is it right to bring children into the world at this time? To begin with, there is all the nervous tension of a war-devastated world, which brings its accumulation of strain on the mother. Her husband perhaps is just back from the war, and trying with difficulty to fit himself into the old niches; there are the cramped housing conditions and threat of strikes – all make her fear the added burden of child-bearing.

'But whatever may be these superficial fears and dreads there is nothing that completes the home like the wee babe's cot or the toddler clinging round one's knees.'

The Australian Army Chaplains' Department issued pamphlets to the girls.

'The vocation of the majority of young women is that of the HOME BUILDER and their share in the spreading of God's Kingdom.

'The girl of today is the BRIDE, the WIFE and the MOTHER of tomorrow. She may type for 2, 3, 4 years, but children and work in the home is her LIFE'S WORK.

'The crux of the question is this: who will come forward tomorrow to build up what has been destroyed and heal this war-torn world? Who but your son and mine?'

Posters based on the 1930 Papal Encyclical about 'Christian Marriage' were sent to the girls with accompanying texts. And so the tracts and pamphlets continued, extolling the delights of 'your wee Jennifer or John', concluding with: 'If we lack noble mothers we lack the first element of racial success and national greatness. Suffering and sorrow are but fires that try the gold of motherhood. We must give our life to our sons and dedicate them to God's purpose.'

After her AWAS officers had been discharged, Sybil Irving wrote to each of them, thanked them for their service to their country and their loyalty to her, their leader, and asked after their welfare and what they were doing in the post-war world. She was, as always, anxious to keep the spirit of comradeship and service alive.

After two to three years in the army, the answers given by the girls were varied. In many cases, surprisingly enough, it seemed the army years had not changed a woman's expectations or accustomed role one jot – a thing that would have pleased their Colonel, who had refused permission for her girls to fire anti-aircraft guns. 'They will be the future mothers of Australia and one would not wish them to have the spilling of the blood of other mothers' sons on their hands,' she told me.

The return to civilian life and the loss of the great companionship they had known for the first four years of their adult lives affected a great number of discharged servicewomen. 'A period of idleness is really essential on discharge, for it affords the gradual mental adjustment to civilian identity. I hope when I return to Sydney, to have an opportunity to engage in some type of voluntary work among ex-servicewomen or others, and so turn to good account some of the things I learnt.' Others said: 'I get so bored with being an isolated civilian after the army life and friends'; and 'The only thing I do miss acutely is the companionship of the other girls . . . I am still at the stage of not knowing what to do with myself. I think there are a good many others passing through that stage . . .'

Lois Schultz, writing to Sybil Irving in 1946, says of Darley Training Camp: 'It was always such a thrill to me to see the new recruits arrive in, looking such an odd and often untidy mixture and then, at the end of the course, watch them march out looking so alert and trim. To me it was a good indication of what army life was to mean to them.'

One girl made a telling comment about men: 'Sometimes I think the future looks very murky, but surely if the girls are prepared to pull their weight as they have been through the war years (and the men are prepared to let them!), we should achieve something out of the horrible mess.'

A few of the girls were obviously going to make full use of the freedom they had worked for. From Cairns, an ex-officer wrote that she and another ex-AWAS had 'sunk our deferred pay in a new venture: a boat named *Voyager*. Fishing, trochus and pearling expeditions.' Another, in South Australia, told of 'an orange grove of 750 trees, 2½ acres of vines, 90 fruit trees and 1000 chickens', which she and her husband owned.

Lucy McGlover of Perth was managing to place ex-servicewomen in jobs. 'Some come to me for help, others just to talk about their little problems as they used to do when I was in the service.' Another had moved beyond Australia's shores. 'You asked me to let you know my final rehabilitation. I have been appointed by the Retail Traders' Association of New Zealand to organise training for retail staff throughout the two islands. It is a new venture for New Zealand and should be very interesting.'

Letters from every state told of plans for running various businesses, although there were difficulties sometimes with obtaining loans. 'Poultry farming with another girl was what I planned for the future, but we have met so many obstacles and were unable to get any assistance from the army by way of a loan. We are now trying to do business through a private bank.' Others were pre-occupied with more domestic interests. 'The AWAS life taught me to be very hygiene conscious. Dirty corners and drains are now my natural enemies – you should see me go to work on our kitchen sink!'

Many of the married women in the services had waited anxiously for the return of a husband or son from the battlefields or prisoner of war camp. 'My husband arrived home in excellent health and spirits and does not seem to be affected in any way by his terrible experiences in Changi and on the Burma–Thailand Railway. We have a dear little house and garden and later this year are having a baby! So all my fears and anxieties of the war years are being made up for a hundred-fold. I only wish it could be so for the hundreds of girls who gave up their husbands for their country.'

'I was married quietly and my husband is due back in Malaya on duty in May. I tell my husband that my army experience has made me a good campaigner and capable of adapting to any conditions.'

'My husband and I have both settled down happily in civilian life and Ray is almost his old self again, except that ... he hasn't yet regained the few stone he lost in New Guinea. There will be an addition to our household in the end of August.'

'It was a very strange feeling to be leaving the Service after so many happy associations. John is just out of the army after six years service and we have come up to Rockhampton and he is in his element back again with horses and cattle. The only drawback is we cannot get a house. The housing position here is even more acute than in the larger cities ... I'm busily making small garments and we are both gloriously happy at the thought of having a baby of our own.'

'I am hoping Robert will be a civilian by the time of the arrival of our baby. With the early end of the war we will now be able to put the foundations under the plans which up to this time have only been our dreams.'

'I am excited at present because my fiancé, who was in a German prison camp for four years, is now in England and we expect him home before long.'

The following letter from an NCO is simple and from the heart: 'Dear Madam, Pardon the liberty I am taking in writing this letter to you. I did wish to say thank you and goodbye before I leave the AWAS. My duty has given me the pleasure of meeting you, your cheerful attitude, understanding and little acts of kindness believe me has lightened the burden of my work and suspense in waiting for news of my boys. I know you will be pleased to know both are safe. Ted will be discharged any time now and Len, who has been a prisoner, I hope to have home soon. He is now in hospital in India. It is with a feeling of regret that the time will soon come for us in the service to go our separate ways. Goodbye and God bless you, guard you and make you happy. Very, very sincerely, D. Hoyling.'

Wives and mothers of men who served in World War I always said, 'No man returned unmarked from that war.' But that can be said for all wars. 'My job in PWA [Prisoner of War Association] continues to be full of interest, although at times terribly sad. Some of our ex-servicewomen have a difficult future ahead, particularly those young lasses who are married to POWs.'

And letter after letter from former AWAS referred to the leader of the service in terms of deep pride of having served under her. In this, the women were the equal of the men who for two wars had been loyal to the depths of their hearts to that person holding authority over their well-being and safety. 'That honour to work under your leadership is what we appreciated – what you did for us, improving conditions and regulations and always keeping a personal interest with those you came in contact with.

'The standards set by you, madam, I am sure, will be reflected upon all who had the honour to serve in your Service. I shall endeavour to maintain in civilian life the high standards and ideals which you have always set.'

'At all times I was proud to wear the uniform of the AWAS. I feel without your guidance, and confidence at all times, I could never have carried out my duties.'

'Any help I gave was a pleasure and I hope that if the necessity arises again I shall be able to lend a shoulder to the wheel.'

Edna Gale and Pat Oram, who met while serving in the AWAS, teamed up again after the war. The *Bairnsdale Advertiser* of 25 January 1951, gave them front page headlines: 'Two Ex-AWAS Transport Drivers – leave on truck journey around Australia with their Queensland heeler "Dilly". Miss Gale has been a member of the staff of Bairnsdale Post Office, Miss Oram a Sister in the Bairnsdale District Hospital. The two were stationed in northern Queensland during the war where they had much practical experience in truck driving and carrying out general repairs on army vehicles. They have prepared their own truck for the journey, and built a comfortable cabin on it to cope with all kinds of weather. Their mechanical knowledge covers motor bikes as well as trucks and if all kinds of motor transport were to fail, then they can both ride horses. They are also skilled in the use of firearms.'

All remembered the arduous years the leaders of the services had spent during the war. 'May I wish you a long and pleasant rest shortly from the ... heavy responsibilities you have borne since the AWAS was formed.' But the comment which best summed up the firmly held belief of all who served under Sybil Irving was written by Betty M. Jess in September 1946: 'You were Captain of a great team, Madam. I'm honoured to have been a player.'

These letters were as varied as the women themselves. How could it have been otherwise? In this largest social experiment with women to have been carried out in Australia every class, type and variety of young woman in the land was represented. It is the fact that they were *young* women that makes the statistics appear to show little change in outlook or behaviour from that of girls before the war. There is a preponderance of talk of marriage, settling down, having babies and domesticity. And why not? Their men had come home, some after an absence of six years.

One might have expected talk of emancipation from women who had done more to prove the equality of the sexes than any before or after them. But one must remember that war is but an aberration, it is not seen as life by those swept along by it. 'When the war is over,' is the cry of the serviceman and woman. 'When we get home again.' As the great wireless-telegraphist Vi McKenzie said on her death-bed, 'We showed them women are as good, or better than men.' They had broken through the barrier, but now they wanted to get on with living; they were weary from the long hard years of their effort.

What they achieved was more remarkable when one considers the era in which they grew up. Women had been 'active' for four decades before World War I. The Women's Suffrage Society was founded in 1884. The last state to give women the vote (Victoria) capitulated in 1908.

Between the two world wars a small, brave band fought for equal pay, status and opportunity for women, but there was never a more inopportune time for such a cause than in those hungry years. Brave words went unheeded amid the worst depression the land had known. If the young men who were scarred by the Depression seemed to welcome the war as a release, we girls and young women were in no way different from them. We too had heard the bugles in the valleys and the trumpets on the hills and recognised reveille calling us.

It had taken women a long time to taste the sweet sugar of a little freedom, but by the outbreak of World War I they had made more progress in the preceding two generations than they were to do for another twenty-five years. The miserly hand of the Depression quashed every hope of advancement for all but the favoured few.

The women who had been tried by fire in Depression and war would step forward after World War II and work for, and demand, opportunities for daughters, as well as sons.

When asked, 'What did you do in the war?' they can truly say, 'I served.'

# *Appendixes*

## *Appendix I*
## *Classifications: Women's Services*

**AWAS**
These classifications included:
Draughtswoman; mechanic (telecommunications anti-aircraft, coast artillery and fixed defences): laboratory assistant; photographer; photowriter; wireless telegraph operator; senior cook.

Adding machine operator; accounting machine operator; camouflage modeller; clerk Grade II; comptometrist; cook; fabric worker; hairdresser; instrument operator in coast artillery and anti-aircraft (including fire control, height taker, plotting room number, predictor number, telescope number, height computer, plotter); optical mechanic; seamstress; signaller (coast artillery); signal woman (personnel performing the duties of male personnel grouped as operators – signals, wireless, line and switchboard); stenographer; store-keeper Grade II; tailoress; transport and motor driver.

Canteen attendant; clerical assistant Grade I; despatch rider; equipment repairer; film examiner; rangetaker (coast artillery); store-keeper Grade I; store assistant; telephonist; teleprinter operator; textile refitter; typist.

Messwoman; office orderly; salvage worker; stewardess; waitress.

**VAD/AAMWS classifications:**
Dental mechanic; dispenser; laboratory assistant; radiographer; senior cook; telephonist (monitress); clerk; cook; operating theatre assistant; optical mechanic; seamstress; stenographer; store-keeper; tailoress; clerical assistant; dental clerk; dental orderly; nursing orderly; refrigerator operator or sick quarters attendant; store-keeper Grade I; store assistant; typist; telephonist; kitchen hand; messwoman; office orderly; waitress, ward orderly.

## WAAAF

War Cabinet approved the following musterings open to WAAAF:
Telegraphist; cook's assistant; cook; fabric worker; dental orderly; meteorological assistant; photographer; cipher assistant; fabric worker's assistant; clerk (general); signals; armament assistant; armourer; shoemaker; electrician; wireless assistant; hygiene inspector; fitter; wireless maintenance mechanic; radar mechanic; clerk; storekeeper; stores' clerk; tailor; office orderly; draughtsman; instrument repairer; caterer; postal clerk; canteen steward; librarian; aircraft hand; trainee technician; cinema operator; flight mechanic; laboratory assistant; recorder; instrument maker; accounts assistant; education assistant; steward; teleprinter operator; pay clerk; sick quarters attendant; telephone operator; X-ray technician; radar operator; nursing orderly; equipment assistant; tracer; radio telephone operator; postal assistant; anti-gas instructor; dental mechanic; flight rigger; assistant medical orderly; hairdresser; medical clerk; medical assistant; linguist.

## WRANS

Classifications for the WRANS are harder to define. Because of little interest, bordering on disdain, with which senior officers of the RAN at first treated the suggestion of women serving, these musterings just grew with the service.

In the WRANS women worked as telegraphists; coders; writers (typists and clerks); transport drivers; car drivers; office orderlies; dental mechanics; cooks; sickberth attendants; stewardesses; press relations officer (which included escorting the press to sea on trials); boarding officer; almoners; dome teacher operators (visual aids used for instruction and entertainment); education officers; vocational guidance; sea transport officers; air liaison officer (moving RAN officers and ratings to all parts of the globe).

There were harbour messengers; an accountant officer; supply assistants; medical, clothing and general stores; postmaster; postal clerk (including delivering mail to ships in port and on anchor); watch keepers.

There were WRANS working as Translation Interpreters in the Allied Translation Section of General MacArthur's main 'Order of Battle'; some worked on the degaussing range (assessing the magnetic attraction of vessels as they crossed the degaussing range); they worked in ciphers; visual signalling; signals and communications; radio telegraphy plotting; and as messengers. Others were with Radar Counter-measure and Allied Intelligence Bureau.

They were at the Gunnery School, small arms range; and one handled all Safe Hand Mail for the busy port of Sydney, while yet another corrected and issued charts (to both merchant and naval ships' masters), and one was Assistant to the Staff Officer (Operations) Brisbane and another to the Director of Victualling.

Many WRANS were engaged on technical duties of a secret nature, working long hours under exacting conditions. For many, this meant absolute silence about their work, even after demobilisation, while the end of the war meant that others were released from secrecy. While the most senior men were adamant that WRANS would not work as mechanics, they did indeed work in ordnance artificers' workshops.

Several women wore WRANS uniform merely for convenience or safety against the event of their being discovered and, as a civilian, being treated as a spy. One such was the coast-watcher, Mrs Boye of Vanikoro Island.

## *Appendix II*
## *Enlistment Figures for Women 1939–45*

| | | | |
|---|---|---|---|
| AANS | 3 477 | WAAAF | 26 704 |
| VAD/AAMWS | 8 485 | RAAFNS | 616 |
| AWAS | 24 082 | Physiotherapists | 150 |
| WRANS | 3 122 | Australian Land Army | 3 068 |
| RANNS | 82 | | |
| | | *Total* | 69 786 |

## *Appendix III*
## *Number of Civilian Personnel in War Work*

When the Japanese entered the war on 7 December 1941, there were 554 000 Australian men and boys and 74 000 women and girls involved in direct war work (out of a population of 6 700 700).

By March 1943, these figures had increased to 1 172 000 men and

184 000 women. Of that number of women 40 260 were in the Defence Forces, 38 200 were in munitions, ship-building and aircraft works and 106 000 in defence works.

The number of women working in factories making goods for civil use fell from 128 000 in 1941 to 82 000 in 1942 as women moved out of the traditional 'unskilled' work to 'war' work, and the numbers of women in rural work went up from 25 000 to 55 000.

(From a population of roughly 6 7000 000 there were in 1943 3 341 000 people employed in both civilian and war work.)

# Bibliography

## Books

Baume, Mollie (ed.). *Australian Women at War*. Introduction by Kathleen Fitzpatrick. Research Group of the Left Book Club, Melbourne, 1943.

Bettison, Margaret and Summers, Anne. *Her Story: Australian Women in Print 1788–1975*. Hale & Iremonger, Sydney, 1980.

Blocksedge, William. *Australia's Dead*. Gordon & Gotch, Brisbane, 1919.

Burke, Eric Keast (ed.). 'The Australian Nurses in India', in *With Horse and Morse in Mesopotamia: the Story of Anzacs in Asia*. Arthur McQuitty & Co., 1927.

Butler, A. G. (ed.). *The Australian Army Medical Services in the War of 1914–1918*. Australian War Memorial, Canberra, 1930–1943.

Curtis, M. et al. *WRANS*. The Naval Historical Society of Australia, NSW, 1975.

Curtis-Otter, M. *WRANS: the Women's Royal Australian Naval Service*. Naval Historical Society of Australia, Garden Island, NSW, 1975.

Devanny, Jean. *Bird of Paradise*. Frank Johnson, Sydney, 1945.

Dunant, J. Henry. *A Memory of Solferino*. Cassell (for the British Red Cross Society), London, 1947.

Fitzgerald, Robert D. *Australian Poetry 1942*. Angus & Robertson, Sydney, 1942.

Giel, Hermon, G. *RAN 1939–42*. Australian War Memorial, Canberra, 1957.

——. *RAN 1942–45*. Australian War Memorial, Canberra, 1968.

Harris, Joe. *The Bitter Fight*. Queensland University Press, St Lucia, 1970.

Hasluck, Paul. *The Government and the People 1939–41*. Australian War Memorial, Canberra, 1952.

Jauncey, L. C. *The Story of Conscription in Australia*. OUP, London, 1938.

Kingston, Beverley. *My Wife, My Daughter and Poor Mary Ann*. Nelson, Melbourne, 1975.

Long, Gavin, *Greece, Crete and Syria*. Australian War Memorial, Canberra, 1953.

Mellor, D. P. 'Ammunition and Explosives', chapter 16 from *The Role of Science and Industry*. Australian War Memorial, Canberra, 1958.

Mills, Frederick, J. *Cheer Up: A Story of War Work*. Body of Management of the Cheer Up Society Inc., Adelaide, 1920.

Moberly, Gertrude, F., RRC. *Experiences of a 'Dinki Di' RRC Nurse*. Australian Medical Publishing Co. Ltd, Glebe, NSW, 1933.

Monie, Joanna. *Victorian History and Politics, European Settlement to 1939. A Survey of the Literature*. Vol. 21. Borchard Library, La Trobe University, Bundoora, 1982.

*Official History of Australia in the War of 1914–1918*. Vols. III–XI.

*Official History of the Australian Army Medical Services, 1914–1918*. Vol. III.

Robertson, E. M. *WAAAF at War: Life and Work in the Women's Auxiliary Australian Air Force*. Mullaya, Canterbury, 1974.

Teale, Ruth (ed.). *Colonial Eve: Sources on Women in Australia 1788–1914*. OUP, Melbourne, 1978.

Walker, Allan S. *Clinical Problems of War*. Australian War Memorial, Canberra, 1952.

——. *Mid East and Far East*. Australian War Memorial, Canberra, 1953.

——. *The Island Campaigns*. Australian War Memorial, Canberra, 1953.

——. 'Australian House of Representatives Parliamentary Debate' quoted in *Medical Services of the RAN and RAF*. Australian War Memorial, Canberra, 1961.

Walker, Allan S. et al. *Medical Services of the RAN and RAAF*. Australian War Memorial, Canberra, 1961.

PARLIAMENTARY PUBLICATIONS

Senate, *Debates* 1958, vol. S, no. 10. 'Women's Services, WWII'.

*Digest of Decisions and Announcements*, no. 85, part V (the relevant section of the Economic Organisation Regulations re pegged wages at 10 Feb. 1942).

*Digest of Decisions and Announcements*, no. 91, pp. 8–9. Statutory Rules, no. 149, 12 Oct. 1944.

*Facts and Figures of Australia at War*, no. 2.

*Facts and Figures of Australia at War*, no. 3.

ITEMS FROM THE AUSTRALIAN WAR MEMORIAL LIBRARY WITH CALL NUMBERS

Provost Corps for Women. 10 February 1944, V28/8/1.

Red Cross Society Annual Report 1918–1919 (incl. VADs) 84/3.

VAD Newsheet 1943–47, 86/33.

Employment of VADs in Military Hospitals, 1025/2/3.

Medical History of the WAAAF, 1025/1/2.

Lecture on Sex Hygiene, 1025/1/48.

Morotai Muthers, 1007/2.

Salvation Army, YMCA, 1945, 195/4/1.

Salvation Army, 1943, 1007/2/1.

NSW Women War Workers, 1007/4/1.

VAD Memoranda, 1007/3/1.

Red Cross up to 1943, 1007/3.

Red Cross, 837/3/2.

Nancy Bird, Women's Air Training Corps WATC, 549/109/24.

BOOKLETS, JOURNALS AND PAMPHLETS

*Aircraft.* June, July 1941; May, December 1943.
*Australian Highway*, 'Women in Industry', vol. 2, no. 1, March 1920.
*Australian Women's Land Army News-sheet* from Victoria, Tasmania, South Australia, Queensland, New South Wales, Western Australia.
Clark, A. C. & Cook, P. H. *Personnel Practice Bulletin*, vol. 5, no. 1, March 1949.
Commins, Kathleen. 'Women Air Trainees: the Australian Women's Flying Club NSW, *Home*, vol. 22, no. 11, November 1941.
Commins, Kathleen & Short, Gordon. 'The Sydney WANS and their Training. *Home*, vol. 22, no. 10, October 1941.
Crisp, Helen. 'Women in Munitions', *Australian Quarterly*, September 1941.
*Guinea Gold*, 24 October 1945.
'A Working Day with the VAD', *Home*, vol. 22, no. 8, August 1941.
Australian Army Nursing Service. *Lest We Forget*. Melbourne, 1944. Commemorative booklet of the Service in 1939–45 war.
Minogue, Noreen. 'The Red Cross 1914–1975: Years of Change'. *Victorian Historical Journal*, vol. 47, no. 1, 1976.
Osborne, Ethel E. *Industrial Hygiene As Applied to Munition Workers*. Australiasian Medical Publishing Co., Sydney, 1921.

O'Sullivan, E. F. *Discrimination Between Males and Females in Australian Public Services*. Council for Action for Equal Pay, 1938.
*RAAF News*, January–February 1971.
'Women's Auxiliary Australian Air Force', *Royal Historical Society of Victoria Newsletter*, no. 97, June 1966.
'Are They Feminine? who, and why are the AWAS?', *Salt*, vol. 7, no. 12, 14 February 1944.
*Salt*, vol. 8, no. 2, 27 March 1944.
'WRANS on Watch', *Salt*, vol. 8, no. 5, 8 May 1944.
'Maids of All Work', *Salt*, vol. 9, 15 January 1945.
*Union Records*, 9 July 1942, Sydney.
*Victorian Historical Journal*, vol. 47, no. 1, February 1976.
*Wings*, 8 June, 22 June and 20 July 1943.

NEWSPAPER SOURCES

*Australasian*, 8 December 1900.
*Advertiser*, Adelaide.
*Argus*, Melbourne.
*Courier-Mail*, Brisbane.
*Mercury*, Hobart.
*Sydney Mail*, 20–27 January 1900.
*Sydney Morning Herald*.
*West Australian*, Perth.

PRIVATE PAPERS & RESEARCH MATERIAL

Material on WWI AANS collated by ex-AANS Beryl Trigellis-Smith, Victorian Army Nurses' Club.

Papers of the late Sybil Irving, the late Kathleen Deasey and the late Kathleen Best, all in the author's collection.

Vernon, H. M. The Health and Efficiency of Munition Workers. Thesis.

UNPUBLISHED MANUSCRIPTS

Kitchen, Alice. Diaries, 1914–19. State Library of Victoria.

# Some Abbreviations Used in Text

*Enlisted Women's Services*
- AANS — Australian Army Nursing Service
- AAMWS — Australian Army Medical Women's Service
- AWAS — Australian Women's Army Service
- VAD — Voluntary Aid Detachment (unofficially called VAs: this service later became the nucleus for the AAMWS)
- WAAAF — Women's Australian Auxiliary Air Force
- WRANS — Women's Royal Australian Naval Service

*Enlisted Men's Services*
- RAMC — Royal Army Medical Corps (British Army)
- RAN — Royal Australian Navy
- AIF — Australian Imperial Forces
- RAAF — Royal Australian Air Force
- AMF — Australian Military Forces
- RAA — Royal Australian Artillery
- VDC — Volunteer Defence Corps

*Decorations*
- ARRC — Associate Royal Red Cross
- MBE — Member of the Order of the British Empire
- FNM — Florence Nightingale Medal
- MID — Mentioned in Despatches
- MM — Military Medal
- RRC — Royal Red Cross
- GM — George Medal

*General Service Terms*
- WWI — World War One
- WWII — World War Two
- W/T — Wireless Telegraphy
- AWL — Absent without leave (AWOL is the American equivalent)
- OIC — Officer-in-Charge
- 2 IC — Second-in-Charge
- POW — Prisoner of War
- OR — Other Ranks
- MP — Military Police
- NCO — Non-Commissioned Officer

| | |
|---|---|
| WO | Warrant Officer |
| Lt-Col | Lieutenant-Colonel (immediately below a full colonel) |
| GOC | General Officer in Command |
| AAGWS | Assistant Adjutant-General Women's Services (Lieutenant-Colonel K.A.L. Best) |

*Medical*

| | |
|---|---|
| AGH | Australian General Hospital |
| CCS | Casualty Clearing Station |
| RAP | Regimental Aid Post |
| MI | Medical Inspection |
| PT | Physical Training |

*RAAF and WAAAF Terms (not used by other Services)*

| | |
|---|---|
| F/Lt | Flight Lieutenant |
| D/WAAAF | Director, WAAAF (Miss Clare Stevenson) |
| Rookies | Newly enlisted |
| MAETU | Medical Air Evacuation Transport Unit |
| MRS | Medical Receiving Station |
| ACW | Aircraftswoman |

*WRANS*

Most naval terms are described in the text. CPO (Chief Petty Officer) being the term non-naval people most confuse.

| | |
|---|---|
| SBA | Sick Berth Attendant |
| Jaunties | Naval Police |

In naval parlance one does not get demobilised at the end of a war. A naval person is P/T (Put Away).

*General*

| | |
|---|---|
| AAMC | Australian Army Medical Corps |
| DDMS | Deputy Director Medical Services |
| MO | Medical Officer |
| NOK | Next of Kin |
| Abluts | Ablutions Blocks |

Service hours run from one minute to midnight – 2359 hours – onwards, i.e. 0945 = a quarter to ten a.m.; 1430 = half past two p.m.

Officers' and NCOs' ranks changed during their time in the services and to attempt to list their promotions in the text would have been confusing to the reader. Because of this, ranks are omitted unless essential to the work.

Women's names are often – but not always – changed by marriage. This again is confusing to the reader; where possible, the name of the servicewoman at the time of enlistment is used.

# *Acknowledgements*

Many women and some men helped with this book. The late Sybil Irving, leader of the Australian Women's Army Service in World War II, talked to me in 1971 and encouraged me to write about the women who have participated in the various wars in which this country has been involved. Others who helped were Clare Stevenson (WAAAF), Sheila McClemans (WRANS) and Margaret Curtis-Otter (WRANS), Dorothea Skov and Elizabeth Lucas (AWAS), Sister Beryl Trigellis Smith (AANS), May Douglas (AAMWS), Joan Dowson (VAD), Jean Wood (Girl Guides), Barbara Clinton, Noreen Minogue (Red Cross) and the various ex-servicewomen's associations.

On the production side of the work, Sue Ebury advised and encouraged me; Jenny Carew, as always, helped with much of the research and Ann Pheloung assisted me in Western Australia. Sandra Zarbo typed the manuscript – often. Barbara James, Darwin (NT) generously gave me her original research, oral history and writings on the Territory during World War II. The librarians and picture librarians of the following libraries assisted me generously: the Mitchell Library, Sydney; the La Trobe Library, Victoria; the John Oxley Library, Queensland; the State Archives of South Australia; the Battye Library, Perth, Western Australia; and the State Archives of Tasmania. Ken Thornett and Kym Faehse gave generous assistance.

The Australian Army Nurses' Club, Melbourne, assisted me most graciously and finally I thank the Moreton Club, Brisbane, for the hospitality given me and ex-servicewomen who met with me there to discuss the contents of this book. Without the help of all these people my work would have been much more arduous than it was and the years would not have sped by so swiftly.

# Index

AAMC  *see* Australian Army Medical Corps
No. 2 AAMC training battalion  120
AAMSW  *see* Australian Army Medical Women's Service
AAMWS Nursing Orderlies Training School  120
AANS  *see* Australian Army Nursing Service
abortion  95–6, 210–11, 214
ACTU, and equal pay  239
*Adamant*, HMS  171
Adam-Smith, Isabella  65
Adam-Smith, Patsy  96–7, 139
Adams, Brigid  65–6
Adams, Sheila  139
Adelaide River  145, 261
*Agamemnon*  21
aircraft production  247–8
air-raid shelters  252
Alice Springs  145, 263, 264
Allied Intelligence Bureau  163
Amboina  108
Anderson, Sister M., GM  119
Anna Plains  265, 267
Anzac Day March  124
Appleford, Major Alys, MM  141–2
*Aquitania*  124
*Ark Royal*, HMS  104
Armistice Day  60, 90

army numbers  205
*Australia*, HMAS  153
Australia, operational areas  119
Australian Army Chaplains' Dept  272
Australian Army Medical Corps  9, 11, 19, 25, 120, 144, 151, 155
Australian Army Nursing Service  2, 18, 19–35, 118–24
 first nurses, WWI  20–35
 in Greece  26, 118
 in Middle East  21–4, 118
 Malaya  118
 New Guinea  120, 145
 prisoners of war  119
 rank  120–1
 Singapore  119
 Tobruk  121
 *see also* Conyers, Matron Evelyn
Australian Army Medical Women's Service (VADs)  139–49
 AAMS auxiliary  140
 civilian members  146
 duties  142
 fundraising  146
 in New Guinea  144, 145, 147
 overseas service  140
 postings  145
 to Middle East  140
 training  143

uniform  143–4
VADs 'If'  149
Australian Comforts Fund  41–7, 64, 253–4
  state divisions  41
  fundraising  44–5
  see also charitable organisations
No. 1 Australian Orthopaedic Unit  143
1st Australian Signals Training Battalion (AWAS)  202
2nd Australian Signals Training Battalion (AWAS)  203
Australian Women's Army Service  1, 115, 144, 186–201, 271, 272–6
  and Girl Guides  186, 188, 191, 192
  as drivers  115–16, 193, 198
  duties  198, 200
  first officers  144, 189
  in New Guinea  198, 200, 201, 224
  opposition  195–6
  postings  198
  recruiting  115, 188, 190, 197
  regulations  196, 197
  training course  196
  uniforms  189, 192, 195, 197
Australian Women's Land Army  4, 226–31
  accommodation  227, 229
  attitudes to  227
  AWLA Auxiliary  227, 228
  camps, hostels  229–30
  peak enrolment  228
  recruitment  227
  shock troops  229
  uniform  228

wages  228, 230
Australian Women's National League  74–5, 81, 82–3, 88
Australian Women's Service Corps  46–7
Avery, Betsy  166
AWAS  see Australian Women's Army Service

Baker, Stella  49, 54
Bardia  101, 253
Bassingthwaighte, Beverley  115
Batavia  148, 169
2/22nd Battalion, on Rabaul  106
Bayer, Lou  84–5
Beagle Bay  226
Beale, Howard  158
Beattie, 3rd Officer Sue  162
Beaufort Bombers  247, 248
Bell, Matron Jane, RRC  24–5
*Benalla*  21
Bender, ACW  180
Benghazi  101
Best, Lt-Col. Kathleen, RRC  119, 144
Bicknell, Sister Louise  28
Bidmead, Sister  10, 11
billeting  252
biochemists  155
Bird, Frederick  21
Blake, ACW Imelda  183
Blamey, Gen. Sir Thomas  117, 197
*Bloemfontein*  2, 8, 9–10, 12–15
blood and serum units  150–4, 244
  transport  152, 153–4

Boer War  2, 7–17
  Australian troops  7, 10
  and disease  9, 12–15
  official records  10–11, 12, 15, 16–17
  sanitary problems  14–15, 16–17
  see also nurses, Boer War
Bombay  148, 149
Borneo  145
Bougainville  145
Boxall, Cpl Georgette  198–9
Boye, Olive BEM  163
  see also Coastwatching Service
Bradley, Mrs Kath  253
bride ships  84–6
Brisbane  252
Brittain, Vera  140, 147
Broome  264–5, 266
  bombed  264
  casualties  265
  evacuated  264–5
Brown, Lt-Col. M. A. Groover  175, 223, 224
Buick, Margaret  139, 173, 178
Buick, Victoria  139, 173
Bull, Sgt  180, 181, 182
Buna  145
Burma–Thailand Railway  274
Butler, C. A.  158
Byrne, Maj. Lorna  190, 198

Cadd, Gwen  233
Cairns  162
Callawa  267
camouflage nets  256
Campbell, Alison McArthur  122–3

Carey, Charlie  127
Cassidy, Sister A. E.  31
casualties  22–4, 26–7, 83, 90, 103, 108, 125, 265
Cavite  169
*Cecilia* (hospital ship)  21
*Centaur*, sinking of  120, 125–30
  rescue  129
  survivors  127–9
*Cerberus*, HMAS  170
Ceylon  118
Changi  274
charitable organisations  36–40, 48–62, 63, 70–1
Chatterton, Cpl  182, 183
Cheer-Up Our Boys Society  48–62
  Cheer-Up Hut  55–60, 61
  Cheer-Ups' Tent  52
  fundraising  52, 57, 58
  slander  56–7
  uniforms  52
Cheney, Second Officer Muriel  162
Chirnside, Audrey  20
Citizens' War Chest Fund  41–6
  comforts  41, 42, 43, 45, 46
  recruiting  43
  sock department  42, 43–4
Clinton, Barbara  195, 237
Coastwatching Service  163–5
  Olive Boye  163
Cockrane, Alex  126
Coleman, Oliver  86
*Commissaire Rainel*  253
Commonwealth Serum Laboratories  150, 151
conscription  3, 73–8, 79–80

anti-conscriptionists 77, 80
referenda 73, 76–8
Conyers, Matron Evelyn 25–6
  appointed first matron-in-
    chief 25
Coomalie Creek 134
*Coonawarra*, HMAS 169
Country Women's
  Association 256–7, 258
Cox, 2nd Officer Josephine 162
Craig, Sister Marie E. 143–5
Crete (evacuation WWII)
  103–04
Crighton, Lily 84–5
Crisp, Helen 244–5
Curedale, ACW 183
Curtin, John 108, 114, 125,
  126, 174, 249
Curtis-Otter, Margaret 160–1,
  162, 175


Daly Waters 133
D'Ambrosio, Ted 262
Darley Training Camp 144, 273
Darwin 250, 252, 261
  bombed 107, 120, 264
  casualties 108
  evacuation 262–4
Davis, Matron Gertrude RRC 29
Davis, Vi 185
Deakin, Vera 38
Deasey, Maj. Kathleen 190, 192,
  271
death, notification of 65
degaussing 162
Dell, Betty 185
D'Emden, Gwen 184
Denholm, Fred 253

Denholm, Mrs F. 253
Depression 2, 91–6
dietitians 155
6th Division 99
7th Division 99
8th Division 108
9th Division 99, 222, 259
Dodwell, Capt. J. F. 158
Doig, Dr and family 87–9
domestic work 113–14
Douglas, Grace MID 26, 28
Douglas, Lt-Col. May 144, 192,
  193
Dowson, Joan *see* Richardson,
  Joan
Drew, Vice-Admiral T. B.
  170
Dudley, Lady 20–1
  field hospital, Wimeraux 20
Dunant, Jean Henri 36
Dunkirk 100


*Echo* 165
Eddy, Nancy 262
egalitarianism 253
Egypt 7, 25, 118
Ekert, P/O Eva 163
El Alamein 119
Elmore, Mrs W. A. 253
Elmore, Private MM 253
*Elora* (hospital ship) 31
*Empire Star* 119
employment, women 239, 240,
  245, 247
  discrimination 245–6
enlistment of women 111, 112,
  113, 114
  and ACTU 113

rates of pay  112
enteric fever  12–15
Eritrea  118
*Euryalus*  10
Ewarth, Bill  248, 258

Farrow, Lt-Col. T. J.  203
Fields, Gracie  100, 201
Finlay, Matron Mary McKenzie RRC  27–8
Finney, Ellis  108–9, 123–4
  see also physiotherapists
Finschhafen  145
Fitzpatrick, Kathleen  245–6
'fleatraps'  258–9
Flinders Naval Depot  159, 166
Forde, Hon. F. M.  111, 115, 116, 196, 256
*Formidable*, HMS  146, 147
Fortune, Dr C. (AAMC)  150, 153
Fremantle  153
fundraising  4, 44–5, 52, 57, 58, 63, 82–3, 233, 255
Furley, Leading Telegraphist Joan  162

Gale, Pat  276
Gallipoli  21–4, 26–7, 28, 29
  casualties  26–7
  Mudros  21, 29
Gapper, ACW  181, 183
Garden, Nurse Effie MID, ARRC, FNM  142
*Gascon* (hospital ship)  21, 22, 23
Gibson, Sister Elsie  21

Gilmore, Mary  107, 108
Girl Guides' Association  186, 188, 191, 192, 243, 255
Glenie, Sister  10, 11
Glover, Hannah  19–20
Gold, Capt. E.  158
Goldstein, Vida  3
  see also conscription
*Gorgon*, SS  168
Gorman, Maj. Eugene  254
Gould, Lady Superintendent Ellen Julia  9
Gould, Matron E.  26
Grant, Mary  184
*Grant*, USS  262
*Grantully Castle* (hospital ship)  21
Greece (WWII)  99, 118, 119
Gregory, Capt.  263
Growse, Jocelyn  123–4
Gugeri, Kit  267

Halls Creek  145
Halsey, Admiral W. F.  165
Hansom, Sgt  182
Harris, Sister  10, 11
Hatfield, Joyce  121
Hatfield, Nancy  121
Hatfield, Ruth  121
Hazell, Writer J.  163
Heagney, Muriel  239–40
*Health and Efficiency of Munition Workers*  179
Heighway, Capt. W. D.  158
Heine, Ferdinand J.  79
*Herman*, HMAS  156, 157
Herring, Squadron Officer Audrey  216

Hill, Second Officer
  Dorothy  *162*
Hines, Sister  *10*
Hobbs, Sister Victoria  *121*
Hoggins, Trevor  *129*
Hollandia  *145*
Hornsby, Capt. Mona  *194, 195, 201*
hospital ships  *126*
  *see also* individual ships, *Centaur*
Howle, Squadron Leader  *133*
Hoyling, D.  *274–5*
Hughes, the Hon. W. M.  *156*
Humphery, Lt-Col. R. C. V.  *203, 204*
*Huon*, HMAS  *170*
Hurley, Air Vice-Marshal  *131*

*Indian* (hospital ship)  *21*
Indian Army  *148*
International Women's Relief Committee  *20*
Irving, Brigadier-Gen. G. G. H.  *186, 188*
Irving, Col. Sybil (AWAS)  *1, 172, 186–8, 189, 190, 191, 192, 196, 197, 200, 218, 224, 252, 271, 272, 273, 276*
Irving, Freda  *196, 209*
Isaacs, Sister Nellie  *30*
Ising, Helen  *230*
Ivey, Sister  *10*


James, Barbara  *261, 264*
James, Wendy  *262, 263–4, 268*
Japan  *104–09, 145*
  attacks American fleet  *105*
  bombs Darwin and Broome  *107, 264*
  bombs Katherine  *264*
  invades Rabaul  *106*
  Port Moresby  *109*
  seizes Amboina  *106*
  war in Pacific  *106–09*
Jess, Betty M.  *276*
Jewell, Matron S. A.  *130*
Jewish refugees  *88*
Johnson, Mrs A. E.  *127*
Johnstone, Winifred  *38*


Kaarlund, Brenda  *165*
Kahan, Douska  *39–40, 150, 153*
Kahan, Harry  *39, 40, 150*
Kahan, Jean  *150–3*
Katherine  *145, 264*
Kelly, Sister, V. E.  *137*
Kelly, Toni  *viii*
Kempton, Alec  *266*
Kendrick, Senior Sister N. I.  *134*
Kennon, Audrey  *263*
King, Kathleen 'Peg'  *166–8*
King, Sister  *128*
King, Sister Alys Ross MM  *see* Appleford, Major
Kitchen, Sister Alice  *22, 23–4*
Knowles, Leah  *122*
Kokoda Trail  *124*
*Koolinda*  *264*
*Kuranda*, HMAS  *169*
*Kuttabul*, HMAS  *169*
*Kyarra* (hospital ship)  *21, 37*


Lacey, Gray  *264, 265–8*
Lacey, Harley  *264, 265*

## Index

Lachlan, P/O Messenger Bessie  170
La Delle, Capt. M.  158
Lae  145, 201
Laidlaw, Matron A. I.  136
Land Army  *see* Australian Women's Land Army
Lang, Matron-in-Chief  131
Larrakeyah Barracks  261
Larrimah  145, 264
Lawler, Leading Writer Julia  162
*Leeuwin*, HMAS  158, 166, 170
Legge, ACW  182
Leighton, A. E.  240
*Lonsdale*, HMAS  159, 170
Loughran, Matron Mary McLean RRC, MID  29–30
Lucas, Elizabeth  192
Lucas girls (Avenue of Honour, Ballarat)  71
Lyon, Delcie  238
Lyons, Phillip  109

MacArthur, General Douglas  108, 109, 175, 252
McCarthy, Matron Maud  25–6
McCarthy, Pat  205–06
McClemans, Sheila (D/WRANS)  158–60, 217
McDowell, Sister E. RRC  20
McGlover, Lucy  273
McKenna, Rita  241
McKenzie, Florence Violet  156–8, 168, 276
 forms Women's Emergency Signalling Corps  156, 157
 and RAAF  157
McKenzie, Lady W. I. E. MB, BS  155
McKenzie, Nurse Lily  32
McKnight, Capt. Keith  158
Madden, Maj. Dora  192, 193
*Magnetic*, HMAS  169
*Maidstone*, HMS  171
Makin, Mr (Minister for the Navy)  160
Malaya  99, 274
manpower requirements  5, 239
 regulations  257
*Manunda* (hospital ship)  137
Marble Bar  265, 268
Martin, Melva  202, 203, 204
masseurs  16, 30, 122
 *see also* physiotherapists
Mataranka  145
Mawson, Sister Beatrice  32–3
Medical Air Evacuation Unit  134
Michelmore, Maj. Jean  192
Middle East  99, 118, 119
military regulations  121
Miller, Emma  8
Mills, Muriel and Roly  63
Milne Bay  137
*Mindari*, HMAS  169
Miningarra  266
Moate, Ronald  127
Moloney, Hazel  115
*Mongolia*  32–3
Montgomery, General  99
*Moravian*  9
*Moreton*, HMAS  162
Morgan, Stan  127
Morotai  145

Morphett, Audrey  241, 242, 243-4, 255
Moule, Trooper J.J.  63-4
Mountbatten, Lord  168
Mountjoy, Lt C. E.  199
Mt Isa  145
Mullewa  237
munitions  239-46
  ACTU  239
  deaths  244
  expenditure  240, 243
  health problems  241-2
  Maribyrnong  240, 241, 243
  safety  240-1, 244
  St Mary's  241
  Salisbury  241, 243, 244
Murray, Captain G. A.  127

Nakagawa, Capt. Hajime  130
National Register cards  239
National Defence League  256, 257
Naval Information Service  161
Newman, Commander J. B.  156
Nixon, Sister Elizabeth  9
NSW Nursing Service
  Reserve  *see* nurses, Boer War
nurses, Boer War  9-12, 15-17, 26
  attitudes to  9, 15-16
  conditions  11, 14-15
  NSW  9, 12, 15
  other colonies  15
  SA  10-11, 15
  Vic.  10, 15
  *see also* Australian Army Nursing Service

occupational therapists  155
O'Dwyer, Matron Ida RRC  31
Oram, Miss  19
Oram, Pat  275
*Oranje* (hospital ship)  130
Order of St John of Jerusalem  140
*Ormonde*, RMS  21
O'Rourke, Nurse Mary  30-1
O'Toole, Alice  204, 205-6
Outridge, Dr Leslie  129


Padres' Few Bob Fund  258
Page, Jean  247, 248
Palestine  118
parachutes  177-8
Paterson, 'Banjo'  20
pathologists  155
Pearl Harbor  105, 111, 161, 261
Pearson, Capt. W. A.  158
Pepper, Pte Higham  64-5, 67-70
*Perth*, HMAS  103, 108
pharmacists  155
physiotherapists  30, 123, 155
  Australian Physiotherapists' Association  123
  overseas service  30, 123
Pocock, Sister Mary Annie  9
Port Hedland  264, 265, 266
Port Moresby  109, 145, 147, 152, 250
Pratt, Sister Rachel MM  28
pregnancy  211, 213-20
*Prince of Wales*, HMS  106
prisoners of war  104, 232-3, 234, 275

Australian nurses  119
Provan, P/O Frances  162
Pye, ACW  181

Queen Alexandra Imperial
  Military Nursing Service  21,
  29, 121
*Queen Elizabeth*  21, 170
*Queen Mary*  123, 170

RAA  200
RAAFNS  131–5
  Darwin  131, 132–3
  uniform  131, 134
  in New Guinea  131–2
  effect on men  132
Rabaul  106, 108
RAFNS, uniform  131
rail journeys  237–8
railway stations  251, 252
RAN  161
RANNS  136–8
Rapke, S/O Betty  270, 271
rationing  3, 251, 257
Rats of Tobruk  99, 101
Rawson, Sister  10
Reay, Sister A. V. C.  31
Red Cross  21, 36–40, 146, 148,
  186, 188, 232–8
  Blood Transfusion
    Service  151–2, 232, 233
  convalescent homes  38
  Field Force  233, 234, 237
  field personnel (WWI)  38
  first Australian branch  36
  forms VADs  139
  fundraising  38, 233

Junior Red Cross  39, 233
  transport section  235–8
Red Cross War Book  232
Redman, Sister Ella  33
refugees, Dutch  264–6
rehabilitation, women  270–6
  and churches  272
*Repulse*, HMS  106
Ribe, Writer Coral  171
Richardson, Frank  147
Richardson, Joan  146–9
Ritter, Mrs E.  79
Robertson, Matron Muriel  21
Robertson, Philadelphia  36
Roll, Edith and family  87–9
Ross, Matron, G.  30
*Rushcutter*, HMAS (anti-submarine
  school)  169
Russia  100, 104

Sache, Herbert  183
Sage, Matron-in-Chief A. M.,
  RRC  120
Salvation Army  217, 219, 254
Sargent, Winnie  264
Savage, Sister Eleanor  127–9
Saxton, Mrs C. R.  93
Schultz, Lois  273
Scott, Mrs Len  252
Scrivener, ACW  181
Seager, Mrs A.  48, 49, 50, 51,
  52, 53, 56, 58, 59, 60, 61
Secrett, Poppy Octavia  263–3
sex, attitudes to  207–12
  pregnancy, in women's
    services  211, 213–20
signallers  202–06
  living conditions  202–03

shifts  *204, 205*
training  *202, 203, 204*
see also Women's Emergency Signalling Corps
Simon, Capt. Derek  *158*
Simper, Vinnie  *234, 235–6, 237*
see also Red Cross
Singapore  *101, 169*
fall of  *107, 119*
*Skaubryn*  *238*
Skov, Maj. Dorothea  *115, 195, 218, 219*
small arms manufacture  see munitions
Smart, ACW  *181, 182*
Smith, Bridget  *90*
Smith, Dr Julian  *151*
Smith, ACW Mona  *182*
Smith, Sister I. M.  *132*
Smith, Robyn  *viii*
Solly, Elsie  *206*
Sowden, William  *49, 54, 46–7, 58*
Spry, Mrs  *266, 268*
Stack, Dr Ella  *259*
Stancke, Maj.-Gen.  *187*
Stevenson, Clare G. (D/WAAAF)  *172, 175, 177, 185, 216–17*
Street, Hon. G. A.  *110*
Stutter, Jack  *127*
Swallow, Sister Beryl  *137*
Sweet, ACW  *181, 182*
*Sydney*, HMAS  *100, 101, 104–05*
Syria  *118, 119*

Tambling, Edna  *262–3*
Tambling, Ern  *262–3*
Tame, Sister J. E. W.  *137*
Taylor, Capt. P. G.  *158*
Tennant Creek  *145*
Tobruk  *118, 121, 259*
see also Rats of Tobruk
Torney, Sister V.  *119*
*Torrens*, HMAS  *170*
Townsville  *162, 180*
Trundle, ACW  *182*

*Ulysses*  *68*
US servicemen  *221–5*
US WACs  *223–4*
and GIs  *223*
see also Brown, Lt-Col. M. A. G.

VADs  see Australian Army Medical Women's Service
Vaille, 2nd Officer Margaret  *162*
VE Day  *269*
venereal disease  *207–12, 216*
Victoria League  *258*
Victory Parade (WWII)  *160*
VJ Day  *269*
Voluntary Blood Donors' Association  *232*
see also Red Cross

WAAAF  *172–85, 208*
achieve enlisted status  *175*
fabric workers  *177–8*
formed  *173*
living conditions  *177*
medical officers  *211–12*

musterings  *176*
officers  *177, 180*
recruiting  *174*
scandalous tales  *214, 216*
'sex hygiene'  *208–11*
signallers  *173–4*
training depots  *177*
WACA ground and AWAS  *194*
Wallal Downs  *264, 265–6, 268*
Walsh, Molly  *261, 264*
Walter and Eliza Hall Institute  *150*
War Bond Drive  *183*
war brides
  WWI  *84–6*
  WWII  *225, 234, 238*
war, expenditure  *250*
Warrrawagaine  *268*
Waterson, Jim  *129*
weddings  *146, 225*
Wedgwood, Lt-Col. Camilla  *192, 200, 201*
Westhoven, 3rd Officer Mollie  *169*
*Weston*, HMAS  *169*
Westwood, Robert  *128*
white feather  *78–9*
White, Lady *see* Deakin, Vera
White, Principal Matron Jessie McHardy MBE, RRC  *26*
Whitely, Judy  *243*
Whitworth, Joyce  *203*
Willard, Mr S.  *255*
Williams, Misses E. and V.  *66–7*
Williams, W/O  *127*
Wilson, Capt. J. J.  *158*
Wilson, Matron Grace RRC, FNM  *28, 120*
Wilson, Strella  *259–60*
wireless telegraphy branch (WRANS)  *156–8*
  *see also* Women's Emergency Signalling Corps
Woinarksi, Sister Valerie RRC  *32*
women
  accommodation  *245*
  discharge  *269–70*
  enlistment  *111, 112, 113, 114*
  and franchise  *8*
  in 'male' jobs  *112, 248*
  in the workforce  *239–40, 247–8, 256, 259*
  pay  *245*
  and responsibility  *258*
Women's Australian National Services  *111, 226*
Women's Auxiliary Australian Air Force *see* WAAAF
Women's Auxiliary of the Australia-Soviet Friendship League  *257–8*
Women's Auxiliary for the Fighting Services  *115*
Women's Auxiliary Transport Service  *116, 226*
Women's Emergency Legion  *see* Women's National Emergency Legion
Women's Emergency Signalling Corps  *156, 157, 168*
Women's Employment Board  *113*
Women's National Emergency Legion  *116, 165*
Women's Voluntary National Register  *110, 111*
Wood, Merv  *158*

Woods, Maj. Jean  *191, 192, 193, 203*
WRANS  *156–71*
  discipline  *159*
  enlistments  *156, 159*
  occupations  *160, 161, 162*
  recruitment, officers  *158–9, 162*
Wright, F. Sgt Bette  *183*
Wurth, W. C.  *230*

Wyndham  *264*

*Yarra*, HMAS  *108*
YMCA  *42*
YWCA hostels and clubs  *116, 258*

*Zealandia  261*